ML

D1588224

30

Cash flow accounting

Series on International Accounting and Finance
Edited by C. W. Nobes

Cash flow accounting
International uses and abuses

Gabriel D. Donleavy

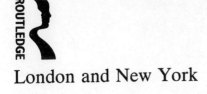

London and New York

First published 1994
by Routledge
11 New Fetter Lane, London EC4P 4EE

Simultaneously published in the USA and Canada
by Routledge
29 West 35th Street, New York, NY 10001

© 1994 Gabriel D. Donleavy

Phototypeset in Times by Intype, London
Printed and bound in Great Britain by
Mackays of Chatham PLC, Chatham, Kent

British Library Cataloguing in Publication Data

A catalogue record for this book is available from the British Library

Library of Congress Cataloging in Publication Data

Donleavy, G. D. (G. Douglas)
    Cash flow accounting : international uses and abuses / Gabriel D.
Donleavy.
        p. cm. – (Routledge series on international accounting and
finance)
    Includes bibliographical references and index.
    ISBN 0–415–08677–9
    1. Cash flow–Accounting. I. Title. II. Series.
HF5681.C28D66 1993
657'.72–dc20
                                                                    93–18904
                                                                    CIP

Contents

Tables and figure

Acknowledgements

This book was facilitated by the constructive and rigorous appraisals of Professor S. J. Gray, the encouragement of the series editor Professor C. J. Nobes, early discussions with Professor R. G. Walker and Mrs Sonia Newby, and the extended patience and forbearance of Mrs Lilian Donleavy during many evenings and weekends.

1 The history and usefulness of accounting

INTRODUCTION

It is strange that although accounting predates all other recorded human activity, debate continues right up to the present about what it is and what it ought to be.

> Hindsight facilitates hypercriticism. While some may jest that accounting is the second oldest profession, intellectually it is in its infancy (or emerging therefrom). . . . It has never been regarded as a philosophy fundamental to human welfare. It has not had an Adam Smith or a John Stuart Mill.
>
> (Gaffikin 1987 pp. 25–6)

In this chapter the historical forces shaping present day Anglo-American accounting are outlined. Next we discuss what is meant by usefulness of accounting reports and how usefulness is recognized. Then we consider the ways in which international accounts appraisal differs from regular accounts appraisal. Finally we consider if any particular place can be said to be particularly appropriate as a base from which to analyze international accounts without unduly heavy domestic accounting pressures.

HISTORY

Prehistory

Pictographs have been found on clay tablets in the Middle East dating back as far as 12000 BC. Also found were clay tokens whose shape and markings represented both a type and quantity of livestock. Tokens are believed to have been transferred along with the livestock they represented as evidence of ownership transfer. Clay tablets replaced tokens as it became clear that pictographs on the envelopes containing the clay tokens did away with the need for the tokens themselves (Schmandt-Besserat 1979).

By about 3000 BC early records are recognizable as accounts. They are mostly inventory lists, lists of commodities used for payment and simple journal entries. The invention of money is attributed to the Chinese around 2000 BC who also appear to have pioneered budgetary control and governmental accounting and auditing. However, it was the scribe of Mesopotamia who was most readily identifiable as the predecessor of today's accountant. 'At school special emphasis was placed on learning commercial terms and phrases. In fact, in Latin and many languages the standard phrase for parsing is *amo* (I love), but in Mesopotamia, the aspiring young scribe parsed with "I count" ' (Green 1930 pp. 29–30).

The Greeks possessed a sophisticated system of public affairs accounting and auditing and enterprise management accounting, according to the Zenon papyri. Virtually nothing of Roman accounting survives, since they kept their records on perishable wax tablets (Most 1982a).

Medieval history

In 1178 the merchants of Genoa advanced money to their government in a series of transactions that created the Bank of St George, the earliest Western bank (Littleton 1933).

In 1202 Leonardo of Pisa introduced to Europe Arabic numerals and zeros.

> It should be noted however that the rules of the bankers' guild invariably prescribed the use of Roman numerals in making ledger records. The idea prevailed for a long time that such numerals made fraudulent alterations more difficult. But there was nothing in this restriction by the guild to preclude other informal uses of Arabic numbers.
>
> (Littleton 1933 p. 21)

Although the medieval banks may have invented double entry, the oldest surviving record reflecting its principles is the Giovanni Farolfi branch ledger in Salon, France, for the year 1299/1300. Luca Pacioli is considered the father of modern accounting because his 'Method of Venice' became the model for subsequent textbooks on accounting. In 1494 he published his *Summa de Arithmetica* which contained two chapters ('de Computis et Scripturis') describing double entry bookkeeping. In 1514 Pope Leo X appointed him to the Chair of Mathematics in the Sapienza University in Rome. The first professional organization of accountants was founded in Venice in 1581, and so the method of Venice was spread throughout the world by a combination of translation, plagiarism and trading. By 1775 double entry had spread to Germany, Belgium, Holland, Britain and Iberia (Most 1982a).

The rise of the company

The earliest companies were royally chartered monopolies like The Russia Company (1555), the East India Company (1600) and the Hudson's Bay Company (1670). Among the reasons Irish gives for the Tudor and Stuart preference for monopolies in international trade, particularly striking is the following (Irish 1947 p. 483):

> The peoples of distant countries did not distinguish between individual merchants. As all Chinamen look alike to us, so all Englishmen or even all Europeans were alike to them. An unscrupulous trader, who cheated, robbed, or killed a native, escaped the consequences of his crime and left them to be borne by his countrymen who sought later to carry on the trade. The home government could not punish such offences, and it should not let them continue. It required, therefore, that a man proposing to trade in a distant country should have an interest in the permanent welfare of the trade, by making him contribute money to the association, and subscribe to its rules.

At the end of each voyage accounts were taken out, distributions made and each particular venture liquidated. The balance sheet thus began life as a liquidation statement (Irish 1947).

In 1613 the East India Company had its capital subscribed for four years, instead of as previously by venture subscriptions. In 1657 its new charter established the principle of permanently invested capital, while preserving a limited right to transfer individual shares without an intricate liquidation of accounts on each transfer. Permanent capital changed the previous liquidation basis of accounting whereby each subscriber received a sum at the end of each venture without any need to partition it between income and capital components. Irish quotes Littleton (1947 pp. 138–9) on the separation of ownership from active control, thus: 'meant that statements separate from the books would soon be highly desirable because of the number of people who had contributed capital and who would desire information about their venture'.

The industrial revolution moved large scale production beyond the reach of most single families, and also sharpened greatly the difference between the time period needed for production and that needed to amortize equipment. The demand for capital involved increasing numbers of investors and savers so that the finance function became separate from the management function, this phenomenon being sometimes termed the managerial revolution. It created the divorce between internal and external accounting (Most 1982a).

The Victorian era

Four factors contributed to financial secrecy in the nineteenth century:

1 No tradition of publicity
2 Belief that information would benefit competitors.
3 Belief that *caveat emptor* applied to securities as if they were *sui generis* with general goods and chattels.
4 No belief in any public right to corporate information.

(Hawkins 1963)

The first break came in the UK when the 1844 Companies Act required directors to supply shareholders with an audited balance sheet annually (Most 1982a).

Limited liability itself arrived with the 1856 Companies Act and the 1862 Act enabled it to be available to any who elected to have it. As case law evolved, the preservation of capital and protection against fraud on creditors and investors became outstanding features. Legal decisions and business practice combined over time to produce conventions rather than principles concerning the income capital boundary (Irish 1947).

Originally, English company legislation called for the preparation and filing of accounts for the protection of creditors and for the information of shareholders. The English Act of 1844 enunciated minimum requirements for the books; it made definite rules as to audit, and provided for due publicity through the publication of the balance sheet. Emphasis was placed on the prevention of fraud and on accounting for capital, rather than on a true determination of income. In fact, no profit and loss account was required.

Proper books of account were not mandated until the 1929 Companies Act required money payments and receipts, assets and liabilities, all sales purchases and stock in trade to be recorded in the books. It also prescribed the annual publication of a P and L account but not its contents (Irish 1947).

US developments

The process of acceptance of the 1894 reporting standard for balance sheets agreed at the meeting of the American Association of Public Accountants was slow (Previts 1984 p. 4). The resolution was 'that the method of stating should be in order of quickest realization', the reverse of the British order. A comment by Robert Montgomery, US born auditing author and early leader of the certified public accounting (CPA) profession in the USA, at the 1904 World Congress of Accountants, on a paper by Arthur Lowes Dickinson, UK born managing partner of the US offices of Price Waterhouse, indicates the continuing UK influence. Montgomery said the UK order was 'hardly the general practice' and that the proposed US order 'conveys the status of the business better'. This implies a comparatively greater interest in the USA in liquidity since the proposed order puts liquidity literally first. This greater focus on liquidity in the position statement may be an early factor leading to the eventual *absence* of focus thereon in the all financial resources basis of the SCFP (Statement of Changes in Financial Position) in the USA which was prescribed by Opinion number 19 of the Accounting Principles Board covering accounts published between 1973 and 1987.

Dickinson's paper at the 1904 Congress greatly influenced the format of the US income statement at its earliest stage of development (Previts 1984).

Paton in his *Accountants' Handbook* noted (1922 p. 109) the increasing importance of the income statement 'and the present-day tendency to regard the balance sheet as the connecting link between successive income statements'. Irish (1947 p. 71) thought this

> arises largely from the basic truth that there is an increasing separation of the personalities of ownership and administration. It is further affected by the growth of some corporations to miniature empires in which so many people have a direct or indirect interest.

The New York Stock Exchange required from 6 January 1933 that companies seeking a listing must henceforth provide audited financial statements.

On 29 May 1933 President F. D. Roosevelt requested Congress to enact a federal securities bill which would add 'to the ancient rule of caveat emptor, the further doctrine, "let the seller also beware" '. Congress signed the Securities Act on 29 May with the long title of 'an act to provide full and fair disclosure of the character of the securities sold in interstate and foreign commerce' (Edwards 1956).

During the forties, the income statement overtook the balance sheet in importance, in the USA. George O. May (1943) called the balance sheet a collection of 'nonhomogeneous residuals' and this to Taggart (1953)

> comes near to being the truth. If stocks are LIFO while debtors are near liquid, then the whole is meaningless. The meaning of certain balance sheet items is still comprehensible, but the balance sheet as a whole now fully deserves the suspicion in which it has always been held by those non accountants who feel that the monotonous balance of the two columns of figures is just too slick to be anything but phony.

Solomons (1961 p. 283) observed:

> just as in the first half of this century we saw the income statement displace the balance sheet in importance, so we may now be de-emphasizing the income statement in favor of a statement of fund flows or cash flows . . . my own guess is that so far as the history of accounting is concerned, the next twenty five years may subsequently be seen to have been the twilight of income measurement.

This very wrong prediction does nonetheless capture the extent to which the funds statement was seen in the fifties and 1960s as having promising information content. Thereafter, measurement corrections rather than supplemental disclosures or reformulations came to be viewed as more effective solutions to the shortcomings of the income statement.

In 1958 the AICPA Special Committee on Research Programs recommended the formation of the APB and of a research basis for its deliberations. The Sprouse-Moonitz study appeared at the end of April 1962 as APB 1. In the Foreword was a statement by the APB that the study was a valuable contribution to accounting thinking but 'too radically different from present generally accepted accounting principles for acceptance at this time'. It did accept *An Inventory of Generally Accepted Accounting Principles* in March

1965 as a desirable piece of codification. Principles were induced from practice rather than deduced from any a priori conceptual framework (Moonitz 1974 p. 28).

The Wheat Committee (AICPA 1972) was charged to consider the feasibility and desirability of establishing a Commission to study and recommend an organizational structure for advancing the formulation and modification of GAAP and for the issuance of authoritative pronouncements concerning the application of such principles (AAA 1971 p. 174). It recommended the establishment of the FASB. Soon after that the Trueblood Study Group concluded that the basic objective of financial statements is to *aid in economic decision making*. This has been cited as the primary objective of accounting reports ever since 1973. Financial statements, per the Trueblood Report, should do three things, namely:

1 Assist in predicting, comparing and evaluating the earning power of enterprises.
2 Report both historical cost and current values which differ significantly.
3 Separate information which is factual from information which is interpreted (Previts 1984)

Early theorizing in the USA

Historically there have been three approaches to the development of accounting theory, namely:

1 Personification theories which ascribed to an account the qualities of a person who received and gave, treated each account as an extension of the proprietor's and/or regarded each account as a clerk receiving or ceding value on behalf of the proprietor.
2 Proprietorial theories which classified accounts into personal and real, for persons and owned objects respectively. As the P and L account developed, real accounts spawned the subset nominal accounts for the period phenomena. In 1795, Edmond Degrange in 'La Tenue des Livres Rendue Facile', published in Paris, divided real accounts into five classes: cash, goods, bills receivable, bills payable, and profits and losses. Followers of his were known as the 'cinq-contistes' or five account school.
3 Entity theories, which have become the conventional wisdom.

Vatter (1947) attacked the proprietary view of accounting as untenable when share capital is recorded at anything other than its current stock market value. 'The simple notion of profit expressed as the personal gain of the proprietor cannot be applied to the corporate situation in which owner-stockholders are constantly moving in and out of the area of proprietary interest' (p. 6).

The entity theory, that the company has a life and accountability of its own, is a view he attributes to Paton and Littleton (1940). He quotes one of its critics: 'Accounting theory would probably be more realistic if it accepted as its basis the fact that the corporation is an association of flesh and blood persons who enjoy special privileges because they have complied with certain legal requirements' (Husband 1938).

Husband's (1938) article asserts that although the entity theory is the dominant accounting paradigm, the practising accountant is quite happy to shift to the proprietary theory 'when it suits his convenience'.

One of the first attempts in this century to provide a sound theoretical framework for accounting was Sprague's *The Philosophy of Accounts* (1907). He saw accounting as a branch of mathematics whose principles were thus determinable by a priori reasoning 'and do not depend upon the customs and traditions which surround the art.' (p. ix). The main significance of this work was its recognition of the need for the development of a more formal methodology for the long term development of the discipline. Previously, accounting rose no higher than technical manuals (Gaffikin 1987).

Paton's *Accounting Theory* (1922) searched for the analytical and empirical premises on which accounting rests, and included a whole chapter on the formal assumptions of accounting. His 'assumptions' tended to be his own view of what the accountant assumed, in his opinion (Gaffikin 1987).

Canning's *The Economics of Accountancy* (1929) presented an economist's critique of accounting and moved inductively part of the way towards building a model usable both by accountants and economists.

During the 1930s there were several theoretical efforts (AAA 1936, Scott 1931) of which one of the most systematically empirical attempts to induce principles was made by Sanders *et al.* (1938).

Littleton (1933) thought the 'antecedents' of bookkeeping were:

1 A Material (something which needs to be reworked)
   (a) Private property (power to change ownership)
   (b) Capital (wealth productively employed)

(c) Commerce (interchange of goods)

(d) Credit (present use of future goods)

2 A Language (a medium for expressing the material)

   (a) Writing (a means of making a permanent record)

   (b) Money (medium of exchange, common denominator)

   (c) Arithmetic (a means of computation)

These elements when energized by favourable economic and social conditions produce:

3 A Methodology (a plan for systematically rendering the material into the language).

The appearance of the Paton and Littleton (1940) monograph, *An Introduction to Corporate Accounting Standards* added importantly to the emerging academic framework for accounting. It was based on the fundamental assumption that accounting was an allocation process, guided by a matching concept, and principally oriented to the historical cost valuation model (Previts 1984).

After the Second World War, the academic community explored alternatives to proprietary and entity orientations although only Vatter's (1947) fund theory of accounting attracted any significant attention.

A very influential attempt at theory had been provided by Paton and Littleton (1940), the more so as Paton was an a priori deductivist while Littleton was a historically oriented inductivist. Littleton's *Structure of Accounting Theory* (1953) was strongly inductive albeit yielding only 'low level empirical generalizations' (Gaffikin (1987 p. 23) interpreting a criticism by Deinzer (1965 p. 56)). However, it can be seen as a turning point in accounting academics' attitudes to methodology which has ever since been largely inductive.

European work to 1960

As for the UK, Gaffikin (1987 p. 24) observes: 'In Britain, accounting was not considered worthy of academic status. Accounting education thus stressed technical and legal procedures; "theory" was superfluous'. This had ceased to be true by the early 1970s, arguably up to ten years earlier, but this section is only concerned with outlining the historical context in which present day funds statement formats were forged, and they were already in their present form by around 1960.

René Delaporte was arguably the most important French theorist. He stressed the importance of the accounting equation and saw accounts as showing value derived from legal rights or discharge of legal obligations (Delaporte 1936).

The major German theorist was Eugen Schmalenbach who founded both business economics and what he called dynamic accounting, as described in his 1916 book of the same name. He said that too much reliance was placed on the balance sheet whose ingredients, even when accurately valued, did not add up to the total value of the firm. The P and L account should be developed and become the main report, with the balance sheet becoming merely the step between two income statements.

Anticipations of agency theory

Berle and Means (1933), writing on the increasing separation of ownership from management, observed that such separation increased the importance of the stewardship function of accounts.

Apropos the separation of ownership from control, Vatter (1947 pp. 107–8) wrote:

> In this situation management is indeed far removed from the application of neat theories of authority delegations following the lines of property rights; management is not the servant of the proprietors but rather the conciliatory agency between two or among several of these groups.
>
> All business units are but parts of a greater whole; vice versa, most business units are themselves but combinations of smaller units. A thing or situation which may be a most useful and workable unit of business from one point of view is likely to prove awkward and unsuited to other users and conditions. In the last analysis the notion of a unit of business is but a means of specifying the area of attention – a delimited and prescribed set of activities which give rise to the kinds of data with which accounting is to deal. Some such unit must serve as the basis for accounting: but it must be a unit devoid of personal implications and at the same time sufficiently definite to make clear just where its boundaries lie; it must be one that may be applied to various forms of organization and different kinds of activities; and it must be one that has definite relation to the processes and the results that accounting is expected to achieve. Such a unit is to be found in the concept of a fund.

He acknowledges the terminological difficulty and favours a definition that really amounts to a sinking fund: 'a segregation of assets for a given purpose' and this involves 'a partial recognition of the set of separate operations which pertain to those assets'. However, this vagueness is quickly made worse.

> In fund accounting a fund is not mere cash resources, and it is more than a mere collection of assets set aside for a particular purpose. The accounts of each fund recognize not only all the asset items but also all the equities that pertain to that fund; in addition, there are also present complete classifications of revenue, expense and income accounts. These, taken together, provide a general ledger trial balance complete in all respects as to the operations covered by the definition of the fund.
>
> (Vatter 1947)

What is being attempted in the above is a justification of fund accounting on proto agency theory grounds. It militates against an all financial resources view of funds as such an aggregate cannot by definition have a particular purpose in any tactical sense.

This, then, was the course of accounting history to the emergence of the funds statement in the early 1960s. Chapter 4 will continue the story. We now turn to discussing the idea of usefulness of accounts.

USEFULNESS OF ACCOUNTS AND HOW IT IS DEMONSTRATED

In everyday language, the word 'usefulness' has no mystery or ambiguity. It means possessing the quality of helping us to improve our well-being in some way, usually a concrete and practical way rather than an abstract and spiritual one. Some useful things do not become useful, however, until we learn how to use them. Examples of such usefulness which has training as a prerequisite are computers, electric corkscrews, microwave ovens, cars and cheque books. In fact, without some training in their use, many modern inventions would be useless. The funds statement is just such an invention; yet its usefulness, like the usefulness of accounts in general, is hardly ever studied with adequate attention to the level of training of the accounts 'user'. Instead, the research literature generally makes either or both of the following assumptions about accounts 'users'.

1 If people are not using the information in a statement, the statement is *ipso facto* useless.
2 Accounts are presented to participants in efficient markets so market reaction to information is itself a sufficient measure of real usefulness.

Assumption 1 reflects an extreme of pragmatism purged of almost all value judgements, a mindset necessary for accounting academics to get published in the top three or so academic journals, on which their careers may depend. We will consider in Chapter 3 the human information processing literature on accounting which has built a rather elaborate set of structures around assumption 1. For the moment we will introduce a distinction between *potential* usefulness which depends on profiting from adequate training and *kinetic* usefulness which merely mirrors use actually made.

Assumption 2 is to accounting research what the Immaculate Conception is to Christianity. Non-believers do not get excommunicated for they are generally not allowed into refereed communion in the first place. An efficient market is one which rapidly and 'accurately' translates news into buy, sell or hold decisions. Imperfectly efficient markets allow some 'rank insiders' to make greater returns over a sustained period than the average for the market. Of course, the 'accurate' translation of news into trading decisions automatically implies trained and sophisticated market players. This sweeping assumption is called the efficient market hypothesis and it is widely believed in the USA where the evidence suggests it is more nearly true than anywhere else in the world. This is elaborated and challenged in Chapter 2, but right from the start we need to be aware of the so-called joint hypothesis problem. When we test whether a stock market reacts to a piece of news such as the news in a new set of accounts, our interpretation of abnormal stock price movement is usually that the news had 'information value', i.e. had usefulness. Actually, however, two hypotheses are inextricably involved in such tests: one, that the news was useful; *and* two, that the market was efficient in its reaction to the news. Unless we first measure efficiency, we can attribute no meaning whatsoever to abnormal price movements apparently associated with the news release. When belief in market efficiency is general enough for it to be an uncontroversial assumption, then we can save ourselves the bother of measuring efficiency. It will be enough to ensure publication of our results merely to cite authorities who showed that the market was efficient when and how they looked at it. Let us look briefly at a few of these studies, bearing in mind that in Chapter 2 a much fuller discussion and analysis will be presented.

Benston (1967) found a significant but small relationship between rates of change in accounting data and rates of change of stock prices. Ball and Brown (1968) (hereafter BB) carried out the study which became the exemplar for all subsequent studies of accounts usefulness to investors. BB tested a null hypothesis that earnings reported in accounts had no information content (because of measurement errors and because of the availability of alternative, more timely information sources). They assumed market efficiency, so prices would incorporate all available information. To find out if accounting earnings were within the description 'information', they investigated the association of variation in stock prices with variation in earnings or with the announcements of earnings. Using a simple proxy for investors' expectations, comprising last reported firm earnings and its previous association with an aggregate market index of earnings, they assembled two portfolios. In one were those firms whose actual earnings exceeded 'expectations' (positive forecast error); in the other those whose actuals fell below 'expectations' (negative forecast error). The shares with positive forecast error tended to generate abnormal returns of more than the market average; the negatives generated less. Moreover, such movements were apt to begin well in advance of earnings announcements and to have only a minority of their total movement left in them by announcement time. This implied that little benefit would be gained by studying the accounts once they were made public (Ball and Brown 1968). This study invented the abnormal performance index for isolating price movements capable of being associated with a specific piece of news. The tendency of prices to move in advance of news is due to correct anticipation of the news by outsiders (improbably) and to insiders like employees and directors acting on news before it is made public (probably). To curb the latter activity, all major capital markets made insider trading a punishable offence in the 1970s and 1980s.

Kinetic usefulness, then, is often measured by the abnormal performance index, but such usefulness concerns only investors (as opposed to creditors, tax collectors or society at large) and its measurement depends on the accuracy of the efficient market hypothesis at the time and place of measurement.

INTERNATIONAL ACCOUNTS APPRAISAL

Accounts appraisal is taught in all accounting and finance courses. Profitability is captured through the return on capital employed ratios, indebtedness through gearing/leverage ratios, liquidity through the current and acid test ratios, business volume through the activity ratios, pricing:costing profile through the margin ratios and productivity through some measure of volume divided by head-count. Less often taught but rather left to be learnt by experience interacting with osmosis is the act of reading the final accounts. It is generally assumed that if students can write accounts correctly, they must obviously be able to read them. In Chapters 3, 7 and 9 we deal with this assumption by way of exposing the gap between the potential and kinetic usefulness of accounts.

Accounts appraisal in an international context is often done by translating foreign accounts into a domestic format and then applying the usual ratios that the analyst applies to accounts produced in his/her own country. If the foreign accounts have been prepared under similar conventions and standards to those that govern domestic accounts, then there will be little distortion involved in the analysis of such accounts as if they were domestic. As a broad generalization, British, Australian, New Zealand, South African, Singaporean, Malaysian, Zimbabwean, Irish and Hong Kong accounts are prepared under similar conventions. American, Canadian, Korean, Taiwanese, English versions of Japanese, Thai and Philippine accounts are prepared under American conventions with assets marshalled in the reverse order on the balance sheet from the British Commonwealth order, with the boundary between provisions not being as sharp as for Commonwealth accounts and with the notion that compliance with GAAP was at least as important as providing a true and fair view. France, Germany, Switzerland and native language Japanese accounts do not share Anglo-American accounting assumptions in some important respects, and this affects their fair interpretation in an Anglo-American context. First, these countries do not take it as axiomatic that accounts are to help shareholders but rather they are to conform with detailed legal regulations, and if anyone is to be helped by accounts, it is the tax inspectorate. Secret reserves are permitted in these countries, especially for financial institutions, and this means that income statements convey much less information about the firm's performance than Anglo-American statements do, since transfers to or from secret reserves can be used to smooth income without being obliged to disclose the size of the transfer. Chapter 5 addresses the problems of cross national accounting with particular reference to the funds statement and the cash flow statement.

In this book Hong Kong is often given a certain amount of prominence which some readers will find odd. International accounting is more easily done and more easily studied from within a geographically tiny but financially large jurisdiction than from one with a strong domestically established accounting framework. Relative to the USA, Canada, Australia, New Zealand, Britain and Singapore the territory of Hong Kong is economically and financially not subject to national constraints, assumptions or solipsisms. It is therefore rather a good base from which to undertake international accounting studies. Its political identity crisis only serves to strengthen its usefulness as a relatively unbiased standpoint for reviewing the accountancy products of the rest of the world. China's nascent accounting profession and academic advisors at the time of writing are engaged in just such an exercise.

In the next section we briefly survey East Asian accounting to show how different it is from Anglo-American. The same title and apparent format of accounts can conceal quite different assumptions about the meaning, reliability and construct validity of the terms employed.

ASIAN ACCOUNTING STRUCTURES

Eastern Asia overview

Regional markets have grown far faster than the quality of public accounts: 'Statutory disclosure and regulatory supervision vary from stringent in Singapore to abysmal in Indonesia.' A region-wide effort to improve the quality of accounts is nonetheless under way, driven by a combination of Anglo-American investors, the local affiliates of the big six accounting firms and interventions by the Korean and Singaporean governments. Escalating insurance premiums following the Carrian and Panelectric scandals, both of which involved as yet unsuccessful negligence suits against the auditors, have been a factor in the new activism (Friedland 1989).

Japan has lagged far behind other advanced countries in standardizing its accounting. The first year that Japanese consolidated accounts were mandated was 1989. They are still not required in Indonesia, Taiwan, Thailand or South Korea. The standard of public accounts in Indonesia, Taiwan and Thailand has failed to keep pace

Table 1.1 Regional disclosure requirements

Country	Consolidation	DR*	RPT†
Hong Kong			not yet
Indonesia	sometimes	no	no
Japan	supplement	no	sometimes
Malaysia			
Philippines	sometimes	no	
Singapore	sometimes		intercorporate
South Korea	sometimes	no	sometimes
Taiwan		no	no
Thailand	sometimes	no	intercorporate

* Directors' Remuneration
† Related Party Transactions

Source: Friedland (1989)

with the exponential growth of their stock markets: 'In terms of standards and practices, the Commonwealth countries and Hong Kong are the most advanced.' Standards and practices based on the US model prevail in Indonesia, the Philippines, Korea, Thailand and to a lesser extent Japan and Taiwan where accounting is driven mainly by tax considerations. 'The US model is considered more rigorous than British accountancy standards and less flexible in its application to local conditions' (Friedland 1989 p. 71).

Table 1.1 highlights some key areas of underdisclosure in Asia.

India has recently decided to open its capital markets to foreign investors but its own GAAP are not fully codified, especially in the key areas of inventory and depreciation where there is not yet comparability inside the country (Khambata and Khambata 1989).

Japan

The basic postulates of accounting in Japan were laid down in 1949 by the Ministry of Finance (MOF) in its still applicable *Financial Accounting Standards for Business Enterprises*. They comprise the consistency, going concern, historical cost and matching principles. In 1963 the Commercial Code and Securities and Exchange Law prescribed the annual presentation of a position, income and appropriation statement together with supporting schedules including changes in capital, changes in bonds, changes in fixed assets, etc. There was and is no need to aggregate the schedules into an SCFP. Notes (trade bills) are the normal mode of credit trading so they tend to exceed receivables and payables on the balance sheet. A uniquely Japanese feature of the income statement is its classification of all items between ordinary and extraordinary (JICPA 1987 pp. 20–8).

The Ministry of Finance (MOF) is advised by the Business Accounting Deliberation Council (BADC) whose members come from a variety of backgrounds in industry, accountancy, government and the universities. The BADC prepares standards called Business Accounting Principles in response to specific requests from the MOF who then publishes them. They bind all companies that have to report to the MOF under the Securities and Exchange Law. BADC members tend to have accounting backgrounds so the Principles stress income measurement and shareholder protection rather than asset valuation and creditor protection to a greater extent than the Justice Ministry Code. Publicly listed companies prepare two sets of statements, to comply with the different requirements of the two different ministries. Net income will be the same, fortunately, under both procedures.

Japanese companies rely heavily on debt rather than equity as their principal source of finance, mainly provided by banks. Short term finance largely comprises fixed interest 90 day promissory notes and longer term finance may consist of an informal agreement to roll over these notes for a number of years. Short term debt often finances a substantial proportion of fixed assets (which include intangibles and investments). In many cases banks own a large, even the largest, slice of the firm's shares. Shares tend to be held on a long term basis, and this, together with the importance of the banks, means there is less focus on short term earnings information than in Anglo countries, (i.e. countries whose accounting has been influenced by the UK or the USA) (Campbell 1985 p. 8).

> The banks have direct access to their clients' accounting information, and so have relatively little influence on external financial reporting.

Indeed it might be argued that the banks have an interest in minimizing such disclosure, thereby preserving information asymmetry in their favour.

The Commercial Code requires companies to transfer an amount equal to at least 10 per cent of their declared dividends to a legal reserve until the reserve reaches 25 per cent of the capital stock account. This resembles but exceeds French and German legal reserves, and it may not be distributed but may be capitalized. This is to protect creditors from the possibility of a profligate dividend policy.

Ministry of Justice staff, who are responsible for administering the Commercial Code, tend to be trained in the law rather than in accountancy. Consequently, as in Germany, the protection of creditors assumes as much importance as the protection of shareholders, reflecting 'the apparent belief of the legal profession' (Campbell 1985 p. 155) that this is the proper state of affairs.

There is no requirement to publish a funds flow statement but extensive cash flow information is obligated in the non-financial supplementary schedules filed with the MOF. The statement makes no attempt to provide a link between the annual profit and the changes in liquid funds. Instead it provides a summarized quarterly receipts and payments account (Campbell 1985 p. 167). In 1978 JICPA's Committee on the Financial Reporting System recommended that an SCFP be produced as did study groups of the Japan Accounting Association in 1985 and 1986. About 20 per cent of Japanese companies provide SCFPs in the English versions of their accounts. Only three IASs had been accepted in Japan by mid–1987: no. 1 on disclosure, no. 3 on consolidations and no. 10 on post balance sheet events (Kozuma 1987).

Investment advice as a profession only arrived in Japan in 1965 and is still far more reliant on institutions than individuals for its customer base (JICPA 1987 p. 18).

Japanese auditors work much more closely with their clients while still preserving their independence, but the biggest difference from the West is in the numbers of accountants: only 8,579 in Japan compared with nearly a quarter of a million in the USA. 'The problem is that the profession had to start from scratch with the CPA law of 1948 and the tough set of examinations has had a failure rate in excess of 92 per cent' (Holloway 1989 p. 75). These are not circumstances supportive of extensive accounting rule making and policing.

The problem is that there is no pressure for greater corporate disclosure in Japan. Outside shareholders are simply not interested in that kind of information. It is the Ministry of Finance which is entirely responsible for pushing companies to cough up more financial information. . . . Since Japanese accountants already have more business than they can handle, the drive for greater disclosure will have to come from the MOF – or from overseas.

(Holloway 1989 p. 75)

Table 1.2 Comparative ratios

Ratio	USA	Japan
Current	1.9	1.2
Quick	1.1	0.8
Debt:equity	0.5	0.8
Interest cover	6.5	1.6
Return on net worth	0.14	0.07

The effects of US–Japan accounting differences exaggerate the real underlying economic differences, as shown in the comparative ratios in Table 1.2 taken from Choi (1980).

The higher debt:equity and lower liquidity in Japan is sustainable where banks are major providers of finance and are closely related to their customers.

Large Japanese MNCs prepare English language versions of their accounts. These generally have to comply with the regulations of the stock exchange on which the shares are listed, which means that English language Japanese accounts reflect Anglo-American GAAP rather than normal Japanese practice.

China

Chinese accounting received its first state backing during the Ming Dynasty, more specifically 1408, when Emperor Yung Lo ordered merchants to keep proper books for tax purposes and to prevent fraud. Government officials were apparently reviewed monthly. The minimum disclosure requirements were: name, tradename and nationality of ships, credentials and quantity of merchandise (Jong 1976). Thus, right from the start, accounting was to the Chinese a burden imposed by a dictatorial state rather than, as in Venice, an organic outgrowth of trading and management practice.

Popular command of literacy and numeracy was sufficiently diffused by the nineteenth century to enable most urban shop apprentices and an indeterminate minority of peasants to keep accounts (Rawski 1979).

> Lacking numerical place notation and relying on the abacus as a computing crutch, the Chinese failed to create a double entry system of book-keeping. Lacking a separation between household and business activities, their so called 'closed' family firms rendered 'accountability' unnecessary.

> (Weber 1961)

However Western double entry bookkeeping was introduced in 1875 under Emperor Kwang Hsu. Even then, transactions were not logged in chronological order but grouped at random before being posted to ledgers which were never reconciled. One book, the Hung Chang, served as a master ledger which yielded an annual trial balance but that did not in turn yield final accounts (Jong 1976).

Chan (1977) contrasted the pioneering role of the banks in fostering Anglo-American accounting procedures with the reluctance of pre-republican Chinese merchants to accept dividends below 7–10 per cent on equity which made equity scarcely distinguishable from loans.

In addition to internationally accepted accounting principles, PRC accountants apply other unique principles including: the principle of control by the masses and the principle of indicating specific funds for specific purposes (Zhou 1988). Joint ventures prepare one set of accounts for the capitalist investors and one for the PRC Ministries, neither conforming necessarily or consistently to any particular GAAP (Yam 1986).

In Hong Kong, accounting closely follows British practice, but as we shall reconfirm in Chapter 5, the cultural underpinnings of accounting in the territory are nothing like the British. The result of the mismatch is a relatively low threshold of accounting information overload, as we shall see in Chapter 9.

CONCLUSIONS

This book is about funds flow statements and cash flow statements. It is concerned with investigating their kinetic and potential usefulness to users anywhere in the world. If their usefulness is limited and if there is a large gap between kinetic and potential usefulness, then this book will consider the main reasons why.

In this first chapter we have considered some important contextual issues. Historically we have seen that although accounting is older than writing itself, modern accounting reports are inventions of the industrial revolution. Accounting theory has followed and largely resulted from accounting practice, until the recent past when academic opinion led some professional accounting bodies to adopt inflation accounting. This was not altogether a happy experience and it remains the case today that accounting academics only rarely have a direct influence on accounting standards and practices. The replacement of funds flow statements by cash flow statements is a rare example of just such an influence; for there is little doubt that the major agent of the change was the University of Washington's Professor of Accounting Loyd C. Heath, as is illuminated in Chapter 4.

We have introduced the concept of usefulness in an accounting context, differentiating between actual use, which we call kinetic usefulness, and the use that could be made by a trained reader, which we call potential usefulness. The term information content is widely used in the literature to mean kinetic usefulness, but it tends to have a restricted meaning of kinetic usefulness to equity investors, and we explore this in some depth in Chapter 2. Usefulness of published accounts to actual and prospective loan creditors is reviewed in Chapter 3 where we will see that studies of individual creditors are the norm as opposed to the mass market studies in Chapter 2. In this chapter we review the usual tools of accounts analysis and in Chapter 3 we will see if these are the tools loan creditors actually use.

We have introduced in this first chapter the difficulties of accounts appraisal across national boundaries, because such difficulties present barriers to the translation of potential usefulness into kinetic usefulness. We shall see in Chapter 4 how the funds statement developed in the USA, in Chapter 5 how it spread round most of the world and in Chapter 6 how and where it has been replaced by the cash flow statement. In Chapter 7 we review some real life statements to experience for ourselves the difficulties of reading other countries' accounts, even after translation into English. We will then be in a position to assess for ourselves the potential usefulness of funds statements and cash flow statements. It is expected that most readers will be aware of a considerable gap between the potential and kinetic usefulness of the statements.

Chapter 8 considers the arguments of full cash flow accounting advocates who feel that cash flow statements do not go nearly far enough in the direction of cash baseness to be useful. We consider if the hyperinflationary economies' accounting practices offer any insights into those arguments.

Chapter 9 discusses whether information overload is a plausible explanation of any part of the gap between the potential and kinetic usefulness of funds statements and cash flow statements. After all, if the problem lies in insufficient training in accounts analysis, then we should see clear symptoms of information overload on the part of their users.

Chapter 10 concludes the book with a review of what we have discovered, a discussion of the usefulness of the statements in the light of our discoveries and a set of tasks to be done in future by those who would like to increase the kinetic usefulness of the statements. By then we will have touched most of the bases in modern international accounting literature and thought.

2 Information content of company accounts to investors

INTRODUCTION

R. S. Kaplan once began a conference presentation on the subject of the information content of accounts with these words (Kaplan 1978):

> When I was first asked to do a paper surveying empirical research in accounting, I found it difficult to believe the world needed yet another survey on this topic. I sometimes think there are more surveys on empirical research than there are papers to be surveyed.

Fifteen years after Kaplan said those words they still seem timely. This is especially so for empirical work on equity market responses to accounting reports in the USA. To Kaplan's (1978) list featuring Gonedes and Dopuch (1974), Beaver (1972), Hakansson (1973) and Lev (1974) can be added Lev and Ohlson (1982 p. 261) who conclude their survey with the assertion that earnings have been shown to have information content robustly 'across statistical methodologies, time periods, and stock exchanges in which shares are traded'.

The thrust of all these studies is that the US market is efficient in the semi-strong form, so that the study of accounts will not enable an investor to maintain investment profits beyond the market average. Even in the USA there has been some evidence challenging this by now conventional wisdom (Black 1973, Jaffe 1974, Downes and Dyckman, 1973) but not enough to subvert it until the very recent work of Fama (1991) and others which is described later in the chapter.

In this chapter, the main studies of stock market efficiency and information content of equity-oriented accounts are reviewed. The rationale for the review is that the term 'information content' is embedded in such studies and the 'usefulness', especially the kinetic usefulness, of any accounting report has usually been operationalized to mean 'information content'. The chapter contrasts the American semi-strong stock market context with weaker overseas markets. It discusses the consequences of market inefficiency for accounts information content, and concludes with a critical review of recent work on this topic. The main thrust of this chapter is that it is necessary to establish that accounts in general have kinetic or potential information content before it is meaningful to consider the more particular question of whether funds statements have such content. The question of how far any information content ascribable to equity readers of accounts is also ascribable to creditor readers will be considered in Chapter 3.

INFORMATIONAL EFFICIENCY

The most authoritative definitions of stock market efficiency at its three different levels could well be those given by Fama in his 1970 paper which has become the most cited paper in the literature on the efficient markets hypothesis. An efficient market is one

> in which prices always fully reflect all available information . . .
>
> First, weak form tests, in which the information set is just historical prices. . . . Then semi strong form tests, in which the concern is whether prices efficiently adjust to other information that is obviously publicly available (e.g., announcements of annual earnings, stock splits, etc.). . . . Finally, strong form tests concerned with whether given investors or groups have monopolistic access to any information relevant for price formation. . . . We shall conclude that, with but a few exceptions, the efficient markets model stands up well.
>
> (Fama 1970)

Tests of market efficiency are relevant to the general question of whether or not accounts have information content. In a fully efficient market in the strong form, accounts should confirm *ex post* the anticipatory movements of the disseminating firm's stock price. In semi-strong form markets, accounts should not only do that but also prompt further price movement, as some investors will view the accounts as relevant new information while others will use the accounting numbers to adjust their previous expectations of the firm's prospects. In a weak form efficient market and in an inefficient market, accounts constitute new information to all except insiders and prices will react strongly (but not necessarily quickly) to information within the accounts. However, it is possible for a market to be efficient in any form while the accounts it receives are devoid of information content. In such a case the release of new accounts will be largely ignored by the stock market. This implies that tests of accounting information content are valid only if market efficiency has already been demonstrated by some means other than reactivity to accounts. Conversely, tests of market efficiency using accounts are really testing a joint hypothesis both that the market is efficient and that the accounts have information content. As Boatsman (1977) put it, 'the EMH is virtually a tautology and hence nearly irrefutable'.

Gonedes (1974) replicated the Ball and Brown (1968) (hereafter BB) study using a set of financial ratios together with earnings per share (EPS) to form the proxy for market expectations. He found that EPS alone captured nearly all of the information content of those accounting numbers in his set.

Patell (1976) replicated BB on a set of firms for which he had management's estimate of earnings for the coming year. The improvement these figures provided over the BB proxy for expectations was only slight, in terms of the actual earnings level itself and also in terms of basing a trading strategy on actual rather than proxy expectations. However, he also found, as had Beaver (1974) and Niederhofer and Regan (1972) before him, that the magnitude of forecast error was almost as important as the direction of the error in explaining abnormal performance.

Collins (1975) found that the 1970 SEC requirement for sales and profit reporting by product line segment was beneficial to investors in firms that had not previously volunteered such information. Segment-based trading strategies were also more profitable than consolidation-based ones. Thus it appeared that the new disclosures possessed incremental information content.

With regard to the information content of the earnings announcement itself, Beaver (1968) found that the stock price change variance was 70 per cent higher, and the stock trading volume 30 per cent higher, in the week of the announcement than at other times of the year. This suggests that the public announcement itself has significant information content even with semi-strong efficiency. The Beaver findings have found continuing support since their first appearance in 1968. Hagerman (1973), McNichols and Manegold (1982), Morse (1981), Patell and Wolfson (1979) and Bamber (1983) are further confirmations of the importance of earnings announcements on the US market.

Grant (1980) linked the volume of information signals to firm size. The inverse correlation of size with market responsiveness to earnings announcements was supported by the work of Banz (1981), Keim (1983) and Reinganum (1983).

Basu (1977) found low price earnings ratio (P/E) stocks outperformed high P/E ones to some extent, but did so with a slowness not consistent with semi-strong efficiency.

Jaffe *et al.* (1989) reviewed the studies by Banz, Basu and Reinganum just cited for their contrasting impressions of whether the P/E subsumed size or vice versa, a confusion which they attributed to the relatively short time periods and the failure to segregate January effects in the previous studies. Their study of movements for all months from 1951 to 1986 (with January segregated) showed inconsistencies with the previous studies just cited. It was, however, consistent with the previously published results of Cook and Rozeff (1984) who found stock returns jointly related both to P/E and to size. However, Jaffe *et al.* (1989) found this joint determination was strong only for January whilst the other months show only P/E to be of any significance.

Harrison (1977) found accounting changes of form rather than substance did have significant positive price responses, in contrast to the conclusions of Gonedes and Dopuch (1974 p. 91) and of Kaplan (1978 p. 314), both of which were based quite heavily on the empirical work of Sunder (1973). Stewart Brown (1978 p. 27) found abnormal returns associated with forecast errors to such an extent and with such a long time lag (almost 45 days) that he felt able to conclude as follows:

> The excess returns from purchasing the qualifying securities at the time of publication of the EPS number substantially exceed transaction costs. The adjustment process, rather than being instantaneous, is rather lengthy. Thus, with respect to this particular sample [of 158 firms] of securities, the market exhibited inefficiencies.

Although studies such as Ou (1984) could be seen as confirming Brown's findings, other studies such as Lee (1987) found transaction costs to exceed gains from fundamental analysis.

Functional fixation has been advanced as a plausible explanation of why some studies such as Harrison (1977), Kaplan (1978) and Brown (1978) described above find cosmetic accounting to be effective in raising stock-market returns. Abdel-Khalik's small sample study of analysts (Abdel-Khalik and Keller 1979) illustrates this. The analysts understood the FIFO and LIFO effects on profits and cash flow but disregarded their own understanding in reacting to the earnings number results of the inventory valuation policy. They were fixated on earnings as such.

ACCOUNTING AND SYSTEMATIC RISK

The dominant paradigm in finance since the late 1960s has been the capital asset pricing model co-invented by Sharpe (1964), Lintner (1965) and Mossin (1966). It supplies the measure of 'accuracy' in the efficient market hypothesis tests. Efficient markets translate new data into trading decisions both quickly and accurately. In the model (hereafter abbreviated to CAPM) higher returns are earned by securities with higher systematic risk, also called higher beta. Defining an accounting beta to be the correlation of the firm's net income with a market index of earnings, Beaver, *et al.* (1970) found it and other accounting-based risk measures to show significant correlation with the market model risk measures including, but not confined to, beta. Accounting beta also seemed to predict future market beta better than the usual beta stationarity assumption did. Assuming the CAPM's beta is a reliable and valid explicator of the rates of return on shares, this result suggests that accounting numbers are associated with investors' information sets. In other words, accounting is relevant to investors' trading decisions in practice as well as in theory.

However, Gonedes (1973) found no such strong association and attributed the association reported in the previous paragraph to those researchers' use of market price to scale the accounting numbers, which introduces a spurious correlation of accounting numbers with market numbers. Brenner (1977) in his thesis argued that Gonedes had mis-specified beta and that all previous work on the accounting predictability of systematic risk was flawed by mis-specification.

Beaver and Manegold (1975) responded to Gonedes's implied challenge by applying a range of different specifications for both accounting and market betas. Again they found significant correlations between the two betas, especially at the portfolio level where measurement errors of firm accounting beta would largely average out. This result still applied when non-market measures were used to scale the accounting numbers.

Gonedes (1975) recast his earlier study with a different index of market earnings, and this time he too found a significant correlation of accounting with market beta estimates although not such a large correlation as Beaver and Manegold had found.

Hammad (1983) found no significant improvement in ability to predict market beta arose from replacing earnings by cash flow.

Collins and Simmonds (1989) found events specific to the firm led to changes in the risk measures specific to the firm.

At this point it might be appropriate to sound a cautionary note. The last four studies mentioned show that accounting numbers can generate useful estimators of a share's systematic risk. That is very far indeed from claiming that investors do in fact use accounting numbers for such a purpose.

Brown and Kennelly (1972) applied the BB approach to quarterly earnings announcements and found that they possessed incremental information content to the extent of improving by 30–40 per cent EPS's ability to predict stock price changes. Beaver (1974), May (1971) and Kiger (1972) confirmed that interim earnings announcements did display incremental information content.

Since studies such as those already mentioned suggest that accounting is relevant to stock price, and since studies of market movements from Bachelier (1900) to Fama (1970) and beyond suggest a virtually random movement in stock prices irrespective of time lag, then this raises the possibility that earnings themselves follow a random walk over time. Studies by Lintner and Glaubner (1972), Brealey (1969) and Ball and Watts (1972) all found that earnings time series patterns could indeed be approximated by a random walk, since such serial correlation as did exist was extremely small.

THE INFORMATION CONTENT OF ACCOUNTING CHANGES

The next question addressed is whether investors in the semi-strong efficient market find accounting reports to have so much information content that they can be fooled into raising P/E by accounting cosmetics. Even as firm a believer in the efficient market hypothesis as Keane felt constrained to point out that the assumption of market efficiency yields 'only limited scope for deciding what information is most useful' (Keane 1983 p. 141). Chambers went rather further:

The EMH entails that stock prices adjust rapidly to new information as it becomes available. But it says nothing about the quality of that information.

(Chambers 1974)

Efficiency is thus no guarantee that purely cosmetic data will *per se* be regarded as useless.

While writers such as Ball (1972) have found that merely cosmetic accounting changes failed to elicit share price changes, some (Patz and Boatsman 1972, Jacobs and Kaplan 1975, Hong *et al*. 1978, Abdel-Khalik and McKeown 1978, Arbel and Jaggi 1978, Beaver *et al*. 1980, Freeman 1981, Ro 1981) found that *even substantive accounting changes also failed to elicit share price changes*. Still other writers found that the share price effects of accounting changes were strictly mediated by any cash flow effects (usually arising from tax burden changes) (Beaver and Dukes 1972, Kaplan and Roll 1972, Sunder 1973, 1975).

THE CONTRIBUTION OF AGENCY MODELS

The motivation of firms to attempt to use form to conceal substance has been addressed by the agency theory literature. In essence, agency theory posits that the directors of a company are agents for its shareholders who will only act in the interests of the shareholders if agency costs such as monitoring (audit) and bonding (pay, perks and share options) are incurred. Their incurrence in turn creates the so-called 'moral hazard' that the very existence of the 'insurance' provided by monitoring will make it more likely that directors will act in their own interests rather than the shareholders'. As for accounting, agency theory supposes directors wish to disclose as little as possible to their principals who therefore must incur agency costs to ensure they receive the information they need. Also it is supposed that directors will prefer disclosures to be 'noisy' which means there will be a lot of words, numbers and pictures but they will not contain much of real value to the reader. Ng (1978) found risk averse managers preferred greater noise in the reports they gave out than owners would like. This noise was thought by Choi (1985) to increase the variability investors attribute to the firm's performance. This is consonant with the belief that managers have an incentive to manipulate their reported performance as reflected in the earnings number so as to maximize their own subjective expected utilities, as proposed by Gordon (1964), Williamson (1967) and Watts (1977), *inter alia*. Smith (1976) found manipulative income smoothing in his 110 firm sample for the period 1954–62 to be significantly higher for manager-controlled firms than for owner-controlled ones. Other studies which are reviewed in Ronen *et al.* (1977) indicated that most income smoothing attempts fail to convince the stock market. Salamon and Smith (1979) found the number of accounting changes to be inversely associated with stock price performance for manager-controlled firms but not for owner-controlled ones. They also found support in their results for the view that investors perceive earnings reports of manager-controlled firms to be noisier than those of owner-controlled firms. Choi confirmed all of these discriminants between owner- and manager-controlled firms, and did not find firm size as such to be important.

Foster (1981) showed that the earnings release of one firm significantly impacts the stock prices of other firms in the same industry. Such information transfer is most pronounced for the larger earners in the same line of business as the reporting firm.

Reviewing from an agency theory perspective the entire work to date on the impact of new accounting regulations, Chow (1983) concluded that new regulations had a weak and inconsistent tendency to transfer wealth from equity holders to bondholders. This tendency was considerably stronger for firms carrying restrictive debt covenants.

EFFICIENCY OUTSIDE THE USA: PROPOSITIONS

Most of the studies of stock markets outside the USA point in a common direction: statistical tests of the efficient market hypothesis have not supported efficiency in most non-US markets.

Many non-US markets can be characterized as thin. Trading volumes are small and frequently discontinuous. Exchanges are less elaborately organized technically; information flows are slower; accounting requirements are formally less stringent, causing poorer disclosure processes. Privileged information channels exist along with shares which are poorly marketable because little is known of them by active traders. The net result of thinness is that only a small number of shares may be bought or sold before a price change occurs. Thinness can contribute to return variances by reducing liquidity and by causing a clientele effect for various stocks (Cohen *et al.* 1976).

Wai and Patrick (1973 p. 271) found that the average number of exchange members in a less developed country was 128 as opposed to 404 in fully developed countries. The average number of listed companies was 172 in less developed countries and 644 in fully developed countries. The market value of listed shares was one-seventh of the gross national product or one-half the primary money supply in less developed countries as opposed to equalling the gross national product or being twice the primary money supply in fully developed countries. The small size of most security markets makes them susceptible to legal and political factors because governments are often dominant market participants, and to manipulation and speculation because of the monopolistic powers of various financiers.

Both governments and financiers are able to limit the operations of security markets especially easily when the necessary conditions for efficiency are not fully met. These conditions are a culture with an investment psychology, a monetized economy for savings, a large supply of securities and new issues, a pool of buyers and sellers willing to deal, and a network of supportive monetary and financial institutions (Arowolo 1971).

The results of organic, institutional, technological, structural and expedient deficiencies are market imperfections. Transaction costs are high and liquidity problems are manifest. There is an over-whelming lack of public information so that the cost of accurate information is inordinately high. Limited regulation is matched with inadequate accounting standards. Investors are discouraged by the lack of tax incentives for security investments and by the general uncertainty about future events. Finally, of importance to the efficient market hypothesis type of testing is the presence of techni-cally deficient market indices and of interest rates pegged below equilibrium levels (Maniatis 1971).

In the next section, evidence concerning the efficiency of stock markets outside the USA is reviewed.

EFFICIENCY OUTSIDE THE USA: EVIDENCE

General

A fairly recent study compared the informational efficiency from 1971 to 1984 of the US, Canadian, Japanese and UK stock markets in anticipating rather than following the announced movement of measures of real macroeconomic activity. The USA was the most efficient in this sense, but Canada and Japan were also leaders rather than followers. The UK was an inefficient follower (Kamarotou and O'Hanlon 1989).

In a survey of three European countries plus Japan, the USA

and the UK, Barrett (1976) found disclosure levels to be positively and significantly associated with market efficiency.

Australasia

Australian studies show small inefficiencies but in no case do they pass Keane's (1983) exploitability test beyond the end of a single trading day (Praetz 1969, Officer 1975, Ball 1978, Ball *et al.* 1978, Brown and Hancock 1977). A comment by Brown (1970) is borne out by the later Australian studies of accounts usefulness in generating superprofits:

> There appears to be no point to waiting until the audited details of profits are published . . . because by then all adjustments have been made and it is too late.

> (Brown 1970 p. 282)

Finn (1982) makes the interesting observation that although, in general, security analysts' forecasts do not enable superprofits to be made, this improves significantly when a forecast is revised in the wake of a company visit by the analyst – such a visit presumably generates inside information of a price sensitive nature.

Emanuel (1989) provides recent New Zealand evidence that asset revaluations for current cost accounting purposes do not produce significant share price revisions. He had previously shown that the time series movement of New Zealand earnings numbers is consistent with a random walk (Caird and Emanuel 1981).

UK

In the UK, semi-strong efficiency was evidenced in the work of Brealey (1970), Firth (1974, 1976), Fitzgerald (1974) and Marsh (1977). Maingot (1984) found that earnings announcements produced sharp price responses with some anticipatory reaction in the week preceding announcement.

One of the most interesting studies on the impact and use of accounting data in the stock market, which looked at the share recommendations from 35 British brokerage firms, was by Fitzgerald (1975). He found large positive returns on day 32, when returns on brokerage house share recommendations could first be realized. This is not consistent with semi-strong form efficiency because it suggests that the information in brokerage house recommendations was not immediately reflected in share prices. It indicated that high research activity in the British stock markets can succeed in generating returns which significantly outperform the market in the short run.

Europe

Pogue and Solnik (1974) used the difference in average betas for daily and monthly returns to measure the importance of adjustment lags. The USA had almost no lags; Belgium and Switzerland had very large lags; while Germany, the Netherlands, Italy, France and the UK had smaller lags. They further noted that the data from the UK and Italy exhibit such interperiod correlations of alphas that it would be possible to earn subperiod portfolio returns greater than the market price of risk by selecting stocks whose alphas have significant statistics in the price period. Pogue and Solnik (1974) considered that semi-strong form inefficiencies exist in European stock markets either because of thin trading or because of slow information absorption.

Studies of the capital markets in France (McDonald 1973), Germany (Modigliani *et al.* 1972) and Spain (Palacios 1975) found substantial evidence of inefficiency.

Canada, South Africa and Japan

In contrast, the market model appeared to be useful as early as two decades ago in forming portfolios from securities traded on the Tokyo Stock Exchange (Lau *et al.* 1974). Portfolio alphas were close to zero and the ranking of the portfolios corresponded to their prior period betas (Pinches 1974).

The Deakin *et al.* (1974) study of the Tokyo Stock Exchange found significant volume effects from the release of the firms' tax data but no price effects.

Deakin and Smith (1978) tested for price effects on the Johannesburg and Toronto Stock Exchanges. Only the Johannesburg stocks showed abnormal price changes in the week of the annual earnings announcement. Toronto stocks were devoid of any unusual changes in any week, and the Johannesburg stocks showed neither anticipation of nor adjustment to the annual earnings number except in the week of release. Fowler *et al.* (1977) reported that Canadian insiders make abnormal profits when dealing in frequently traded securities. Belkaoui (1978) and Drury (1979) offer limited and somewhat massaged evidence in favour of the opposite view: that the Toronto market has no exploitable weak form inefficiencies.

Using the methodology of Fama and MacBeth (1973), Bark (1991) conducted an examination of whether the capital asset pricing model (CAPM) is applicable to the Korean stock market, which is small and relatively underdeveloped in comparison with the US and other advanced nation stock markets. Empirical findings indicate that the Sharpe-Lintner-Mossin CAPM paradigm is not adequate in the Korean stock market. First, the critical condition of the CAPM, a positive trade-off between market risk and return, is rejected. Second, it is found that the residual risk played an important role in pricing risky assets. The inadequacy of the CAPM in the Korean stock market may be attributed to market inefficiency and the highly undiversified portfolios held by the Korean investors.

Hong Kong

Few studies have been undertaken of the efficiency of the Hong Kong stock markets. Wan (1980b) had earlier tested the weak form efficiency of the Hong Kong stock market using monthly prices of 32 index shares for the period January 1970 to December 1972. Later, Law (1982) used the daily closing prices of 56 shares to test the weak form efficiency of the Hong Kong stock market during the period September 1979 to November 1979. Out of 56 stock prices 32 were found to behave non-randomly, and 13 out of the 32 were constituent stocks of the Hang Seng Index. He attributed the absence of randomness to the small size of the stock market, and the fact that only some 20 stocks could be said to have permanently active markets. It is interesting to note that the market was found by Law and Au Yeung (1983) to behave as if it were semi-strong form efficient in its treatment of takeover price announcements. Finally, quite marked effects of interest rate announcements on different stock indices during 1 January 1979 to 31 December 1981 were found by Mui and Law (1983).

Insider trading was evident in the price movements of 11 Hong Kong firms involved in takeovers in 1980 (Law and Au Yeung 1983).

A total of 24 Hong Kong blue chip companies were studied for the years 1986 through 1988 by Li (1990). He found that in Hong Kong prices anticipate profit announcements by 12 to 14 days and steady the day after the announcement, unless the profits have fallen, in which case the price dropped for some time. This suggests good news is more likely to be leaked than bad news through oral networks.

Ang and Pohlman (1978) found serial correlation for bi-weekly price changes in 1967–74. Wong and Kwong (1984), testing 28 major stocks for 1977–1980 by serial correlation and runs tests, could not support the view that the stock market was efficient in the weak form, despite its being the fifth largest in the world by turnover in the period. Dawson (1982) thought he found semi-strong form inefficiency in the ability of the recommendations of the largest local stockbroking firm to outperform the market.

Law (1982) chose 80 per cent by value of all the stocks traded on the Far Eastern Stock Exchange throughout 1978 and 1979 in three-month blocks of daily price changes for weak form testing by runs, serial correlation and regression tests of the market. He found that 52 per cent of the market moved non-randomly, that is, 32 out of the 56 sampled stocks including all the Hang Seng Index constituents and all the property stocks – possibly as a result of manipulation by large operators. Utilities (all regulated by the government's Scheme of Control) moved randomly.

For the period September 1985 to August 1986 5 out of 14 of the most active stocks moved non-randomly, as did 4 out of 10 of the middle active and 7 out of 9 of the least active (Chan *et al.* 1989). Unification of the four old stock exchanges into one new one in April 1986 did not cause any obvious inflection or break in the patterns of serial correlation. Runs tests showed comparable results. The results of the Chan *et al.* (1989) study show that, although the most active sectors approach weak form efficiency, the normal behaviour of the Hong Kong stock market cannot be considered as efficient in the weak form, especially for those securities with a low volume of transactions. The random behaviour of the stock prices appears to apply only to a few securities. Consequently, it seems that traditional technical analysis and fundamental analysis will assist short term investment decision making in Hong Kong, and permit the earning of excess returns (Chan *et al.* 1989).

Previous research done on the betas of Hong Kong securities questioned their stationarity (Wan 1980b, Ip 1982). Some 62 per cent of the betas of the 37 (the most active) stocks studied by Mok *et al.* (1990) for the whole of the 1980s showed non-stationarity. Market risk explained and constituted 60 per cent of overall stock risk. There was a significant effect on industry. The implication is that tests of the capital asset pricing model in Hong Kong would have to deal with error terms possibly large enough to render the tests useless. It follows that efficiency tests will be biased towards an excessive focus on the speed of price adjustments to new information, rather than on the 'accuracy' of such adjustment in asset pricing model terms.

The average annual rise in the Hang Seng Index of 17 per cent from January 1976 to December 1985 was comparable with the average annual growth in GDP of 20.4 per cent nominal and 10.4 per cent real. The P/Es for the sample of 32 of the most actively traded local companies examined by Whitman (1990) varied little over the period from a cross-sectional mean of 15. Dividend yields varied little from a 4 per cent mean. Average returns on equity as per the published accounts were 25.01 per cent compared with returns on the market after accounting for rights, dividends and scrip of 24.91 per cent. This seems to show that returns based on stock market measures and returns based on accounts were measuring the same phenomenon. However, the accounting return showed a 14 per cent standard deviation compared with the market's 9 per cent, and the correlation coefficient between the two sets of annual numbers was only 0.087 with no significance at the 1 per cent level. The coincidence of sequence means was just coincidence.

Whitman (1990) interpreted his findings as suggesting that the information content of Hong Kong accounts for Hong Kong equity investors was not very high.

In conclusion, it can be seen that the Hong Kong stock market combines great activity with great volatility. As an inefficient market, it attracts speculative interest-chasing arbitrage profits from time to time. It is comparatively under-regulated in international terms, and many believe such under-regulation helps explain its level of energetic activity. Earnings announcements are anticipated by insiders and such anomalies as Monday effects are consistently perceptible. In these circumstances, accounts constitute information with potential usefulness in obtaining capital gains beyond the market average, especially if the accounts reader is an insider. The information content of true and fair accounts, therefore, is potentially great, for the market is too inefficient to have fully discounted such information before its release. This makes such second division stock markets as Hong Kong especially suitable for testing the information content of accounts.

If any aspect of accounts has information content, sophisticated analysts in such places as Hong Kong will be rather likely to register the fact. They would do this to make superprofits arising from the combination of their insider status, the inefficiency of the market and the *eventual* price sensitivity of the accounts data they were considering. In Chapter 3 the way in which analysts, bankers and investors process their information sets is considered.

RECENT DEVELOPMENTS IN EFFICIENT MARKET STUDIES

The famous historian Lord Acton said of the Holy Roman Empire that it was neither holy nor Roman nor an empire. Similarly even the US stock markets are not strongly efficient; other markets are too thin to be considered markets at all and the hypothesis of efficient behaviour in such markets is disconfirmed. In recent years, even the USA's efficiency has been under question, as reviewed in the subsequent paragraphs.

Syed *et al.* (1989) examined whether trading strategies inspired by the 'Heard on the Street' (HTS) column of the *Wall Street Journal* could generate abnormal returns. The effect of the HTS column on stock prices was examined using the widely used event study methodology originally used by Fama, *et al.* (1969). The findings clearly support the hypothesis that, in the identified cases in which the HTS information was leaked in advance, the publication of the column had a significant effect on stock prices on the day of publication. If advance information about the forthcoming HTS could have been obtained, then considerable two-day abnormal returns could have been achieved. The findings are *not* consistent with market inefficiency in the strong form.

Fama (1990) showed that 58 per cent of the variance of stock returns from 1953 to 1987 on the New York Stock Exchange could be explained by time-varying returns and by growth rates of real production which alone accounted for 43 per cent of the return variance. The implication is that the stock market captured the real economic performance of its firms. This conclusion was reinforced by Schwert (1990) using an additional 65 years of data.

LeRoy (1990) claims that the statistical evidence that has accumulated since Fama's (1970) survey has raised questions about his conclusion that capital markets are efficient. Stock price volatility has been shown to exceed the volatility consistent with capital market efficiency. Other evidence, such as the small-firm effect and the January effect, points in a similar direction. Analysts have found it difficult to explain stock prices, even after the fact, using realized values of variables that should account for stock price changes.

Fama (1991) reviewed the efficient markets literature and confirmed that: (a) the joint hypothesis problem would mean that precise measures of market efficiency would remain impossible, and (b) no significant evidence has been put forward that inside information is not helpful in earning abnormal returns.

So far, the hypothesis of at least semi-strong efficiency, at least in the USA, is not defeated; but efficiency consists not only of speedy translation of news into buy/sell/hold decisions but also of accurate translation thereof. We have noted that 'accuracy' tends to be proxied by the returns to systematic (beta) risk as sanctified by the capital asset pricing model (CAPM). Both the Roll (1977) critique of the inherent unverifiability of the model and Ross's (1976) postulation of the arbitrage pricing theory as an alternative which is more abstract and more general failed to shake the hold of CAPM's postulates in the efficient markets research literature.

Dreman (1992) reports the astonishing conclusion of Fama and French (1992) that there is no link between risk and long term performance. The beta model takes a number of inputs that seemed to correlate with volatility in the past and states that they will work again in the future. However, the fact that some variables moved in step with volatility for a number of years does not mean that they initiated it. Fama and French indicate that low price-to-book is one measure that produces above-average returns over time. Other criteria are adequate diversification, reasonable debt-to-capital structure, higher-than-market earnings, and the growth of dividends over time. American stock issues that meet these criteria include IMC Fertilizer, Monsanto, and Upjohn Inc.

According to Fama and French, high beta stocks produce no greater returns on average than low beta stocks. Over the long term, value stocks *should* outperform growth stocks and small stocks should outperform large stocks. The data further show that historical *beta*, long accepted in investment management circles as a key measure of the risk of a stock or a portfolio, *has no predictive ability in terms of investment returns*.

The importance of the new study by Fama and French (1992) cannot easily be exaggerated. It means that for some 25 years, academics and market traders have been attributing importance to a construct, beta, that turns out to be devoid not only of 'stationarity' (i.e. reliability and consistency) but also of empirically grounded validity. This raises serious questions about the rationality of stock markets; and no sooner are they raised than along comes a brand new model to address them. It is called the 'Coherent Market

Hypothesis' and was introduced by Vaga (1990). It is outlined in the next paragraph.

The 'Theory of Social Imitation' was invented by Wolfgang Weidlich in Stuttgart to describe the intense polarization of opinions in social groups such as those that arose in the French student riots of 1968. The theory was developed by Earl Callen and Don Shapero using the idea of ferromagnetism. When the temperature of an iron bar falls below a critical point, the magnetic interaction between adjacent molecules becomes stronger than random so that clusters form which draw in surrounding molecules to form a high degree of order. Callen and Shapero suggest people are like molecules in a bar of iron, in that under some conditions individuals act independently but under others they become polarized and subject to 'groupthink'. Recovery is slow and individual from such states of coherence. Transitions from disorder to order tend to share the same macroscopic characteristics in most kinds of systems. Market returns may fluctuate randomly around zero as with a heated iron bar, or exhibit a high degree of polarization as in subcritical temperatures. The stock market equivalent of temperature is sentiment coherence. Below a critical threshold, random walk pertains. Above it, coherent bull or bear markets form but if the fundamentals are mixed, chaotic markets occur. In coherent markets the expected return is over double the standard deviation – a quantitative symptom of a coherent market. The random walk phase tends to display a widening of the probability distribution of returns around normality; but towards the end of the phase bias enters so that moves in one direction become more likely than in the other. As sentiment coherence goes above its critical level, extreme instability exists with very high volatility relative to the returns. Coherent bull markets occur when cash reserves are unusually high and coherence is supercritical with coherent bear markets. Coherent markets provide the best profit opportunities.

CONCLUSIONS

In this chapter, the links between the information content of accounts and efficient market tests have been briefly explored. In the USA, stock markets seem to behave at the semi-strong level of efficiency. This means that accounts have information content before they are made public but most of the price sensitive data in them have been exploited by insiders before the public dissemination of the accounts. However, stock markets in the rest of the world are markedly less efficient than in the USA. For example, in Korea and Hong Kong the stock markets largely fail even weak form efficiency tests. This means that studies of quoted companies' accounts would assist the investor to beat the market, and the corollary of this is that accounts have *potential* information content. If that is so, then funds and cash flow statements should also share in that information content, assuming they really are at least potentially useful to investors. However, if investors turn out to disbelieve Hong Kong and Korean accounts, rightly or wrongly, then such information content as accounts do possess would have to be interpreted as, mostly, indirect signalling or announcement effects. That is, the accounts' price effects would have to do more with market interpretation of the message that management was attempting to convey in its annual report than with any simple and direct response to any accounting numbers. Perhaps the earnings announcement and its accounting context in a risk-tolerant milieu like Hong Kong are like the croupier's announcement of which number the roulette ballbearing actually landed on after all the bets are in.

Chapters 4 to 7 will address the issue of the *incremental* information content of funds and cash flow statements. Chapter 3 will consider the kinetic usefulness of accounts in general to loan creditors.

3 Information content of company accounts to lenders

INTRODUCTION

In this chapter, attention is focused on what constitutes the information content of accounts to loan creditors. The previous chapter concerned information content in a stock market context. It was seen that the market commented on information content at an aggregate level, using the language of share price movements. Information content for loan creditors, in contrast, has been largely studied at the small group or individual level. There is no equivalent of share price movements for unsecuritized loans. Most loans are largely bilateral affairs between a company and its banker. Even with syndicated loans and traded debt instruments, it is the bilateral relationship between the borrower and the leading bank in the issue (or placement) that materially determines the terms and capital costs of the loan. Information content in this situation has been studied by consideration of how bankers process information in considering a loan application. Bankers, indeed, have been among the most frequently used subjects in the human information processing experiments reported in the accounting literature. This chapter reviews the two principal models in that literature, the lens model and protocol analysis. It then summarizes the major empirical tests of these models that have been conducted in the banking, finance and accounting fields. One particular aspect of human information processing, information load, is so germane to this study that it merits its own chapter, Chapter 9. The present chapter opens with a brief discussion of the comparisons made in the empirical literature of lenders' and investors' information needs, and then moves on to its main information processing focus.

ABSENCE OF AN EFFICIENT MARKET FOR LENDERS

An efficient market is one where new information is immediately and appropriately translated into trading decisions to buy, sell or not trade. In the capital markets of the world securities are the objects which are traded. Securities include common stock, ordinary shares, preferred stock, preference shares, loan stock, corporate debentures, bonds, and all their derivatives such as options and warrants. What all securities have in common is their transferability. Anyone able to provide evidence of ownership of a security, for example by proffering a share certificate in his/her name, is able to sell it at the prevailing market price through a duly authorized agent. A security is a legal entitlement to dividends or interest while the issuer stays in business. Securities entitling the owner to interest are collectively referred to as bonds. Corporate bonds are often termed debentures in the UK and loan stock in the USA. Every bond holder is by definition a lender to the issuer at the original date of issue. After that, a bondholder selling some of his/her holding puts the buyer on the same footing as a lender to the issuer. A buyer of bonds in the capital market or by private contract becomes a lender to the original issuer as if s/he were the original bondholder. The buyer's payment to the seller reimburses the seller for his/her loan to the issuer gross of any capital gain or loss caused by market fluctuations in the value of the bond since the original issue. Every bondholder is a loan creditor of the issuing institution, and there could be as many creditors as there are bond lots (a lot being the minimum number or value of bonds tradable on the particular capital market handling the bond). In contrast, a bank loan or house mortgage has only one creditor. To refinance a bank loan or mortgage the debtor would usually have to repay the original loan with the new loan, and there is no question of the first creditor selling the debt to the second creditor. At the level of the individual loan then, there is no such thing as a tradable and transferable security in practice. Over the last decade or so, most especially in the USA, the practice has arisen of grouping debts into lots, each lot being constituted as a tradable security. This has especially applied to real estate mortgages and the relevant lots are traded as 'fanny maes' and 'ginny maes' in the US capital market. This securitization of loans has not yet occurred to any material extent outside the USA. Within the USA bilateral non-tradable bank loans remain important relative to bonds even for the larger groups.

The market for loans is clearly not nearly so unified as the market for equities in any country in the world. We saw in Chapter 2 that nowhere in the world are equity markets strong form efficient, and in most of the world such markets were not efficient at all. It is therefore not surprising that even the securitized part of the loan markets of the world should be inefficient; for equity holders own the firm, so can order disclosure, but bondholders are merely creditors and have to take the information they are given, if any, by the debtor company. The bilateral part of the loan market, occupied largely by bank loans from single banks to single debtor companies, is not really 'a market' at all in the sense of a unified marketplace where things can be traded, but only a market in the abstract sense used in academic economics.

We have seen that a major contaminant of equity market efficiency is the presence of inside knowledge that leads to insider trading which is very difficult to eliminate even in places where it is a criminal offence with strict penalties on conviction. In the bilateral relationship between a banker and a debtor company, the bank is able to ask for any information it wants. Its ability to be told the information requested depends on the political and economic balance of power between the bank and the client. In the UK companies are much more reluctant to divulge sensitive information to banks than in Germany where the banks are more important as a source of finance to business than the German equity market has been. In Germany, Switzerland, the Netherlands and, until recently, Japan, accounting disclosure rules to the shareholder and general public were weak by international standards. The major supplier of capital was the banking sector and the banks had no interest in sharing with the rest of the economy the information they could demand of their clients. In such a situation there is acute information asymmetry and thus acute information inefficiency in the market as a whole.

As for the securitized part of the loan market, large bond issues are usually placed with a consortium of banks who hold and/or sell on to the investing public. Information similar to that contained in a share issue prospectus is widely required by mature capital market controlling committees or commissions. Once the bonds have been issued, however, no jurisdiction requires any particular public disclosures to be made to bondholders. They have to read the annual reports, framed as they are for the principal benefit of the equity shareholder. The next section addresses the question of how far the information needs of loan creditors differ from those of the equity holders.

DIFFERENT NEEDS FOR DIFFERENT USER GROUPS?

Studies in banking (including Libby 1975, 1979b, Estes and Reimer 1977, Eyes and Tabb 1978, Abdel-Khalik and El-Sheshai 1980, Casey 1980b, Zimmer 1980) have tended to support the view that users' needs are specific and relate to each job, decision making task or environment. No general summary of needs or informational priorities has emerged, with the possible exception of such studies as McCaslin and Stanga (1982b).

Libby (1979a b) in two studies evaluated the communication process between CPAs and commercial lenders and the impact of one type of qualification on the lenders' decisions. Later Libby and Lewis (1982 p. 249) expressed their findings thus:

> Contrary to opinions expressed by some policy making organizations, little miscommunication between the two groups was in evidence. Recognition by the bankers of other sources of information concerning uncertainties appeared to make the auditors' qualification redundant in this situation.

A study was conducted by McCaslin and Stanga (1986) to determine the similarities in the information needs of users of the financial statement. Statistical analysis of the responses by the 59 accountants and 112 chief commercial loan officers disclosed no significant differences in the relevance or reliability judgements of the analysts or bankers for most items. This can be seen as implying that users have similar information needs and that therefore general purpose external reporting is valid. The findings contrast, however, with those of a previous US study by Benjamin and Stanga (1977), but they are consistent with an earlier UK study by Firth (1978). However, both of these earlier studies focused on disclosure needs rather than measurement needs. The present work, also, is more a study of disclosure than of measurement, so we are not entitled to generalize from findings with investment analysts to the bankers making loan decisions.

In partial confirmation of McCaslin and Stanga's study, on the specific issue of materiality, Reckers *et al.* (1984) showed that within-group differences in the evaluation of materiality were very large both for bankers and for CPAs, certainly very much larger than the between-group differences.

The question of overlap and contrast between the accounting needs of equity investors and lending bankers is clearly far from approaching even a tentative set of answers. On the one hand there is the view that published accounts are (or should be made to be) general purpose performance reports to all stakeholders in the firm. On the other hand there is the view that different users have to make different decisions, and so have different information needs arising from the various decision demands. To oversimplify this rather complex matter, the general purpose view is apt to be held by those who (unfashionably) insist on stewardship and accountability as the basic justification for publishing accounts. The specificneeds view sits rather more comfortably with the Trueblood-inspired decision usefulness schools. The traditional stewardship view has received something of a boost with the rise of the agency theory and Watts-Zimmerman approaches to accounting design in recent years, but it remains broadly fair to say that decision usefulness is the aim espoused by standard setting bodies in the Anglo-American accounting communities around the world. Decision usefulness in the lending context critically concerns the probabilities of timely and full repayment of cash. The literature fully reflects that concern as will be especially strongly reflected in Chapters 4 and 5. The decision usefulness philosophy of accounts has been adopted in this work, but with reservations that will be expressed at the appropriate points hereafter.

BANKERS' INFORMATION USAGE AND THE LENS MODEL

Introduction

A prime concern of all human information processing research is to map the individual's judgement policy. This is generally done in an experimental setting where the individual is presented with various combinations of values on several input variables which may be used to form a judgement. The individual's policy is inferred from the relationships between the variables and the resultant judgements. Hofman (1960) deemed such an approach 'paramorphic', by which he meant such studies do not show exactly how information is processed but only what information it is that gets processed and what its apparent importance is in explaining the ultimate judgement.

Paramorphic judgement modelling is frequently done within the paradigm of the lens model first expounded by Egon Brunswik (1952, 1956). In its simplest form it relates an environmental variable to a person's predictive judgement of the size of the variable. Evidence available to make the judgement is wholly partitioned into discrete cues. The correlation between the environmental variable and each individual cue is termed the validity coefficient of the cue, while the correlation between each cue and the personal prediction is termed the utilization coefficient. The closer the two types of coefficient, the more accurate will be the prediction. Einhorn *et al.* (1979) thought that choices are made more difficult when some cues presented to subjects are redundant. Payne *et al.* (1986) reported the effects of manipulating cue values on processing strategy and confirmed an earlier finding by Johnson (1985) that subjects paid more attention to cues with extreme values.

One element of a lens model analysis is the consistency with which an individual applies his/her own decision rules to appropriate situations over time. This is called cognitive consistency. Many studies have shown that high cognitive consistency is so rare that nearly any prediction by an individual is outperformed by the least squares linear regression model of the individual's series of predictions of an environmental variable (Goldberg 1970, Dawes and Corrigan 1974). The superiority of the individual's longitudinal regression model over any one product of that model is matched by the superiority of the cross-sectional model derived from regressing the decisions of a group of people at a single point in time. The cross-sectional model is sometimes termed (in lens model research reports) the composite judgement. Ashton (1982 p. 42) made the following claims about it:

> It can be shown analytically that the accuracy of such mean (i.e. composite across a set of individuals) judgements will be greater than, or equal to, the mean accuracy of the individuals' judgements. Thus the mean accuracy of the individuals' judgements is a lower limit for the accuracy of the composite judgements.

However, empirical research within the lens model framework has shown composite judgements to be substantially more accurate than this lower limit. Hubbard Ashton (1984) found that when predictions by subjects were adjusted for mean systematic bias, the results were more accurate than their regression models on a case by case basis. Libby and Blashfield (1978) found that the majority of the incremental accuracy to be gained by forming composites of all individuals in a group could be achieved by forming composites of only three individuals.

The cognitive consistency of the individual subject is balanced against the consistency with which the environment behaves, and this is referred to as its environmental predictability. The greater the role of random events, accident and genuinely new phenomena in the environment, the lower will be its predictability and the less purpose will be served by model building. The success of a model in predicting the state of the environment is gauged through the matching index, which relates the *ex ante* optimal prediction derivable from available cues to the individual's regression model. In contrast, absolute success in predicting what actually did turn out to occur is gauged through the rather less decision useful achievement index, which is little more than a record of predictive hit rate. The achievement index absorbs compensatory virtuous error whenever cognitive inconsistency happens to be reinforced by environmental unpredictability – a phenomenon some business people call 'gut feel'.

Because many cues may be mutually correlated, the regression of utilization and validity coefficients may produce distorted final regression equations for the cue make-up both of the environmental variable and of its predictive estimate. ANOVA (Analysis Of Variance) is not distorted by multicollinearity but rather tends to reflect it through the size of interactive effects. Although Ashton (1982 p. 24) stated ANOVA had been used only for policy capturing studies, which look only at the right side (cognitive consistency side) of the lens model, there is nothing inherent in the technique to perpetuate that limitation. He further maintained (p. 25) that interactive effects in studies before his had not been very significant. This he linked with the relative insignificance of non-linear terms in the regression approach to information processing.

Lens model studies have been applied to auditing (e.g. Ashton and Brown 1980, Weber 1978), materiality judgements (Messier 1979, Firth 1979), and bankruptcy prediction (which is drawn on in subsequent subsections).

Bankers' cue processing with specified priors

Libby (1975) had 43 experienced loan officers use 5 financial ratios to predict if each of 60 actual firms had or had not failed, after being told that the failure rate was 50 per cent. Environmental predictability was 51. That is, 51 out of the 60 firms could be correctly predicted from a discriminant model using only the 5 cues; 40 of the 43 subjects performed at a level better than random. If the majority predictions for each firm were taken (the 'composite judge' method), 49 out of 60 were correct. The linear regression model of the subjects' individual predictions gave 52.9 correct scores, which exemplifies the tendency for the results of a person's decision model over time to outperform any one result emerging from it. Libby (1976) suggested some reasons for this phenomenon in the particular context of predicting bankruptcy. First, the environmental variable, business failure, is well defined and reliably measured. Second, bank officers are experts at the task of prediction. Finally, the distributions of the actual ratios used were very skewed, which made prediction that much easier.

Zimmer (1980, 1981) replicated Libby's study with 30 Australian loan officers, 42 firms and 5 ratios. Environmental predictability was 37 firms, 28 of the officers did better than random with a mean of 32.4 correct while the composite judge produced 36 firms. He obtained virtually identical results a few months later with 30 students.

Cue processing without specific priors

Casey (1980b) reported results apparently worse than, and inconsistent with, those of Libby (1976) and Zimmer (1980, 1981). For 30 firms the mean predictive accuracy was only 17 while the composite judge was hardly any better than this mean. The explanation was that subjects in this study were not told before they started that the sample of firms was equally divided between failed and non-failed. It seems as if subjects used their own subjective prior probabilities which were rather optimistic.

Abdel-Khalik and El-Sheshai (1980) asked 28 loan officers to predict default for 32 firms, using cues they themselves 'bought' from the researchers' catalogue of 18 possible ratios. Subjects were only told that 'some' firms had failed. Environmental predictability optimized at 90.6 per cent while individual predictive accuracy was 62.5 per cent, as was their decision model. This suggests the importance of priors when man is outperformed by the model. This study also reported the surprisingly high predictive ability of a current ratio of over 2 (84 per cent) and of a debt-to-equity ratio of over 1 (72 per cent).

Reviewing the Abdel-Khalik and El-Sheshai (1980) study where cues were purchased from the researchers, and noting the 23 per cent improvement in accuracy associated with replacing subjects by their regression model, Libby and Lewis (1982 p. 246) commented: '[It] suggests that the choice of cues is crucial while the weighting is of lesser consequence. This conclusion is consistent with that of Dawes and Corrigan (1974), Einhorn and Hogarth (1979) and others.'

Findings by Danos *et al.* (1989) suggest loan officers reach a high level of confidence early in the lending process based on summarized accounting and other background data. When, later on, factors concerning firms' financial plans or underlying assumptions are varied, then lenders adjust their decision in the appropriate direction even if it goes against an earlier judgement.

Loan officers from eight banks were used in the Danos *et al.* study. It was decided to focus on their medium-sized clients since larger ones could be evaluated from publicly available data, and data from smaller ones were apt to be inconsistent and unreliable.

> Decisions regarding existing borrowers were based heavily on track record and interpersonal relationships, making it difficult or impossible to isolate the effects of accounting information and creating serious internal validity problems.
>
> (Danos *et al.* 1989 p. 236)

For new clients, the procedure consisted of the following three steps:

1 look at public data to form a preliminary impression,
2 make contact with key personnel and visit the borrower's place, to size up operations and plans, and
3 perform detailed credit analysis and evaluation of both historical and forward data, to evaluate the repayment probabilities.

The Danos *et al.* team used two cases, one strong, one weak: 48 out of 52 bankers agreed on the weak case, 47 on the strong case. Accounting data seemed to be used to signal managerial competence. 'Providing well grounded forward looking data for lender examination seems to signal creditworthiness.' (Danos *et al.* 1989 p. 245).

In settings without quick and clear feedback of the outcome, even with experienced professionals, decision makers displayed extreme and inappropriate confidence in the quality of their judgements (Einhorn and Hogarth 1978, Oskamp 1965) and ignored subsequent disconfirming evidence (Elstein *et al.* 1978, Lord *et al.* 1979, Koriat *et al.* 1980). However, bank loan officers do have to defend their decisions before a loan committee. 'Such a setting has been shown to enhance peoples' memory of cues and to incorporate more cues in their judgements (Ebbesen and Konecni 1975)', as cited by Danos *et al.* (1989 p. 238). It also means they can detect and respond to subtle variances in routinely analysed data (Danos *et al.* 1984).

Schepanski (1983) claimed that studies previous to his showed considerable evidence that creditors use financial statements in judging commercial loan applications (Miller and Relkin 1971, Beckman and Foster 1969, Cole 1984, Clemens and Dyer 1982, Collins 1966, Cohen *et al.* 1966, Beckhart 1959, Hodgman 1963). Since a majority of most auditors' clients consist of small or medium firms with closely held ownership, creditors may be the main external users of firms' financial statements (Schepanski 1983).

The literature shows that the main traits bankers rely on to evaluate prospective borrowers are payment record, financial condition and quality of company management (Schepanski (1983) citing the same references as in the preceding paragraph). Schepanski asked 25 bank trainee subjects to rate on a 19 point scale, for each of the 3 traits, the prospects of 79 firms. The judgement model emerging from this was non-linear with a geometric averaging rule and conditional monotonicity (whereby the rank effects on the dependent variable of a change in any one cue remain the same, irrespective of the fixed values of the other cues).

An individual's ability to express the relative emphasis she places on cues when forming judgements is called self-insight in the HIP (Human Information Processing) literature. In accounting and business contexts, research has found relatively little self-insight with frequent and large errors in the estimation of important cues (Ashton 1974, Joyce 1976, Savich 1977, Slovic *et al.* 1972, Wright 1977, 1979, Mear and Firth 1987).

Content cues

In an interview, Robert E. Wilkes (1985), Executive Vice-President of First Jersey National Bank, discussed what his bank looks for when evaluating a loan request. For the first loan, the list of priorities includes:

1 adequacy of capital,
2 debt service capacity, and
3 integrity of the people.

When monitoring loans to small companies, factors which are reviewed concern:

1 adherence to repayment schedules,

2 receiving current financial information regularly, and
3 trend analysis.

This probably conforms to a common sense view of what laymen would expect bankers to be interested in. Empirical research on bankers' actual processing of loan requests, however, casts some doubt on the realism of this view.

Hoshower and Versaggi (1985) reacted to a 1983 *Wall Street Journal* article which had stated that few bankers and investors are sophisticated enough to understand accounting procedures, and may thus make ill-informed decisions. They devised a comprehension test of accounting by lenders and investors. Bank vice-presidents and certified financial analysts were selected to complete a questionnaire on accounting definitions. The results showed that many users of financial statements failed to interpret correctly the results of some familiar accounting procedures.

Rogers and Johnson's (1988 p. 6) study selected the current ratio, the net margin ratio and the debt/net worth ratio to develop their cue model because 'a number of studies point out their significance as indicators of loan approval (Miller 1972, Cole 1984, Van Horne 1980)'.

Dyckman *et al.* (1978 pp. 63–6) reviewed the literature to report that decision makers were not much interested in inflation-adjusted numbers. Similar results were reported for bank managers by Eyes and Tabb (1978) and for life insurance investment managers by Benston and Krasney (1978). Enis (1988) found CCA (Current Cost Accounting) led to lower accuracy and consensus than historical cost (HC) in investor prediction of stock price movements. Finally, Berry *et al.* (1985) discovered that US bankers operating in the UK still find HC possesses more information content than CCA but they do not ignore CCA altogether.

Epstein (1975) found that financial statements were little used in making investment decisions but respondents to Most and Chang (1979) *felt* they were very useful in such decisions. These differences of result could reflect instrumentation differences only.

Presentational cues

Main body of the accounts vs footnotes

Welsh (1987) found that the manner of presentation affected the accuracy of students and analysts in predicting stock prices. Subject achievement was significantly increased by the placement of data in the body of the balance sheet rather than in a footnote, both for the novices and the experienced analysts.

Yallapragada and Breux (1989) found that it was a widespread practice in both the UK and the USA to transfer clients' accounts onto in-house spreadsheets which were used to output ratios for credit analysis purposes. Donleavy (1991) found the same practice to be widespread with bankers in Hong Kong and thought this contributed to the relatively low level of average ability to read the SCFP with much perspicacity.

Chernoff faces

Moriarity (1979) asked 227 undergraduate accounting majors to classify 22 discount stores, 7 of which had failed, but this was not revealed to any of the subjects. Instead, half the subjects received their financial cues in the form of Chernoff faces where the size and shape of features represent distinct financial ratios (Chernoff and Rizvi 1975). Those who received the faces with explanations showed by far the greatest prediction accuracy while those who received only financial ratios performed the worst.

Functional fixation on constant cues

Relevant to the present work are studies of functional fixation. An individual fixated on accounting numbers will be unable to change his/her utilization of those numbers when the underlying methods that generate those numbers change. Ashton (1976) supplied 106 MBA student subjects with sets of information for setting selling prices of 30 products. Some students were then given data prepared on a different costing basis and so advised. All students were given a second group of prices to set. Multiple regression was used to extract each subject's decision model from the first exercise, and that model was used to predict the prices that a totally fixated student would have used in the second exercise. About half of the students given data on a new costing basis did not change their prices by any more than the students whose costing bases were unchanged. This result meant a 'sizable proportion' of subjects were functionally fixated.

Swieringa *et al.* (1979) replicated Ashton's study with a tighter control of confounding influences, and broadly supported his results. They also found, however, that the *more* information that was supplied to the students about the changes, the *less* the extent of the price change, a phenomenon suggestive of an overload effect. A detailed discussion of overload effects is presented in Chapter 9.

Abdel-Khalik and Keller (1979) asked 61 financial analysts and investment officers to evaluate the attractiveness of 6 real but disguised firms as investment opportunities, before and after a FIFO-LIFO switch or the reverse. The results suggested considerable functional fixation.

Information search studies

Payne (1976) found that the proportion of information searched declined both as the number of alternatives available in a decision situation increased and as the number of dimensions (such as cost, revenue, time, energy and personalities) per alternative increased. Also, for 11 of his 12 multi-alternative decision situations, the amount of available information searched was as great or greater for the alternative chosen than for any other alternative in the choice set. This suggests that subjects may have been reducing the amount of information they had to search by eliminating some alternatives on the basis of only a few dimensions: an imperfect 'elimination by aspects' strategy. This in turn suggests the possibility of subjects eliminating alternatives on the basis of only partial information. The verbal protocols appear to support this view. This is consistent with the findings of Shields (1983).

Biggs *et al.* (1985) used 11 loan officers to see how they processed loan candidates, in particular how they conducted the information search. They found that 'task complexity' was related to the depth and variability of the search, and the use of non-compensatory strategies. The percentage of information searched was greater for tasks with similar alternatives while variability of search decreased.

Jacoby *et al.* (1984) observed how 17 security analysts chose stocks for buying. They found the analysts' performance level to be related to the amount of information searched. The depth of search decreased over trials as high performers examined the same amount of information across task trials but low performers looked at fewer pieces of information.

Gul (1987) showed how bank officers' perception of company risk increases when disclosures add 'subject to' qualifications, and such qualifications elicit higher levels of information search. These results are consistent with the earlier arguments of Bertholdt (1979) and Schultz (1979).

Protocol analysis

Introduction

Protocol analysis is the method of detecting how decisions are made, by asking subjects to think aloud as they work out alternative merits and demerits in all the dimensions they deem relevant. Protocol analysis is also known as process tracing in earlier articles.

Byrne (1977) asserted that protocol analysis should be confined to situations where individuals find it easy to verbalize.

Anderson (1985) found that a sharp drop in performance was demonstrated by inexperienced analysts when required to verbalize, thereby demonstrating the distortions inherent in protocol analysis.

Libby (1981 p. 93) admonished thus: 'It cannot be overemphasized that process tracing is not a substitute for theory or a well defined purpose.'

Much of the early process tracing research was done by engineers and computer scientists. They were concerned with building computer programs representative of human information search and processing behaviour as part of a project to replace man by his model. Libby (1981) was concerned that such an orientation showed little concern for reproducibility, parsimony, discriminability or explanatory theoretical structure.

Decision processes

Protocol analysis characterizes decision making processes in the following ways:

additive: this is the *linear compensatory* decision process wherein each alternative is scored for each of its components, which gives rise to selecting the alternative with the highest score.

additive difference: proposed by Tversky (1969), this linear compensatory process compares alternatives directly on each dimension, extracts a difference and finds their sum (taking one pair of alternatives at a time).

elimination by aspects: also attributable to Tversky (1972), this non-compensatory process begins by selecting an aspect or dimension. All the alternatives that do not possess this aspect are eliminated, and a second aspect is focused upon for the second round of elimination. This recurs until only one alternative remains.

conjunctive: an alternative must have a certain minimum value on all the relevant dimensions.

Payne (1976) defines the **lexicographic** strategy as a disjunctive, non-compensatory, non-linear strategy that selects the most attractive alternative on the most important dimension.

Review of recent reviews

Ford *et al.* (1989) have done the most recent review of the protocol analysis literature; 45 studies were identified and coded. The results firmly demonstrated that non-compensatory strategies were the dominant mode used by decision makers. Compensatory strategies were typically used only when the number of alternatives and dimensions were small, or after a number of alternatives had been eliminated from consideration.

The most important previous review of this literature was by Abelson and Levi (1985). Most of the studies reviewed reported the conjunctive model to be the dominant mode of processing decision information. A further conclusion that emerged was that as the number of alternatives and dimensions increase, there is a greater likelihood that the decision maker will use non-linear processing strategies such as the lexicographic or elimination by aspects.

Application of protocol analysis

Four studies applied protocol analysis to the process of financial analysis. The earliest was Clarkson (1962) who attempted to construct a model of a bank trust officer's portfolio selection process. Then, Biggs (1979) extended Payne's approach using 11 experienced financial analysts who thought aloud as they selected the company with the highest earnings power from a group of five.

Bouwman (1980) used protocol analysis to distinguish expert from novice decision making strategies in analysing financial case studies. Although the sample only consisted of 3 professional accountants and 15 students, some differences appeared pronounced enough to be worth mentioning. Students appeared to evaluate information in the order it was presented until a problem emerged. Information was evaluated on very simple trends such as sales are up, and a set of simple relations between data items were formed which were internally consistent but not reconciled to other sets. Once something was identified as a problem, novices made little extra effort to gather relevant new information. On the other hand, the experts appeared to use a standard checklist of questions only as a starting point. Data were often examined in terms of complex trends. A general overall picture of the firm was developed and named (such as 'expanding company') based on the initial information acquired. When the stereotype was violated, an in-depth examination to uncover significant causes would be initiated.

Stephens (1979) asked ten bankers to think aloud while evaluating a commercial lending case. He found that they spent a lot of time computing and analysing ratios and ratio trends. Their failure to adjust for differences in inventory or depreciation methods suggested a degree of functional fixation on earnings.

Protocol analysis by Frishkoff *et al.* (1984) lent support to the importance for 12 financial analysts of earnings per share, return on investment and working capital, but *not* to cash flow. On the other hand, Campbell (1984) reported in his protocol analysis that six bank loan officers found earnings per share not useful.

A protocol analysis by Rogers and Johnson (1988 p. 18) of loan officers' lending decisions found that 'normal interpretation becomes difficult because verbal explanations do not accommodate the impact of remote causes on loan officers'. This is a succinct description of the threat to the internal validity of the protocol analysis method, since self-reporting accuracy depends so much on conscious self-insight and environmental awareness.

Other approaches to information processing

Information economics

The Committee on Concepts and Standards for External Financial Reports (1977 p. 27) noted that information is usually treated as a free good in decision theory. However, information economics 'treats information as a conventional economic commodity, the acquisition of which constitutes a problem of economic choice'. This means that experiments involving information purchase may be inadequately explained without explicit consideration of an information economics approach.

Ceremonialism

March (1987 pp. 160ff) argues on quasi-anthropological grounds that decision process is more important than decision product. Decision making is said to be a sacred ritual involving highly symbolic activities. It celebrates the central values of a society, in particular, the ideas that life is under intentional human control, and that control is exercised through individual and collective choices based on explicit anticipation of alternatives and their probable consequences (Feldman and March 1981, March and Olsen 1984). It reinforces the legitimacy of existing authorities, and provides a basis for interpreting their downfall as appropriate. These sacred values are interpreted and reinforced through the information systems and decision processes of organizations. Individuals establish their reputations for virtue; an interpretation of history is developed, shared and enforced; dissent is nurtured and contained; new ideas are grafted on to old ones or dissociated from them. These ritual, symbolic and affirmative components of decisions and decision processes are not unfortunate manifestations of an irrational culture. They are important aspects of the way organizations develop the common culture and vision that become primary mechanisms for effective action, control and innovation.

Journalism generates accounts of daily events intended to be sold to readers, ostensibly because they find the accounts worthy of their attention. From a decision point of view, however, most of the information generated by journalism is gossip as far as most readers are concerned (March and Sévon 1984). It resolves no immediate decision problems (save perhaps what TV shows are available). And this feature is particularly true of those newspapers that cost the most and have the highest reputations.

> It is perhaps a strange vision of information engineering to say that an accounting report should be a form of poetry, using the language of numbers, ledgers and ratios to extend our horizons and expand our comprehensions, rather than simply fill in unknowns on a decision tree. But it is not an entirely unworthy vision of professions to say that their accounts and reports can be richer in meaning than they are aware or intend, and that they can enrich our senses of purpose and enlarge our interpretations of our lives.
>
> (March and Sévon 1984 p. 165).

This view is diametrically opposite to the Trueblood-inspired decision usefulness criterion for evaluating information value.

Lehman and Tinker (1987 p. 516) quote the suggestion that accounting might be best seen as a 'technology of foolishness: a ritualistic kind of playfulness and experimentation' (Cooper *et al.* 1981, Cooper 1983). Their prescription for what they seem to view as a kind of illness on the part of accountancy to date displays a remarkable lack of the qualities Cooper mentioned.

To be effective, [expounded Lehman and Tinker (1987 p. 517)] a particular discursive accounting string must anchor itself in a discursive field – a complex of sedimented discourses – to warrant itself by resonating with the common stock of knowledge of society (Laclau 1977; Hall 1982 pp. 72–80).

In other words, users need to understand accounts if the accounts are to be 'effective'. This is perhaps a rather uncontroversial proposition. More seriously, an implication of this passage is that foreign accounting practices and assumptions may be ineffective in other cultures.

CONCLUSIONS

This chapter has travelled quickly over a large area of literature, so it will be summarized and integrated at this point. The main purpose of this chapter has been to review studies of how bankers make use of information in appraising loan applications.

The opening section contrasted the way information processing behaviour is studied in market-wide aggregations for equity investors with the single group or single individual focus that prevails in loan information processing studies. Studies attempting to establish that lenders really did have different accounting information needs from equity investors were judged not to have reached their goal. The theoretical reasons why needs differentiation exists are nonetheless persuasive to an advocate of a decision usefulness perspective in accounting, and it is such a perspective that the present study adopts.

The essential elements of the lens model were outlined with its distinction between cue validity and cue usage. Analysis of variance is the preferred technique to apply this distinction to actual decision processes, since it better quarantines the multicollinearity of the cue set through its calibration of any interactive effects of the set's elements.

It was shown that cue processing was done much more efficiently when subjects had prior probabilities to work from than when they had not. The choice of cues was suggested to be much more important than the weighting of cue coefficients in their assembly into a decision model. Danos *et al.*'s (1989) sample, at least, seemed willing and able to modify initial judgements in the light of any later disconfirming evidence, but personal relationships and track record far outweighed accounts as such for new loan applications from existing clients, in their study.

For new clients, the procedure consisted of the following three steps:

1 look at public data to form a preliminary impression,
2 make contact with the key personnel and visit borrower's place, to size up operations and plans, and
3 perform detailed credit analysis and evaluation of both historical and forward data, to evaluate the repayment probabilities.

Since a majority of most auditors' clients consist of small or medium firms with closely held ownership, creditors may be the main external users of firms' financial statements (Schepanski 1983).

The presentation of cues in the main body of the accounts improves performance over their presentation in footnotes.

Functional fixation was found in some major experiments in accounts processing by students and by financial analysts.

Stephens (1979) reported that his bankers seemed to be functionally fixated on ratios and earnings but indifferent to depreciation and inventory variations. Frishkoff *et al.* (1984) found that financial analysts rated earnings high but cash flow low – perhaps because they were concerned with equity investors rather than with creditors. Campbell's (1984) loan officers were unconcerned with earnings per share (EPS). External validity of protocol studies of very small samples is very questionable, but, such as they are, they offer some support to the view that investors and creditors do read accounts for different reasons and hence employ different cues in making their judgements from the accounts.

Information economics treats information as a saleable commodity whose value could be best represented by its price. Ceremonialism treats accounting as a social ritual whose usefulness for economic decision making is largely irrelevant compared with its role in reinforcing power structures.

4 Evolution of the funds and cash flow statements

INTRODUCTION

This chapter describes the history of the funds statement, largely with reference to the USA, since the USA has led and catalysed developments elsewhere in the world in adopting and reforming the statement. This section is the necessary introduction to the critiques of the fund statement and to the discussion of cash flow statements and cash flow accounting. In this chapter, the historical survey may clarify the traditional objectives of the funds statement.

In this and subsequent chapters, the abbreviation SCFP will be used in two contexts. In the narrow context of accounting in the USA, it will be used to designate the Statement of Changes in Financial Position as required successively by APB 3 and APB 19. In any other context, the abbreviation will be used to signify funds statements generally, irrespective of their official title in the region under review. Corresponding remarks apply to the abbreviation SCF for the Statement of Cash Flow. The abbreviation SCF/P means *both* the SCF *and* the SCFP.

HISTORY OF THE FUNDS STATEMENT

Introduction

The AICPA published a research study on funds statements in 1961 and the resultant opinion in 1963 (APB 3). This was the earliest official pronouncement on the subject by a major accounting body.

'The prime reason' for confusion in both the interpretation and the preparation of the statement, per Rosen and De Coster (hereafter cited as RD) (1969 p. 124), 'is that a positive position has not been taken by an authoritative body. Also it seems to the authors that the funds report is being asked to accomplish too much.' This view is echoed throughout almost all published views on funds statements from the 1920s to the 1990s. A striking example of the confusion RD mentioned is provided in one of the historical reviews of the funds statement. Someya (1983) opens his history (which largely derives from RD) with the following strange assertion:

> As the problems of income accounting are embodied in the income statement, so problems of fund accounting are crystallized in the funds statement. Therefore, the development of funds flow accounting is that of the funds statement.
>
> Fund accounting (Vatter 1947) actually has nothing to do with funds flow accounting.

Cole and Finney

The funds flow statement predated Cole's (1908) influential textbook which was the first to note its existence as one of several supplementary statements that were in use. Receipts and payments styles of statement are extant from the accounts of the Northern Central Railroad (1863), England's Assam Company (1862) and the American Bell Telephone Company (1881). The first 'all financial resources' SCFP found by RD (p. 125) belongs to the Missouri Pacific Railway Company and its subsidiary, the St Louis, Iron Mountain and Southern Railway, for 1893.

At the turn of the century, US firms began to provide subtotals for current assets and current liabilities. The funds statement issued in 1902 by US Steel and its subsidiaries may have been the first to begin with net profit and then add back items like depreciation. In 1903, it began to reconcile profit in the statement to net current assets.

Cole (1908 p. 132) reported that the funds statement in various forms began to be adopted by railroad companies about five years earlier. In fact by 1903 at least four different forms of funds statement could be seen: cash, gross current assets, working capital and all financial resources. While the first three can be presumed to portray the causes of movements in one of three definitions of a firm's liquidity, the fourth is argued by RD (p. 126) to have been 'intentionally broadened in scope in order to overcome the narrow perspective of the income statement'. Whilst this explanation seems quite plausible, some evidence in the form of contemporary quotations would have have made it much more so.

Apparently, all four of Cole's influential accounting textbooks (1908, 1910, 1915, 1921) illustrated only the 'all financial resources' format. In these illustrations, general solvency, trustworthiness of the books and liquidity are advanced as justifications for the funds statement.

Seymour Walton recognized, in the 'students' department' of the *Journal of Accountancy* in 1914, the need for a liquidity-oriented statement to complement the income statement. He thought that the only time an accountant would want to use an all financial resources format was when 'he wishes to show that a concern has been increasing its fixed assets at the expense of its working capital' (Walton 1914 p. 231). This view is held by RD (p. 128) to have strongly influenced Finney who led a drive from the war years to the late 1920s to adopt as a major report a working capital oriented funds statement. As editor of the student's department of the *Journal of Accountancy* after Walton, Finney provided model answers to CPA questions. When funds statements were called for, the answer was always formatted to explain changes in working capital. He explained that a funds statement provided 'a clear and comprehensive conception of the change in the financial condition caused by the profits of the period, the dividend payments and any financing program which may have taken place' (Finney 1923 pp. 460–1). The working capital orientation of funds statements originated with Finney (1925). His statement listed funds provided by: (a) net profits before provisions, (b) bond issue proceeds and (c) asset sale proceeds. The funds provided were equal to the funds applied to (a) asset purchases, (b) dividend payments and (c) itemized increases in working capital and deferred charges. His explicit definition of funds, however, was disappointing. 'The term "funds" suggested something more than cash' (Finney 1925, p. 507). He asserted his format was 'in more or less general use' (Finney 1925 p. 497) but concurrent evidence suggests few firms were using any form of funds statement, and the few that were favoured no specific format (Kempner 1956, Anton 1962). RD (pp. 129–30) comment that:

There is considerable evidence supporting the simple explanation that many authors of textbooks, CPA examiners and accounting teachers saw the funds statement primarily as an excellent vehicle for testing a student's knowledge of the mechanics of the accrual basis of accounting. Specifically, the working capital format was a better testing device than the 'changes in all balance sheet accounts' at this time, because the former eliminated the effects of many 'intra-entity' bookkeeping entries, and its definition of funds approximated accrual accounting concepts. . . . Unfortunately over time the pedagogical benefits of the report may have received too much stress, and very little attention seems to have been given to the empirical testing of the merits of the concept of working capital.

A brief controversy flared up in the journal in 1925 between Finney and his critics, particularly Esquerre, who favoured a format explaining changes in total wealth. The controversy seems to have strengthened the desire for uniformity and this favoured Finney's format for essentially political influence reasons.

1925–63

By the end of the Second World War, the statement of sources and applications of funds, also known as the statement of changes in financial position, was usually presented with the annual report, sometimes in the notes (Most 1982). The working capital format remained predominant in the USA through the 1930s to the late 1950s, although several ameliorations were suggested to overcome a number of criticisms. Bliss (1924) had already counselled against a rigid format insensitive to corporate circumstance or user objectives. Mautz (1951) thought cumulative eight year statements would show changes in solvency and how growth had been financed. Kohler and Morrison (1931 p. 379) wanted two non-current accounts to be in the funds statement since:

> Bonds and stocks issued in exchange for assets other than cash, or issued to replace liabilities, may always be regarded as 'funds' received inasmuch as they are paid out in lieu of cash, and the values received are ordinarily expressed in terms of fair cash value.

This shift in the definition of funds to mean purchasing power was adopted by a number of writers (Streightoff 1932, Husband and Thomas 1935, Noble *et al.* 1941, Binkley 1949, Mauriello 1950). Paton (1938) wanted to begin the funds statement with sales rather than profits in order to avoid the confusion attributed to the depreciation add-back, but such a presentation repeated too much information already on the income statement, according to the writers of APB 3.

Moonitz (1943) thought inventory increases were an application of funds, not different in kind from increases in fixed assets, rather than being funds themselves. Goldberg (1951) expressed the view that there was no significant difference between acquiring assets by cash or by securities, but the working capital orientation excluded transactions where securities were the financing means. These external transactions were essential to obtain a proper idea of the true change in financial position.

Moonitz (1956) wanted a maximum definition of funds to be limited to cash and items only one transaction away from cash, so as to exclude inventory and prepayments. Similar definitions were advocated by Anton (1962) and Pautler (1963). Still other concepts have been identified by Mason (1961) as short term monetary assets and net monetary assets and by Yu (1969) (who hoped to see an all economic resources input-output copy of national accounts on a corporate scale).

Cole (1908) had favoured the all financial resources view of funds, Finney (1925) the working capital view, and both APB 3 and APB 19 supported Cole, albeit that the latter wished changes in working capital to be prominently displayed. What can be inferred from this review so far is that the debate between the working capital school and the all financial resources school goes back to the first quarter of this century, and most of the points in favour of either approach had already been published by 1925.

APB 3

The AICPA finished its research on the funds statement in 1961 (Mason 1961) and issued 'The Statement of Sources and Applications of Funds', *Opinions of the Accounting Principles Board No 3* in 1963. This said that a statement of sources and applications of funds was desirable as supplementary information in accounts but not mandatory. RD disliked APB 3 as 'vague', 'confusing', and:

> Unfortunately, the Opinion probably has had the effect of reinforcing the unsatisfactory idea that the 'funds' report should be used to fill all gaps in disclosure.
>
> (RD p. 135)

This means that the funds statement must report changes in some definition of liquidity, reveal all important inter-entity transactions, somehow reconcile the cash (or near cash) and accrual bases of accounting, be flexible, report different perspectives, and readily communicate with laymen. Surely accountants are asking one report to accomplish too much. Clarity cannot result when incompatible (such as cash and accrual) concepts are meshed into one statement.

(RD p. 137).

In 1962, only 39 out of 100 randomly selected Fortune 500 firms provided a funds statement compared with 89 by 1967. About half used the working capital format throughout the period, about a quarter the all financial resources format and no data are given on the rest (RD p. 133). The strong advocacy of funds statements by the New York Stock Exchange and the Federation of Financial Analysts is a possible explanation of the increase in use.

APB 19

APB 3 recommended the statement but did not require it. The SEC began to require it in 1970 (SEC 1970 Accounting Series Release no. 117) and the APB to do so with its Opinion 19 (AICPA 1973).

The AICPA reported the increasing adoption of the SCFP between the publication of APB 3 and APB 19 as shown in Table 4.1

APB Opinion 19, 'Reporting Changes in Financial Position', asserted (para 7) 'a statement summarizing changes in financial position should also be presented as a basic financial statement'. The statement (para 8) 'should be based on a broad concept embrac-

Table 4.1 US companies using an SCFP

Year	No. out of 600	% of the 600 sampled firms
1963	271	45.2
1964	387	64.5
1965	458	76.3
1966	503	83.8
1967	524	87.3
1968	535	89.2
1969	548	91.3
1970	573	95.5
1971	597	99.5
1972+	600	100.0

Source: AICPA, *Accounting Trends and Techniques*, New York: AICPA, 1963–79

ing all changes in financial position' and its title should be the statement of changes in financial position.

APB 19 para 15 restricted the use of the cash concept of funds to situations in which 'all non cash items have been appropriately adjusted'. This means each change in each working capital component has to be reported as a source or use of funds. De Ridder (1980 p. 37) thought that this requirement explained the unpopularity of the cash basis thus far.

APB 19 para 13 required individual disclosure of financing and investing activities without netting off or combining.

The objective of the SCFP per APB 19 was: 'to summarize the financing and investing activities of the entity, including the extent to which the enterprise has generated funds from operations during the period'.

Most (hereafter abbreviated to KSM) (1982b p. 451) wrote, 'This last concept is sometimes referred to as self-financing.'

KSM believed the meaning of funds which best fulfilled APB 19's goals is 'means of payment' from its narrowest denotation as coins and notes to its broadest which includes any resource two transactions away from such a form (one transaction being always the drawing of notes from the bank account).

It may be surmised that the different forms of funds flow statement arose from specific user needs. For example, the financiers of a company which has executed an indenture in connection with its bonded debt, requiring working capital to be maintained at a certain level, will be interested to see the net change in working capital at the end of each accounting period. The directors of a company which has a chronic shortage or surplus of cash will be interested in a funds flow statement which highlights the net change in cash.

(KSM 1982 p. 453)

It follows from the above that cash flows are a part of funds flows and not a surrogate therefor, or vice versa.

Given the great variety of different types of cash receipts and payments, this [one similar to SFAS 95] classification could present as many problems as does accrual accounting. How should a seasonal bank loan received to finance merchandise purchases be classified? It certainly results from operations, but if the borrowing is an annual event, it could be classified as a recurring loan.

(KSM 1982 p. 455)

Spiller and Virgil (1974) compared a sample of reports before and after the effective date for the implementation of APB 19. Many non-complying practices were found to persist, attributable to deliberate violations and to narrow constructions of the opinion's requirements.

Rosen (1974) opined that the SCFP of APB 19 was a return to the funds statement of the nineteenth century except it was now accompanied by financial position and income statements and by notes. He recommended a format variable in content to suit the different needs of different users.

OPINION SURVEYS AND PUBLISHED CRITIQUES OF THE SCFP

Defenders of the SCFP

Only four articles in the journals of the last decade could be found in unambiguous praise of the SCFP. Siegel and Simon (1981) thought that it helps to plot the future direction of a company through contrasting earnings with liquidity, and through interpreting management's choice of financial instruments as clues to future earnings stability.

Byrd and Byrd (1986) argued that the SCFP can be the most useful statement for small businesses in that it can help predict cash flows, enable a better assessment of income quality, of capacity change decisions, of financial flexibility and liquidity, and gives an overview of the firm's financing and investing activities.

Gentry *et al.* (1987) argued on the usefulness of funds statement elements in bankruptcy prediction. In their sample of 33 failed and 33 non-failed firms, investment, dividends and receivables had significance for the failed firms but only size and dividends had any for the successful ones.

Coker (1986) advised loan officers that the SCFP was a useful base from which to project cash flows. The balance sheet was only important if cash flow was inadequate and liquidation might be required.

Critics of the SCFP

That funds statements are gravely unsatisfactory is one of the few propositions that appears to be almost universally held by professional and academic accountants alike.

Han (1981) wrote, 'In my opinion most of the published funds statements are confusing and misleading.' UK critics such as Smith (1985), Holmes (1976), Robins and Mitchell (1985), Taylor (1979), Mason (1983) and Rayman (1971) all criticized the confused and ambiguous nature and purpose of the funds statement but, unlike Lee (1984a) or Lawson (1983), suggested no practical alternatives.

American criticisms of APB 19 for inadequate definition of the term 'funds' and insufficiently clear objectives of the statement itself can be found, *inter alia*, in Clark (1983), Swanson and Vangermeersch (1981), Ketz and Kochanek (1982), Spiller and Virgil (1974) and, rather cogently, in Bryant (1984). The identification of the most useful definition of funds and the best statement format were discussed without strongly supported conclusions by a number of commentators in the early 1970s (Fess and Weygandt 1969, Regazzi 1974, Stark 1975, Warren and White 1975, Rakes and Shenken 1972, Yu 1969, Roberts and Gabhart 1972, Henry 1975).

In Australia, Clift (1979) produced a wide ranging discussion of the purposes and contents of funds statements that reinforced the criticisms made in the British, American and Canadian journals.

Smith (1985) thought management should be free to choose the definition of funds flow most appropriate for the company's situation even to the point of eliminating it altogether if funds information is redundant.

Doughterty (1978) asserted that though banks recognized the value of the SCFP for manufacturers, it was regarded as worthless for evaluating the financial condition of a bank. This view was to be accepted by FASB in SFAS 96 which largely exempted banks from SFAS 95.

Among the constituents most confused by funds flows are writers of accounting textbooks, especially British textbooks in the 1970s and 1980s. In view of the criticisms that have appeared in the professional and academic journals regarding the vague focus and insufficiently clearly defined reporting objectives of the funds statement, it might be expected that college accounting textbooks would exercise caution in addressing the uses and benefits of funds statements. In most texts, the calculation of the numbers in the statement is systematically explained, but as the following samples indicate, interpretation of the statement is not.

Bird (1979 p. 16) asserted fund statements 'do shed some light on the nature of the statement and the items that go into it', the nature of that light being (p. 70) 'The most direct indication of the liquidity and solvency of the company' subject to reservations about the treatment of bank overdrafts.

Reid and Myddleton (1978 p. 211) declared the aim of the statement 'is to show how a company's activities have been financed and the use to which funds have been put'. They criticized the UK's SSAP 1O for allowing netting off and pointed out that the working capital on the balance sheet may not reconcile with working capital changes on the funds statement.

Rockley (1975 p. 93) asserted: 'A complete analysis of a company's financing strategy will be revealed by a study of several funds flow statements' whose object (p. 94) 'is to show how a firm's asset/ liability status has changed during a specified period'. He then moved on to focus on cash flows.

Jaedicke and Sprouse (1965 p. 78) conceded, unlike the textbook writers cited above, 'The term "funds" flow is slightly ambiguous' but then explained the statement using a working capital focus, concluding that such a focus (p. 92) is 'perhaps not the most useful' concept of funds. The all financial resources approach is preferred because of its all inclusiveness but its treatment is 'beyond the scope of this book' for some unidentified reason.

Lee (1975 p. 176) considered 'any transaction' carrying a movement in assets or liabilities is a flow of funds. In his opinion (p. 179), 'There is indeed a strong case for drafting the funds statement so as to show directly the effect of the year's transactions on net short term monetary assets' (debtors, quoted investments and cash) but (p. 181) cash flow accounting 'has a rather defeatist ring about it, and savours to many accountants of throwing out the baby with the bathwater'.

Briston (1981 p. 148) only used funds statements to back ratio analysis and regarded the statement as no more than 'an orderly presentation of the changes in balance sheet items'.

Frank Wood (1975 p. 801) regarded the statement as 'an analysis of the reasons for changes in either the firm's cash resources or its fund of working capital' but only four pages later (p. 805) the statement has been relegated to 'simply a convenient way of describing in concise form the changes which take place over a period of time in those accounts which directly influence working capital and cash flows'.

Glautier, *et al.* (1978 p. 138) had no doubts on the matter: 'to most people the term funds means cash. In accounting the term funds has a restricted meaning and is used to refer to net working capital'.

For McNamara (1979 p. 315) the statement answers the questions 'from where did the funds [cash] come and to where did the funds [cash] go during the period?' but for Samuels, *et al.* (1981 p. 296) 'the statement shows the source of all resources and how they have been used'.

Sprouse (1971 p. 168) attributed to the statement 'a summary of the transactions resulting in changes in working capital' and exemplified (pp. 170ff) how 'the non use of funds is not the same thing as a source of funds'.

The Financial Analysts Federation (1964 p. 9) of the USA went rather further. 'Valuable insight' is given by the statement into 'future dividend policy, the financing of capital expenditures and the extent to which additional debt and/or equities may be issued to finance same, and the ability to meet debt servicing requirements'.

For Barton (1975 p. 263) in Australia, 'Where management does not have perfect knowledge of the more distant future, long term projections are normally made on a funds flow basis rather than a cash flow basis'.

Finally, Bull (1980 p. 461): 'Fund flow analysis seeks to recast the income statement and balance sheet as prepared in accordance with accounting postulates, and describes the events of an accounting period in terms of sources of additional funds, and the uses to which these were put'. Moreover (p. 468) 'A good analyst however can often do a fairly accurate job of deducing what probably took place. Fund flow analysis therefore is a useful managerial tool insofar as it can help highlight reasons for changes in the liquidity of the firm'.

With such divergent views in the textbooks about the content and purpose of funds statements, it is not surprising that teaching and examination of this topic tends to comprise calculation rather than interpretation or analysis. Pratt and Chrisman (1982) showed how calculation itself was improved by imparting interpretative ability, through the direct method in their particular case.

So, the personal opinions of journal and textbook writers seem to be an inexhaustible source of confusion about funds flow statements that surveys of professional views have done little to reduce. The next section surveys how far such confusion is underwritten by the results of previous empirical work on the funds flow numbers themselves.

Some academics feel the confusion as to the exact boundary of 'funds' is one of the problems solved by adopting cash flow accounting. Lee (1982) pointed to its objectivity but Rutherford (1982b) argued it to be nearly as misleading as accrual accounting, especially when segmental reporting is involved. Clark (1983) quoted various American institutional views favouring a cash flow rather than funds flow focus in the relevant accounting statement but Sorter (1982) argued that 'cash' and 'cash flow' are terms no less subject to ambiguity than 'funds' and 'funds flow'. Mason (1961) cites with approval Moonitz (1961) as follows:

> In essence the accrual basis itself developed in an effort to over-come the shortcomings of cash movements as indicators of the results of operations. And yet the newer emphasis on 'fund flows' or 'cash flows' seems to run counter to the movement to perfect an accrual accounting . . . the sophisticated concept is that of accrual accounting, the more primitive one is, of course, the elemental idea of cash movement.

Critics' suggestions

The journals have not lacked suggestions for improving the funds statement. Many of the writers cited above concluded their criticisms with suggestions for reformulated funds statements. Ismail and Rae (1984) wanted funds statements segmented by line of business. Lee (1984b), Ketz and Kochanek (1982), Golub and Huffman (1984), Lawson (1983), Swanson and Vangermeersch (1981) and Bryant (1984) all gave examples of reformulated funds statements they argue to be more meaningful than conventional formats. Heath (1978a, b) argued that replacing the funds statement altogether was the best policy and recommended a 'statement of financing and investing activities' that separated these two activities clearly. McMonnies (1984) went furthest of all critics in wanting to scrap all published accounts as lacking value for all users and believed narrative reports would be more effective in communicating financial information. This view had been moderated by 1989 (McMonnies 1989).

Giese and Klammer (1974) criticized the add-back format sanctioned by APB 19 for funds from operations and recommended a direct approach.

Henry (1975) noted that the purpose of a funds statement was to report the financing and investing activities of a firm, but thought disclosure of operating flows would be better done on a direct basis rather than on an add-back one.

Coleman (1979) proposed separating internally generated funds from externally generated funds, reconciling to cash rather than working capital, and categorizing capital expenditures into replacement and improvement, expansion and compliance categories.

Hooper and Page (1979) proposed a new statement beginning with cash increase or decrease over last year end, and adjusting the cash flow at three levels to end with net income. Level 1 adjustments are receipts and payments on capital account, broadly the same as financing and investing activities. Level 2 adjustments are accruals and prepayments including sales not yet paid. Level 3 adjustments are termed accounting allocations and include depreciation, profit or loss on asset disposals (reported gross in level 1), undistributed subsidiary earnings and deferred tax. They held that their statement 'clearly distinguishes between real transactions, judgmental transactions, and accounting allocations' which correspond respectively to their three levels of adjustment (Hooper and Page 1979 p. 55), but failed to note that such correspondence is not beyond controversy.

Choi and Sondhi (1984), having praised SFAS 52 for enabling consolidated funds statements to reflect changes expressed in each of the currencies of each of the countries in which subsidiaries operate – instead of only in US$ as previously – proposed a funds statement format that would distinguish operations results from exchange rate change effects.

Australia's two-entity controversy

AAS 12 (1983) defined funds as cash and cash equivalents but its section 102 said 'Clearly the concept of funds remains that of all financial resources.' McKinnon *et al.* (1983 p. 83) proposed a two-entity test to clarify the ambiguity thus:

1. The Funds Statement aims to show the flow of resources, capturing the effects of external transactions alone and omitting book entries.
2. The measure of the sacrifice of a resource is normally its recorded cost amount.
3. As not all recorded amounts involve resource flows with external transactions, a two-entity test is proposed, namely;
4. A movement of funds occurs only when an event recorded in the accounting records of one entity is recorded also in the accounting records of another entity.

Robb (1985) commented on the practicality of this test by observing that a firm does not usually know whether or not the other firm has recorded the transaction. Moreover the test would exclude tax provisions, dividends, doubtful debt provisions and reclassifications and revaluations of working capital.

In response, Partington *et al*. (1986) accused Robb of using selective and garbled quotations. As to one party's ignorance of the other party's accounting entries, Partington *et al*. blamed this on accrual accounting rather than on their test. They attributed to Robb a belief that funds flows involve movements if they are really external, but performance of a service to extinguish a debt involves no movement although it does reduce the size of liabilities and passes the two-entity test. However, they did agree that their test is inadequate to deal with all kinds of changes in the components of working capital but added (p. 43): 'If a working capital statement is required, then it is best prepared using the working capital concept of funds' (as opposed, presumably, to the two-entity concept).

In a possible admission of having lost the argument, they concluded (p. 44):

> The two entity test was offered as a possible refinement of the conventional external transaction test for resource movements. Perhaps it will prove to be no improvement, but it has stimulated criticism (mostly adverse) from our colleagues, breathing some new life into this ancient unresolved topic.

Robb (1986) in his final comment read the Partington *et al*. article as tacit acknowledgement of his criticism. However, it was perhaps a victory too easily obtained. Had McKinnon *et al*. not specified the other party as having *actually* recorded the transaction in their books, but had instead stipulated that the other party *should in accordance with GAAP* have recorded it, the two-entity test might well have been seen as a useful step forward in cleansing funds of their unnecessary ambiguities.

Surveys of opinions of the funds statement

Banker's views

Hiltebeitel (1985) found that, for his sample of bank loan officers, there was a significant three-way correlation between perceived usefulness, risk assessment and information needs.

Baker (1987) experimented with surrogates for decision usefulness to bank loan officers, and found the most dependable to be certainty and precision.

The importance, but not necessarily the helpfulness, of the statement of changes in financial position to various users of the statement had been somewhat supported by Summers (1968), Pankoff and Virgil (1970) and Chandra (1974).

Brownlee's (1978) survey found the SCFP to be rated useful both by commercial banks and by bank trusts. The banks used it for determining the appropriateness of a loan applicant's financial policies. The trusts used it to assess the future earnings from the current uses of funds. The statement was seen as a reservoir of information from which users can draw the particular data that suit their needs.

Graci (1982) believed he had found that the SCFP had no incremental information content and did not influence American bank loan officers faced with a short term borrowing application from a retail firm.

Vicknair (1983) found that bank loan officers preferred the APB 19 approach to funds over other alternatives but cautioned (p. 101):

> Usefulness of funds reporting alternatives is not dependent on the particular funds concept selected by chief commercial loan officers as the underlying basis of the statement.

Small firm managers

Chesley and Scheiner (1982) examined the usefulness and understandability of funds statements to owners of small businesses in Canada and the USA. Their sample was 246 Nova Scotian manufacturers and 250 near equivalents in southeastern USA. To their 25 point questionnaire covering both Likert scale ratings of the statement's possible dimensions of usefulness and also questions on a specimen SCFP, they received 95 Canadian and 76 American responses. The only non-response bias detected in follow-up calls was that Canadian non-respondents tended to be from slightly smaller small firms.

The most important results are summarized in Table 4.2.

As a result of this study, the authors determined that the respondents understood the concept of working capital in its general sense, namely as cash resources for the working of their business.

> The accounting definition of this term is very specific and includes assets and debts which vary in their proximity to cash. Unless

Table 4.2 Summary of results

Question and answer	Canada (%)	USA (%)	X^2	alpha
Is the funds statement used?				
Yes	73	82		
No	27	18	1.66	>50%
What statements are prepared?				
BS, IS, Retentions and SCFP	66	84		
BS, IS, RE only	20	16		
Single statement only	14	00	13.64	<0.5%
How useful is the SCFP?				
Very	32	30		
Quite	33	14		
Slightly	29	32		
Not	6	4	11.47	<1%
What changes in the SCFP are suggested?				
None needed	89	80		
Definition of funds	4	11		
Details	6	7		
Price level	1	2	2.11	>50%
Which definition of working capital (*sic*) is most useful?				
Cash	30	12		
Cash & 1 liquid asset less c. ls.	34	20		
Current assets less c. ls.	28	63		
Multiple responses	8	5	21.43	<0.1%
Are you familiar with the concept of working capital?				
Yes	99	100		
No	1	0		
Is your SCFP similar to the specimen supplied?				
Yes	90	97		
No	10	3	15.01	<0.1%
Is the application of funds to paying dividends and debts equal to cash?				
Yes	55	64		
No	7	5		
Not necessarily	38	31		
Are funds from operations equal to cash?				
Yes	31	33		
No	60	48		
Don't know	9	19	24.61	<0.1%

the user understands this point, the working capital funds statement can be misleading. . . . This study provides evidence that users may be misinterpreting the funds statement as a statement of cash receipts and disbursements. To reduce the confusion, perhaps as Heath suggests, three separate statements should be presented.

(Chesley and Scheiner 1982 p. 58)

Australian institutional investors

Anderson (1981) found that Australian institutional investors rated income and position statements three times more important than the funds statement for sell or hold decisions but only twice as important for buy decisions. The study of annual reports was seen as less important than a range of other information sources like tips, brokers, visits to companies, magazines and even government publications.

CPAs

Phillips (1984) surveyed CPAs on their preferred construct of funds but was unable to obtain any consensus, except for the weak conclusion that accounts users were more open to revision of APB 19 than accounts preparers were.

Financial analysts

Rakes and Shenken (1972) found that 134 out of their 151 chartered financial analyst respondents preferred an all financial resources definition of funds over working capital or cash.

RESEARCH ON THE SCFP'S PREDICTIVE ABILITY

Association with other variables

Association of funds flows with market movements

Barlev and Livnat (1986) found a positive association between uses of funds and stock returns for 494 firms included on the Compustat tape for the decade 1971–81. The information content of sources of funds seemed to be directly negative but indirectly positive, although this result is at least partly an artefact of the path analysis method.

Harmon (1984), however, found earnings were more closely associated with stock price changes than were funds flows. This contrasts with Staubus (1965) who had found funds flows (defined as net working capital from operations less taxes) more reliable than earnings in predicting stock prices. However, it supports Ball and Brown (1968) who found funds flows (net operating income before non-recurring items) not as good as EPS or net income in predicting the residual behaviour of stock prices; Beaver and Dukes (1972) who found funds flow (earnings before interest, tax, depreciation and amortization) worse than earnings in terms of a U test of associations with stock prices; and Govindarajan (1980) whose sample of financial analysts' comments on 976 companies showed 86.5 per cent put more importance on earnings than funds flows. None of the above, however, precludes the possibility that funds statements constitute significant *extra* information.

Association with earnings and cash flow

Research on the ability of other currently reported performance measures to serve as proxies for cash flow from operations was done by Thode *et al.* (1986). Twelve hypotheses were tested using data on cash flow, working capital and income from continuing operations for all firms contained in Standard and Poor's 400 Industrials Index during 1973–82. They found that cash flow from operations was not easily inferred from, and not systematically related to, other conventional performance measures or cash flow surrogates.

Seed (1984b) performed a ten-year correlation of operations working capital flow with operations cash flow. R^2 was too small for either to be inferred from the other, so the funds statement is providing unique and at least potentially useful information, a conclusion supportive of previous similar findings and inferences by Gombola and Ketz (1983) and Bowen *et al.* (1984). However, Seed (1984b p. 55) cautioned:

> We stress the word *potential* because the above studies generally ascertained that it is a distinct measure of performance; not that it is a clear determinant of company value or an obvious essential element in decision models used by investors or creditors. Thus, the relevance of cash flow from operations, such as might be measured by statistical association with stock price movements, has not been demonstrated empirically. Rather, what we have is a belief, shared by the FASB and others, that accounting data should be helpful in assessing the timing and amounts of future cash flows and, by implication, that the cash flows themselves are important.

Andrew *et al*. (1985) analysed 112 Singaporean firms in 1983 and 1984, finding funds from operations so closely correlated with profit that they concluded it is not a useful indicator of solvency and does not add to the information in the income statement.

Predictive accuracy

Predicting cash flows

Easton (1984) found accounting earnings to be about equally correlated as share prices were with the theoretical value of a dividend stream. Cash flow predicted theoretical dividends slightly less efficiently than earnings, but both were far better than current dividends or sales revenue. This was held to support the view that accounting had information content in the prediction of *actual* dividend streams.

Costigan (1985) found that working capital funds from operations had a marginally better performance than cash flow from operations in predicting future cash flows.

Wilson's (1985) PhD Dissertation for Carnegie-Mellon University addressed the information content of accruals elements in funds flows in predicting operating cash flows. He distinguished between current accruals and non-current ones, the former being the aggregate of all the working capital changes excluding cash and the latter being the difference between earnings and working capital funds flow from operations (largely comprising depreciation and deferred tax). He found that the total accrual had positive information content but was unable to establish a consistent allocation of such content between the current and non-current accruals.

An analysis by Hassanli (1988) of 29 accounting measures showed that 21 of those variables, mostly funds flow statement items or ratios thereof, are important in predicting cash flows.

Predicting mergers

Ratios derived from the SCFP were slightly superior predictors of whether or not a firm had merged compared with ratios derived from the income and position statements (Barton 1986).

Bankruptcy forecasts

A direct basis for the SCFP resulted in the solvency judgments of professional analysts and portfolio managers outperforming their indirect SCFP-based judgements (Allen 1985).

Amy Lau (1982) was one of the first researchers to use multinomial logit analysis (MLA) to predict four different levels of financial trouble from reduced dividends to full bankruptcy, by means of ranked probability scores for up to three years before the event. Her MLA model outperformed and was more robust than the Altman, Beaver and naive models. The predictive ability of the model was enhanced when operating earnings or working capital funds flows rather than net quick assets or cash flows were input into the model. She concluded (Lau 1982 p. 143):

> This empirical superiority of earnings and working capital flow information is contrary to the advocacy of cash flow which is prevalent in current authoritative accounting literature.

Marlowe (1984), however, found no significant difference between net income, working capital or cash-based funds flow models in using logit to classify firms between bankrupt and non-bankrupt.

Casey and Bartczak (1984) found cash flow data incapable of distinguishing failed from unfailed firms in the five years before failure. Like Casey and Bartczak (1984), Gentry *et al.* (1985b) found cash flow from operations has no incremental classifying information content beyond other cash-based funds flows of which dividends were the most significant.

Gentry *et al.* (1985a) showed dividends to be the most effective funds flow component in distinguishing failed from unfailed firms up to three years earlier. Receivables and investments provided reliable signals, but only in the year before failure. They also found cash-based statements to be a viable predictor of failed firms but not a better one than funds flow (Gentry *et al.* 1985b).

Barton (1986) found that the classification of firms into bankrupt or merged with ratios derived from the SCFP slightly outperformed ratios from the other two final accounts, but ratios derived from all three were significantly better still. Contrary to expectations, cash flow measures were not superior to working capital measures in predicting mergers.

Gentry *et al.* (1987) repeated their demonstration of the usefulness of funds statement elements in predicting bankruptcy. In their sample of 33 failed and 33 non-failed firms, investment, dividends and receivables had significance for the failed firms but only size and dividends had any significance for the successful ones.

Significant differences between failed and unfailed firms were found by Gahlon and Vigeland (1988) for five years before bankruptcy in respect of net cash flow from operations, cash flow after debt retirement and age of trade creditors. These all assume cash flows calculated on the direct basis, as the indirectly based flows will not discriminate quite so well.

Summary of this section

Evidence on the usefulness of funds flows as leading or lagging indicators of stock market price movements is mixed, but there is quite strong support for the importance of accrual-based earnings in such a role.

Funds flows from operations appear to be closely related to earnings but quite far away from operations cash flows; yet funds flows seem to predict cash flows better than do cash flows themselves. Finally, funds flow based variables do at least as well as cash flow, often much better, in predicting or classifying bankrupt firms.

Thus, recently published empirical studies would seem to offer significant support for the notion that conventional funds flow statements have distinct information content.

The Walker study

Walker (1981, 1984) conducted a study, which he termed an experiment, to test hypotheses developed from claims made in the literature about the advantages of presenting data in the form of an SCFP; in particular, the claim that the SCFP assists readers to interpret a set of financial reports by making the reports 'more readily interpretable'.

From literature-based observations Walker formulated four experimental hypotheses, namely:

H1 There is no difference in the time taken by readers of annual reports to assess a firm's position and prospects when they are given financial statements which (a) include funds statements, or else (b) do not include funds statements.

H2 There is no difference in the consensus secured among readers of annual reports who (a) are provided with funds statements or (b) are not provided with funds statements.

H3 There is no difference in the confidence reflected by readers of annual reports who (a) are provided with funds statements and (b) are not provided with funds statements.

H4 There is no difference in the accuracy achieved by readers of annual reports when assessing aspects of a company's financial position and performance when those readers (a) are provided with funds statements or (b) are not provided with funds statements.

In the study 200 subjects were given a sequence of 6 sets of financial reports and questioned on each firm's financial position, performance and prospects.

Financial report pages were colour coded and presented to participants in a predetermined sequence to enable easy recording of the time taken to complete each stage of the exercise. Participants were told it was essential to complete the questions and read the reports in the specified sequence. The responses were so unobtrusively timed that only three of the subjects indicated that they realized that they were being timed at all.

A pilot study with students had shown a considerable learning effect manifesting in considerably shorter processing times for the later stages of the exercise. Walker (1981 p. 6) thought this was also strongly influenced by peer performance, since the pilot test had been administered in a group situation, notwithstanding Chervany and Dickson's (1974) report of no such peer pressure existing in their comparable experimental setting. Walker found this aspect of his pilot test sufficiently serious to justify administering his test on a one-to-one basis. In this, he is imputing external validity to student behaviour in a way not necessarily justified for adult accountants and analysts. Moreover, he is treating peer pressure as a contaminant, whereas it could be argued that its presence enhances the representativeness of the setting. In financial and banking offices, open plan multiple occupation is the norm in Hong Kong, even for credit analysts. Thus, insofar as a group of subjects all doing the same task constitutes real peer pressure, it also constitutes a realistic and representative work setting. It is almost as if Walker wished to slow down his subjects' responses by putting them in solitary experimental confinement. As for learning effects, these are only possible if the task content and requirements hardly vary at all from one attempt at a task to the next. Given the great variety present in the real world population of funds statements, it would have been quite possible to minimize learning effects by sequencing the accounts in an appropriate way.

Reports were selected to minimize the possibility that subjects could base their responses on knowledge of actual case histories, but all reports were Australian and related to firms of similar sizes of total assets. The reports of the firms included a fictitious name for the firm, an illustrated cover, an index, lists of fictitious officers, and reports from directors and auditors. Notes to the accounts were included but edited down. The financial statements themselves were edited enough to standardize the extent, but not the narrative content, of disclosure. The reports totalled nine colour-coded pages each, exclusive of a one-page funds statement.

> To cope with the possibility that the reports of some firms might be more difficult than those of others, the six annual reports were presented to matched pairs of subjects in ten randomly selected sequences, so that within each subject category, a subject provided with funds statements received the reports in the same sequence as a subject not provided with funds statements.
>
> (Walker 1984 p. 130)

The questions accompanying the annual reports were developed from a literature review of what funds statements are supposed to achieve. The following table combines and abbreviates Walker's (1984) Tables 6–1 and 6–2:

Aim	No. of supporting references	Associated questions
A	28 [latest Courtis 1976]	c1 c2 j1 j5
B	22 [latest Spiller & Virgil 1974]	c5
C	10 [latest Courtis 1976]	j2
D	9 [latest The Corporate Report 1975]	j3
E	21 [latest Seed 1976]	c4 j4
F	2 [latest The Corporate Report 1975]	c3

AIMS

A To represent changes in a firm's financing policies
B To depict how a firm's resources have been applied during a period
C To represent changes in the pattern of a firm's investments
D To provide an indication of a firm's capacity to maintain an investment programme (or other activities) with resources derived from business operations

E To depict changes in a firm's liquidity
F To indicate the significance of dividend payments *vis-à-vis* other distributions, or to represent capacity to pay dividends.

CALCULATION QUESTIONS

c1 Has the firm raised new equity capital during the year covered by the report?

c2 Is the firm more heavily dependent upon external borrowings than in the previous year?

c3 Did the firm distribute a higher percentage of its profits in the last year than in the year before?

c4 Has the firm's liquid position deteriorated, relative to what it was a year ago?

c5 Has the firm expended significant sums in the last year on new investments or in replacing productive assets?

JUDGEMENT QUESTIONS

j1 Are the firm's financing and investment policies likely to lead to increasing profitability?

j2 Has the composition of the firm's assets changed significantly during the last financial year?

j3 Would the firm be in a position to finance expansion of its activities from internally generated funds?

j4 Is the firm in a position to pay its debts as and when they fall due?

j5 Have there been any significant changes in the firm's gearing over the past financial year?

The c questions need calculations to be accurately answered, the j questions only require judgements to be made.

> Subjects were required to answer yes, no or not sure to each question. This provided a very crude measurement of confidence. Rating scales were not used, since it was considered that they might lead to some hesitancy or vacillation and so affect response times.
>
> (Walker 1984 p. 133)

In the study 100 subjects were given the c questions, 100 the j questions; but all received three reports with and three reports without funds statements. There were 20 subjects in each of the following categories:

1 first year students,
2 advanced accounting students,
3 academic accountants,
4 accounting practitioners, and
5 financial analysts.

Financial analysts were chosen for their occupational involvement in the interpretation of financial data and because their information needs are thought to influence the design of accounting reports. The selection of other groups was based on the extent to which they were expected to have received relevant training and work experience, although more senior practitioners would not perhaps be as familiar with funds statements as would recently qualified accountants, accounting academics and advanced accounting students. This is because only in 1973 did Australia require listed firms to produce funds statements. First year accounting students were thought to be a surrogate for unsophisticated investors. Some considerable differences in familiarity with funds statements were expected between these subject groups.

The experiment was administered in six rounds. In rounds 1 to 3, one group received a report without funds statements, the other received the same report (in each round) including a funds statement. In rounds 4 to 6, the first group's reports included funds statements, the second group's reports excluded them. The Wilcoxon matched pairs signed ranks test compared the subjects' round 3 scores with their round 4 scores (after the switch from without to with). Financial analysts took longer to answer the c questions, while both groups of students took less time to answer the j questions after the switch. However, no group took less time to answer questions throughout rounds 4 to 6 compared with the time taken for rounds 1 to 3. That is, the learning effects feared from the pilot tests were not found in the main experiment. Around 20 per cent of the time spent reviewing the reports in each round was spent on the funds statement, again with no significant change in this proportion from the early rounds to the later ones. Walker acknowledged that these results could be explained by mere sampling variation (Walker 1981 p. 20).

The mean response time for all subjects answering the c questions was 5.51 minutes and on the j questions 5.48 minutes for the reports without funds statements; and 6.00 minutes for c questions and 5.16

for j questions for the reports with funds statements. No significant time reduction was associated with the provision of funds statements except for the two student groups on the j questions in a within-subject design, but financial analysts showed significant time increases in answering the c questions.

Four of the c questions had correct answers based on calculations. The fifth inadvertently introduced a subjective materiality criterion. The funds statements appeared to make no significant difference to judgement accuracy, but did enhance confidence in answering question c4 concerning liquidity deterioration and question j3 concerning financing expansion from operations when judged by the chi square test, but scarcely at all when judged by the Fisher exact probability test. No consensus effect was found.

Walker thus found all four of his null hypotheses supported but his final paragraph cautioned thus:

> The results cannot be interpreted as reflecting upon the usefulness of funds statements as a means of conveying information not otherwise obtainable from balance sheets or income statements. It is emphasized that the investigation concerned funds statements in the form of 'all inclusive' statements of changes in financial position, and that the findings cannot be related to claims about the usefulness of funds statements containing, for example, information about realized cash flows. These claims remain unsupported hypotheses.
>
> (Walker 1984 p. 144)

Walker's conclusions seem valid as regards their internal validity, since his experiment was designed to minimize contaminants. His study may well also have external validity within Australia for Australian accounting reports, but a mean time of between 5 and 6 minutes for nine- or ten-page annual reports suggests an average time per page of less than 30 seconds to answer all five questions on the question sheets. This seems remarkably fast, especially for calculation questions. Overload effects arising from providing the SCFP on top of nine other pages could explain the lack of increment in accuracy, but such effects would be hard to isolate when the nine other pages already contained enough data to overload subjects working at the speeds claimed by Walker. The purpose of providing full reports rather than just balance sheets and income statements is unclear and was not followed in the present study. Disagreement has already been expressed earlier in this section with Walker's view of the distortions inherent in peer pressure. Apart from these points, however, Walker's approach had some considerable strengths. His derivation of funds statement justifications from a comprehensive literature review is hard to fault. His questionnaire design arising from those justifications is also largely convincing, with some minor reservations. His use of non-parametric statistics to test his four hypotheses seems appropriate, if a little timid, given the robustness of ANOVA to almost every kind of deviation from normal distribution parameters. All in all, the Walker study's strengths were judged to outweigh its weaknesses to a sufficient extent that it was used as a point of departure for the research design of Donleavy's (1991) replication of it in Hong Kong.

Bradbury and Newby

Bradbury and Newby (1989) replicated Walker's work in New Zealand with three differences. First, their questions were developed from the local SSAP 10 (1979) rather than from the general body of the literature. Second, they protocol-analysed actual use of the funds statement as opposed to Walker's contrast of processing in the 'with' and 'without' funds statement modes. Third, they claimed to have studied whether use was made of information only available in the funds statement, whereas Walker had no such information available, this reflecting a difference between the Australian all financial resources statement which simply repackages the other two final accounts, and the New Zealand funds statement which had a working capital approach. They used 30 financial analysts whom they asked the following two judgement (j) and three calculation (c) questions:

j1 Is the company likely to default in repayment of the specified loan during the normal course of business?
j2 Is it likely that the company will pay a dividend next year? (sic)
c1 By what amount has the working capital position changed over the year?
c2 State the amount of liabilities repaid during the year.
c3 State the amount of fixed assets purchased during the year?

Every analyst was given the same annual report, *in full and inclusive of notes*, of 'a small New Zealand manufacturing company'.

Reprocessing their results, some interesting behaviours emerge as follows:

On	Most time was spent reading	Mean total time spent reading for the whole report
j1	BS	9.22 min
j2	BS	56.4 sec
c1	BS	1.24 min
c2	BS	1.95 min
c3	BS	1.36 min

Note: BS = Balance Sheet

It is odd that so much time should have been spent on so-called calculation questions that are really a matter of simply retrieving the appropriate published total or subtotal from the report. Question c2 saw the greatest time spent on the funds statement but even here the BS was more extensively searched, and six analysts seem never to have used the funds statement at all. Judgement questions were answered on a five-point scale from 1=very likely to 5=very unlikely. Respondents also had to indicate their degree of confidence on a five-point scale, thereby implicitly disagreeing with Walker's reasons for not employing such a refinement – its comparative meaninglessness on an intersubjective basis (the well-known Arrow impossibility theorem supports Walker in this reservation). Bradbury and Newby concluded from their study that the funds statement did not enhance judgement accuracy or confidence nor did it enable quicker processing, although working capital calculations for c1 were done somewhat faster when the funds statement was used. Surprisingly, only 7 of the 30 analysts gave a correct answer to c2 requiring 'calculation' of the total liabilities to be repaid. The study may well be justified in concluding that 'there is little point in retaining the SOCIFP as a third financial statement', but with results like those from a group of sophisticated users, the doubt arises as to whether the results say more about the analysts than about the reports. This is a lesser problem with Walker's results, since he used five different kinds of subject. It is interesting that Bradbury and Newby's results support Walker's but with apparently greater variations in speed for their 30 subjects than was shown by Walker's 200. Indeed it is the speed results in both studies that stretch credulity furthest. Particular care, therefore, was taken by Donleavy (1991) to monitor speed with precision.

Conclusions

Throughout the literature, criticisms of the confused nature of the concept 'funds' and the unfocused purposes of the funds statement abound. As mentioned previously, Walker (1984) crystallized the aims of the funds statement as follows:

A To represent changes in a firm's financing policies
B To depict how a firm's resources have been applied during a period
C To represent changes in the pattern of a firm's investments
D To provide an indication of a firm's capacity to maintain an investment programme (or other activities) with resources derived from business operations
E To depict changes in a firm's liquidity, and
F To indicate the significance of dividend payments *vis-à-vis* other distributions, and to represent capacity to pay dividends.

Assuming readers of full reports adopt a search minimization strategy, it is possible that the SCFP might provide an initial indication of the key relationships within the financial data, such as that subsisting between accounting profits and cash balances.

Hence, scrutiny of funds statements would enable readers quickly to identify matters which they might wish to review in detail. Moreover, funds statements could be supposed to enhance the interpretability of annual reports by reducing information complexity. Since individuals vary in their capacity to handle information complexity (Schroder, Driver and Streufert 1967), it might be supposed that the presentation of funds statements would ensure that a wider range of readers would be able to discern relationships reflected in financial data.

(Walker 1984 p. 127)

If SCFPs do achieve these things, then readers should process financial information both more quickly and more accurately than if SCFPs were not available. There should also be more consensus and greater confidence on the part of readers provided with SCFPs compared with those who were not.

The personal opinions of journal and textbook writers seem to be an inexhaustible source of confusion about funds flow statements that surveys of professional views have done little to reduce. The third section here surveyed how far such confusion is underwritten by the results of previous empirical work on the funds flow numbers themselves, and found a rather more convincing picture of the usefulness of funds statements than was demonstrated in the expressions of personal opinion of most of the non-research-based commentators.

Evidence on the usefulness of funds flows as leading or lagging indicators of stock market price movements is mixed, but there is quite strong support for the importance of accrual-based earnings in such a role. Recently published empirical studies would seem to offer significant support for the notion that conventional funds flow statements have distinct information content.

Funds flows from operations appear to be closely related to earnings but quite far away from operations cash flows; yet funds flows seem to predict cash flows better than do cash flows themselves. Finally, funds flow based variables do at least as well as cash flow, often much better, in predicting or classifying bankrupt firms.

Finally, Baker's (1987) most dependable surrogates for decision usefulness to bank loan officers were found to be certainty and precision. This means that fuzziness implies uselessness, and 'funds' excel in fuzziness. The literature has assumed 'cash' is self-evidently sharper and more certain than 'funds'. Chapter 6 will discuss the problems with such a view, and show how SFAS 95 and its overseas equivalents are introducing fuzziness into the notion of cash with the notions of 'near cash' and 'liquid funds'. It would be rather strange if Finney's (1925) definition of 'funds' as 'something more than cash' were to become more than a little appropriate for some of the new approaches to cash itself. The recent history of government attempts in the UK and the USA to define money in order to control its supply shows the naivety of assuming that 'cash', even in its M1 form, is a self-defining, self-evident state of nature. It is perhaps as impossible to draw firm lines round any liquid asset as it is to measure the precise volume of water in, say, the River Clyde at any point in time. It is as if 'liquidity' is inherently and irrevocably 'fuzzy'.

THE EMERGENCE OF THE CASH FLOW STATEMENT

The SEC issued Release Number 117, 'Adoption of Article 11A of Regulation SX', *requiring* cash-based funds flow reports to accompany reports filed with the SEC after the end of 1970 (SEC 1971 *sic*). This did not affect accounts issued to shareholders or to other arms of government, but may well have facilitated adoption of cash-based funds statements by US firms, obliged as they now became to provide them for the SEC.

Arthur Andersen (1976) was one of the earliest elements of the accounting establishment to express a preference for cash over 'unimportant' working capital as the focus of the statement of changes in financial position. However, the probable turning point came when the AICPA sponsored its council member, Loyd (*sic*) C. Heath (1978a), to produce a monograph criticizing existing funds flow statements as the product of unclear, misleading and unattainable objectives. To meet these objectives, three separate statements were needed, namely:

1 a receipts and payments account,
2 a statement of movements on loan and equity financing,
3 a statement of movements on long term asset accounts.

An article called 'Let's scrap the funds statement' by Heath (1978b) summarized his criticisms. A riposte by Largay *et al.* (1979) pointed out four main things:

1 That Heath explicitly adopted the very objectives of APB 19 he had been deeming unattainable.
2 That the replacement of one statement – the SCFP – by three new ones was not readily assessable as an improvement.
3 That a receipts and payments account has limited information content and represents a regression to pre-accrual accounting.
4 That the working capital basis is superior to the cash basis because the former eliminates the timing fluctuations arising from the cash-cash cycle. One might add that this point carries the further implication that working capital is harder to window-dress than is any definition of cash.

At the end of the 1970s, views on credit analysis were changing, as illustrated by the following quotations:

> The early emphasis on working capital did have its shortcomings resulting in a changing emphasis in credit analysis. For example, assuming a firm is a going concern, its working capital probably represents a permanent investment. Thus, repayment of loans will be made from current earnings.
>
> (Graci 1982 p. 23)

This point was earlier graphically elaborated by Arthur Stone Dewing as follows (Dewing 1953):

Bankers learned by tragic experience that there was no mystical significance in the two to one ratio. They observed that in many types of business, under the stress of general disaster, inventories could not be sold, and if such an attempt should be made, not a two-to-one or even a three-or-four-to-one ratio would bring them the immediate payment of their debts. If business failed, the relative amounts of current capital in the days before the failure had little significance in the final liquidation of the bankrupt business.

Sophisticated creditors were alleged by Heath to realize that a firm's ability to repay its debts depends on its future cash generating ability, and future cash inflows do not necessarily depend on profit potential. Heath (1978a p. 78) emphasized this point by stating:

> The financial failures of the late 1960s and the early 1970s drove home the point that debts are not paid out of profits in much the same way that the failures of the 1930s drove home the point that current liabilities are not paid out of current assets.

According to Barlev and Livnat (1986 p. 225), 'Heath's study made a significant contribution to the FASB Discussion Memorandum [1980].'

Braiotta (1984) reported that as early as 1983 57 per cent of sampled executives planned to use a cash-based SCFP compared with 27 per cent in 1980. Of the 1982 reports surveyed by Thode *et al.* (1986) 56 per cent used this approach which had been recommended by the Financial Executives' Institute. The professional notes section of the *Journal of Accountancy* in December 1978 published three of the 'unprecedented number of comments from readers', most of which defended the SCFP. Heath's statement of cash receipts and payments is a sources and uses format with a supporting schedule showing the build-up of cash provided by operations. It looks like this:

Cash provided by operations

Cash collected from customers		783,545
Interest and dividends received		1,417
Total cash receipts from operations		784,962
Cash disbursements:		
For merchandise inventories	457,681	
For admin and selling expenses	264,577	
For interest	6,941	
For other expenses	14,963	
For taxes	13,273	
		757,425
Cash provided by operations		27,537

Heath (1978a p. 104) equated cash and near cash with a firm's debt paying ability. He saw that the danger of overtrading increased during inflation and that the need for a receipts and payments account was correspondingly greater (p. 111). He strongly favoured a direct method of cash accounting for operations and Barber (1981 p. 69) criticized this on the grounds that it failed to highlight the disparity between cash flow and net income. The indirect method, on the other hand, adds back items to net income to arrive at operations cash flow, thereby explaining the disparity. In an earlier paper, Heath (1982) attacked the reconciliation approach of the indirect method on three grounds. First, it assumes that the income statement is *the* statement of operations of a business. Second, it confounds income with receipts. Third, it assumes that the purpose of an SCF or SCFP is to explain what 'happened' to a firm's income.

Net income, the change in a company's net assets, is an abstract number; it is not a physical 'thing.' Or, as the courts are fond of saying, profit is a quantum and not a res. Trying to explain what happened to last year's profit is like trying to explain to a child what happened to the two inches he grew last year. No statement can do that.

(Heath 1982 p. 167)

The point here is that before any country issued any standard requiring a cash flow statement, the principal architect of the new statement put on record the crucial role of the direct method of reporting operations cash flow in distinguishing the future SCF from the past SCFP.

Holly Clemente (1982) reported the results of the Financial Executives' Institute survey earlier in the year. Of almost 1,200 respondents, 79 per cent adopted a sources and uses format, and 57 per cent defined funds as cash and short term investments.

Nurnberg (1983) pointed out that the pre SFAS 95 exposure drafts had not removed the ambiguities left by APB 19 concerning the boundaries between the operating, financing and investing activities of a firm.

An exposure draft from the FASB was issued in 1981 proposing a cash rather than working capital focus. Gibson and Kruse (1984) found that a majority of their 87 sample firms already used a cash focus, reconciling net income to cash flow. This finding was echoed by England and Goodman (1986) who also said most firms were already using the three-section (financing, operating and investing) format.

Braiotta (1984) reported that 56 per cent of his 66 firm sample were already using the cash basis, something that may be connected with the 1982 Auditing Principles Board statement allowing firms to change from a working capital to a cash basis without thereby incurring an audit report qualified for breach of the consistency principle.

Ketz and Largay (1987) unsuccessfully tried to link SCFP numbers with their equivalents in the income and position statements. In particular, the income statement idea of operations differed from that of the SCFP. They recommended the FASB to fuse the two statements into one or at least to impose a common definition of operations. They attribute the move from a working capital to a cash basis statement during the 1980s to 'strong encouragement provided by the Financial Executives' Institute and by publications of the FASB' (Ketz and Largay 1987 p. 10). (The publications to which they refer are FASB (1980) and (1981.)

Heath (1978b) wrote:

> The activities of business enterprises may be classified as operating, financing and investing. Operating activities are those activities directly related to the purchase and sale of raw materials, supplies and merchandise, the conversion of raw material and supplies into finished goods and services, the sale of finished goods and services, and the servicing of goods and services sold previously. Financing activities are those activities directly related to obtaining capital including, for example, the borrowing and repayment of debt, the issuance and reacquisition of a company's

stock, the conversion of securities into common stock, and the payment of dividends. Investment activities include the purchase and sale of securities of various types (excluding a company's own securities) and the purchase and sale of plant and equipment that is used in production, distribution, and maintenance of other goods and services.

(Quoted in Ketz and Largay 1987 p. 996)

Heath conceded that the boundaries between the three kinds of activity are unclear. Nonetheless, the FASB (1986) exposure draft that heralded SFAS 95 largely adopted Heath's distinctions and added to them (paragraph 10) the propositions that 'gain or loss from early extinguishment of debt is generally part of a cash outflow for financing activities' whilst 'gain or loss from sale of assets . . . is generally part of a cash inflow from investing activities'.

Chapter 5 describes the spread of the SCFP and the early adopters of the SCF outside the USA. The development of the SCF itself is reviewed and analysed in Chapter 6.

5 Global reach of the funds statement

INTRODUCTION

The aim of this chapter is to show how and when other countries followed the USA in adopting the funds statement and its successor, the cash flow statement. I will report why such adoption took place for the countries disclosing their reasons in English. Finally I consider whether the trajectory of the SCFP and the SCF sheds any light on the validity of accounting cluster theories in international accounting.

THE DISPERSION OF THE FUNDS FLOW STATEMENT AROUND THE WORLD

The UK

Morris (1974) reported a growth from 7 per cent in fiscal 1968/9 to 39 per cent in fiscal 1972/3 of the presentation of funds statements in published accounts.

Effective 1 January 1976 but approved 15 July 1975, the British SSAP 10 required firms with a gross income of over £25,000 to present a funds statement. The ICAEW survey of 1978 reported the increasing adoption of the statement by 300 sample firms in the immediately previous years, as shown in Table 5.1.

Table 5.1 Adoption of the funds statement

Fiscal year	No. of firms	% of sample
1973/4	153	51
1974/5	219	73
1975/6	256	85
1976/7	289	96
1977/8	300	100

Source: ICAEW, *Survey of Published Accounts*, London: ICAEW, 179–87, 1978

The 1975 Corporate Report thought the needs of all user groups could not be met by general purpose statements and McMonnies (1989 sec 3.8) agreed adding:

> We believe that so far as possible, reports should be framed in such a way that users can get what they want from them without having to turn for advice to an accountant, lawyer, economist or other specialist.

McMonnies' (1989) report for the Scottish Institute recommended two replacements for the funds statement and these are reproduced below:

From McMonnies' para 7.24, 'A Simple Statement of Changes in Financial Wealth'

Financial wealth added by operations	22,874
Increase in values of quoted investments	1,111
Reduction in deferred liability	4,991
	28,976
Decrease in value of tangible assets	(9,011)
	19,965
Distributable change in financial wealth in yr	19,965
Distribution	(6,444)
	13,521
New share capital	10,000
Change in financial wealth for the year	23,521
Movement in market capitalization	48,750

The above would comply, coincidentally, with the USA's APB 19.

From McMonnies' para 7.38 'A Cash Flow Statement'

Opening balance	(6,016)
Generated by operations	18,320
Investments in fixed assets and quoted shares	(19,833)
New finance – debentures	8,000
New finance – share capital	10,000
Closing balance	10,471

This statement, on the other hand, would not comply with SFAS 95, in the above summary format.

Once the USA had replaced funds statements by cash flow statements, the UK became in Adams' (1988) view very likely to follow. The 1980s' economic and political climate under Thatcher in the UK was similar to that under Reagan in the USA. The International Federation of Accountants was headquartered in New York; the International Accounting Standards Committee was headquartered in London. The largest accounting firms in the USA all began life in nineteenth century London. The dissatisfaction with the funds statement was felt as strongly in the UK as the USA; and as we shall see in Chapter 8, Britain has become the home of cash flow fundamentalism, thanks to the work of Lee and Lawson. So little surprise was to be voiced when the last exposure draft of the old Accounting Standards Committee, ED 54, proposed to replace the funds statement with the cash flow statement. The Committee's successor, the Financial Reporting Board, issued its first standard FRS 1 in 1991 requiring British companies to use cash flow statements in place of the funds statement for financial years ending after 1 January 1992. Its format is contrasted with the SFAS 95 format in Chapter 6.

Canada

In 1953 14 per cent of CICA-sampled companies had funds statements, in 1962 31 per cent, and in 1968 95 per cent (Murphy 1979). So when Canada required a sources and applications of funds statement by the 1970 Canada Business Corporations Act, as previously recommended by the 1965 Kimber Report (AG of Ontario 1965), most firms already presented one anyway.

For Canada 91 per cent of 325 companies surveyed were presenting a funds statement by 1967, and 98 per cent by 1970 (*Financial Reporting in Canada*, p. 163, Toronto: Canadian Institute of Chartered Accountants, 1971), following the section 1540 recommendation in the Institute Handbook in 1968. In September 1974 the section was revised to specify that the SCFP be used rather than a sources and uses statement. It remained a recommendation rather than a requirement. Then in 1975 the Canada Business Corporations Act section 46(1) *required* the inclusion of an SCFP. From 1972 all sampled firms presented a funds statement. Paragraph 1540 defined funds as working capital for firms whose balance sheets segregated current assets from current liabilities and as cash and cash equivalents for all other firms.

In 1985 Canada became the first country in the English-speaking world to require the replacement of the SCFP by the SCF. The Canadian Institute of Chartered Accountants' Handbook section 1540 was accordingly amended with effect for financial years ending after 1 July 1986. The format of the Canadian SCF is virtually identical to the American format under SFAS 95, but not quite so prescriptively detailed. Chapter 6 elaborates SCF format differences.

Australia and New Zealand

Of 120 company reports surveyed by Kenley and Staubus (1972) 36 included some form of funds statement. The General Council of the ASA had specifically mentioned the statement as exemplifying the accounting improvements it then wanted. In January 1971 the Australian Institute issued Technical Bulletin F1 which recommended the inclusion of a funds flow statement with the annual report. Its purpose would be 'to materially assist the reader to appreciate the meaning and significance of the reported financial results and the deployment of the resources of the company' when read in conjunction with the two older final accounts. By itself the statement 'enables the reader to understand better the effects of the company's policies in relation to such matters as the financing of trading operations, the investment in fixed assets, the payment of dividends and the repayment of loans'. As to format, although nothing was specified, the statement 'summarises movements in the financial resources, as reflected by successive balance sheets' (Kenley and Staubus 1972).

In January 1971 the Institute of Chartered Accountants in Australia recommended the inclusion of a funds statement in a Technical Bulletin (ICAA 1971). It favoured but did not mandate an all financial resources view of funds, but excluded bonus issues, movements on reserves and asset revaluations from disclosure. In July 1980 ED 16 *Statement of Sources and Applications of Funds* was issued and it was transmuted into Accounting Standard AAS 12 in March 1983 which was amended in March 1985. ED 16 defined funds flow as the flow of resources into or out of the accounting entity as a result of transactions with parties external to that entity. AAS 12 in March 1983, however, defined funds as cash and cash equivalents but its illustrative appendix used an all financial

resources format. The most important of the March 1985 amendments to AAS 12 required total operating outflows to be separately
disclosed from total operating inflows.

In 1986 the Accounting Standards Review Board approved AAS
12 as ASRB 1007 mandating the presentation of a statement of
sources and applications of funds as a primary financial statement.
In response to a number of comments on the exposure draft for
that standard, a new exposure draft (ED 37 1986) was issued. It
sought to require a note to the funds statement analysing cash
flow from operations, as exemplified in section 12 of the ED and
reproduced below.

Cash flow from operations

	19x1 '000	19x0 '000
Operating profit before income tax	250	165
Add: Depreciation	14	10
Long-service leave expense	6	5
Funds from operations before income tax	270	180
Add: Increase in trade creditors	35	15
Carrying amount of noncurrent assets disposed	60	–
	365	195
Less: Increase in debtors (including debtors from disposal of noncurrent assets)	125	60
Increase in inventories	75	25
Payment of long-service leave	5	4
Cash Flow From Operations	160	106

It is not intended to provide a comprehensive list of all accruals
that may need to be considered when reconciling funds from
operations to cash flow from operations.

(ED 37 1986, section 12)

ED 37 evoked considerable controversy and Australia did not
revive the cash flow issue until 1991 when the ASA and AARF
issued a joint standard AAS 28/ASRB 1026 requiring the replace-

ment of the funds statement by the cash flow statement for financial years ending after 30 March 1991.

The New Zealand Society of Accountants strongly recommended the funds statement in 1971 (Cowan 1971) and required it in 1979 by its own SSAP 10 by when it had become an SCFP in name but not necessarily in format (SSAP 10). Funds from operations were to be shown net of tax and of extraordinary items. Asset revaluations and transfers of reserves were not seen as funds flow. New Zealand became one of the first countries to require a statement of cash flow in March 1992 when its FRS 10 replaced the old SSAP 10.

Europe

Mielke and Giacomino (1987) reported that a cash or near cash emphasis in funds statements was not confined to the USA but was also common in Europe in the years 1984–6. Only one of their 45 companies used the all financial resources format and that was an unnamed UK company. Other features are shown in an edited version of their Exhibit 1 in Table 5.2.

Although none of the countries specify a required definition of funds, there seemed to be widespread consensus that cash or working capital was the appropriate definition. Cash tended to include all bank deposits and also short term securities. The relative absence of the all financial resources format may be attributable to

Table 5.2 SCFP reporting practices in Europe

Country	N	E	C	W	O	F	I	B	S
France	4	R	2	2	3	0	0	0	2
Germany	5	M	4	1	3	1	0	0	4
Eire	2	R	1	1	1	0	0	0	2
Italy	(Fiat)	M	1	0	1	0	0	0	1
Nethrlds	8	P	6	2	7	0	0	1	8
Sweden	7	P	7	0	5	0	0	5	0
Switzld	3	M	2	1	2	0	0	1	3
UK	15	R	12	3	12	0	0	0	10
TOTALS	45		35	10	34	1	0	7	30

Glossary of abbreviations used above:
N Number of companies sampled
E Extent of statement provision in country
R Required disclosure
P Predominant practice to supply a funds statement
M Majority practice

the non-occurrence of sales of assets for securities instead of for cash – so commented Mielke and Giacomino (p. 148) but they offered no evidence for this (such as could have been obtained in the notes to the accounts in many cases). They conclude (p. 149) with an interesting reason for inducing the IASC to emulate the USA's SFAS 95:

> This article does not suggest that IASC merely react to FASB's current standard by 'rubber stamping' SFAS 95; however, considering the considerable effort applied by FASB and its staff to the cash flow reporting issue, we believe that it is wise to consider seriously each of FASB's requirements

The SCFP in Hong Kong

SSAP 10 was adopted by the Hong Kong Society of Accountants as entry 2.104 in its Handbook on 1 January 1978. Salient extracts follow.

2.104 SSAP 4 Statements of Changes in Financial Position
Section 1 For a fuller understanding of a company's affairs it is necessary also to identify the movements in assets, liabilities and capital which have taken place during the year and the resultant effect on net liquid funds.
Section 2 The objective is to show how operations have been financed and how financial resources have been used.
Section 3 Long term sources and uses should be distinguished from short term ones.
Section 8 The SCFP should start with the profit or loss for the period.
Section 9 It should link successive balance sheets via the profit and loss account avoiding netting off as far as possible.
Section 12 brings the SSAP into force on 1/1/1978.
2.104 SSAP 4 Appendix
This appendix is for general guidance and does not form part of the SSAP. The methods of presentation used are illustrative only and in no way prescriptive and other methods of presentation may equally comply with the accounting standard. The format used should be selected with a view to demonstrating clearly the manner in which the operations of the company have been financed and in which its financial resources have been utilized.

Example statement of changes in financial position

	$000	$000	$000
SOURCE OF FUNDS			
Profit before tax			1,430
Adjustments for items not involving the movement of funds:			
Depreciation			380
TOTAL GENERATED FROM OPERATIONS			1,810
FUNDS FROM OTHER SOURCES			
Issue of shares for cash			100
			1,910
APPLICATION OF FUNDS			
Dividends paid		(400)	
Tax paid		(690)	
Purchase of fixed assets		(460)	
			(1,550)
INCREASE/DECREASE IN WORKING CAPITAL			360
Increase in stocks		80	
Increase in debtors		120	
Decrease in creditors excluding taxation and proposed dividends		115	
Movement in net liquid funds:			
Increase (decrease) in:			
Cash balances	(5)		
Short-term investments	50		
		45	
			360

China

For joint ventures with entities in China, Joint Venture Accounting Regulations Articles 60 and 62 prescribe the format of SCFPs on a working capital basis. In fact the term funds is scarcely used at all, with working capital being used instead at every stage (Chiu 1992). The blocks are as under:

Sources of working capital
Applications of working capital (including income tax attributable to the year as it is paid in quarterly instalments)
Changes in working capital items: subdivided between increase in current assets and increase in current liabilities

International comparisons

Few countries have specific requirements for the focus of the funds statement but those that do have them tend to prefer net change in working capital (Gray *et al.* 1984 p. 190).

The following countries required such a statement in 1984: Brazil, Chile, Colombia, Finland, Hong Kong, Indonesia, Ireland, Malaysia, Mexico, New Zealand, Philippines, Portugal, South Africa, Thailand, UK, USA and Zimbabwe.

The following countries recommended but did not require it: Argentina, Channel Islands, France, Italy, Spain and Zambia (Gray *et al.* 1984 Table 4.1)

Of the above the following *specified* a net change in working capital focus: Brazil, Hong Kong, Indonesia and Portugal.

However, the following countries recommended such a focus: Argentina, Chile, Finland, France, Italy, Philippines and Spain (Table 4.2(a)). In the Philippines' case, net change in liquid funds is the preferred idea of working capital (4.2(b)). Thailand required the focus to be net change in cash; France recommended it, while Brazil, Hong Kong, Indonesia and Portugal prohibited it (4.2(c)).

Only South Africa required separate disclosure of tax paid and dividends paid while Argentina and Colombia only recommended it. All the others mentioned in the lists above as requiring or recommending a funds statement expected separate disclosure of dividends paid but make no mention of tax (4.3(c and d)). Most also required or recommended that changes in working capital should be analysed into its component parts (4.3(i)).

The results of a more recent survey by Lafferty Publications in 1989 are shown in Tables 5.3–5.6.

The Lafferty 1980 list was similar to the above except then Singapore instead of India was a partial non-producer. It is not known whether the Hong Kong company suffered a qualified audit report

Table 5.3 Incidence of funds statements

Number of companies	AM 65 (%)	EUR 100 (%)	RW 35 (%)	T88 200 (%)	T80 200 (%)
Group funds statement only	85	70	66	73	76
Group and parent company	15	8	3	10	3
Parent only	–	7	17	7	8
Subtotal	100	85	86	90	87
No funds statement	–	15	14	10	13
TOTAL	100	100	100	100	100

AM = North America; EUR = Europe; RW = Rest of the World; T88 and T80 = Totals for 1988 and 1980 respectively
Source: Koch (1989 p. 114)

Table 5.4 Number of companies and countries which did not produce funds statements

Country	No. of companies	% of country sample
Belgium	5	56
Denmark	1	50
France	1	7
Germany	4	27
Italy	2	20
Switzerland	1	10
Spain	2	40
Japan	2	11
India	2	67
Hong Kong	1	25
TOTALS	21	100

for non-compliance with the local accounting standard mandating the presentation of funds statements.

Most companies placed funds statements *pari passu* with the balance sheet and income statement. Six Australian firms (62 per cent of the Australian sample) put them in the notes instead, and all the German firms placed them in the Directors' Report.

Further, 92 per cent of US, 80 per cent of Canadian, 85 per cent of Japanese, 85 per cent of Swedish and 50 per cent of Dutch firms used the SCFP heading; 93 per cent of Australian, 87 per cent of UK, 60 per cent of South African and 50 per cent of Dutch firms used the sources and applications heading.

Although 39 per cent (78) of the sample firms use a liquid funds (cash and marketable securities) approach, only 4 per cent (8)

Table 5.5 Heading given to funds statement

| Heading given | % of region adopting | | | | |
	AM	EUR	RW	T88	T80
Sources & applications or movements of funds	31	45	12	35	42
Changes in financial posn	58	36	74	49	36
Corporate financing	–	3	–	2	8
Statement of cash flow	11	1	–	4	1
No funds statement produced	–	15	14	10	13
TOTALS	100	100	100	100	100
Number of companies	65	100	35	200	200

Source: Koch (1989 p. 117)

Table 5.6 Definition of funds used in funds statement

| Definition | % of companies applying | | | | |
	AM	EUR	RW	T88	T80
Movement in liquid funds	60	34	11	39	16
Movement in working capital	8	18	66	23	50
Sources = applications	26	23	6	20	19
Movement in borrowings	6	10	3	8	2
No funds statement produced	–	15	14	10	13
TOTALS	100	100	100	100	100
Number of companies	65	100	35	200	200

Source: per Koch (1989 p. 123)

described the statement as a cash flow statement. This particular inconsistency was exhibited by all the Canadian and Swedish firms, and by 84 per cent of the US, 73 per cent of the Dutch and 60 per cent of the UK firms.

As regards funds from operations, 62 per cent (124) used profit after tax but before dividends, 23 per cent (46) profit before both tax and dividends, and 4 per cent (8) various other starting points for showing the sources of these funds.

Finally, the IASC's own most recent survey (IASC 1988) included the following remarks (p. 30). After mentioning that the USA, South Africa, New Zealand and Canada now require a statement of cash flows instead of a SCFP, the writer says:

A preference for cash flow information is however not new. A Statement of Cash Inflow and Outflow has been a required disclosure in registration statements in Japan since 1953. Recent proposals have been made, however, to improve these disclosures. A major issue is whether they should form part of the financial statements; the Statement of Cash Inflow and Outflow is presently only supplementary information because of the uncertainty in other countries over the use and status of such information.

In 1985 the Board recognised the growing trend in favour of the preparation of changes in financial position in terms of cash or cash equivalents, rather than in terms of working capital. While viewing this trend with approval, the Board did not believe that the working capital approach should be prohibited at that time.

It is interesting to compare the focus on cash in the above quotations with the views of the IASC a decade earlier, when IAS 7 (IASC 1977) adopted the SCFP title but in its paragraph 4 seemed to adopt the cash idea of funds:

The term funds generally refers to cash and cash equivalents, or to working capital. In a Statement of Changes in Financial Position the particular use of the term is not clear.

Seven countries had by 1988 adopted IAS 7 as a national requirement: Botswana, Cyprus, Malawi, Malaysia, Oman, Pakistan and Zimbabwe. Four countries used IAS 7 as the basis of a national requirement: Jamaica, Lesotho, Singapore and Sri Lanka. Some 39 countries, most of those surveyed in fact, had national requirements or national practices that generally conform with IAS 7. That left four countries whose national practice failed to conform with IAS 7: Belgium, Germany, Greece and Switzerland. This is not wholly consistent with the results of the 1989 Lafferty survey above, presumably owing to sampling bias in either or both. Two countries, Germany and Switzerland, are very creditor oriented; whilst the under-regulated Greek situation results in non-compliance with many other standards besides IAS 7. In the other three cases, especially Germany's, banks are presumed to get all the information they need by direct access to their clients' books, so there is no source of pressure for general public disclosure of funds flow type of information. Still, it seems unlikely that Lafferty picked out the only Belgian, German and Swiss producers of funds statements. It is more likely that the IASC survey relied on the reports of national accounting bodies rather than on inspection of actual published accounts. If this is the case, then conflicts between the two surveys should be resolved in favour, provisionally, of the Lafferty results.

THE SPREAD OF THE CASH FLOW STATEMENT

Chronology of the first adoptions

Table 5.7 Chronology of adoption

Place	ED. no.	Approved	As	Effective date
Canada		1985	sec. 1540	October 1985
New Zealand	ED 39	1987	SSAP 10	January 1988
USA	FASB 1986	1987	SFAS 95	15 July 1988
South Africa		1988	AC 118	October 1988
UK	ED 54	1991	FRS 1	26 March 1992
Australia	ED 52	1991	AAS 28/ASRB 1026	30 June 1992

Canada

Marinucci (1985) described the Canadian adoption of the SCF three years earlier than the USA. The Accounting Standards Committee approved the relevant changes to section 1540 of the CICA Handbook in June 1985, following responses to its November 1984 exposure draft 'Cash Flow Information'. The new recommendations stated that:

1 The SCF should report changes in cash and cash equivalents and analyse them into their components.
2 Cash flows should be classified by operating, financing and investing activities.
3 Cash flow from operations should be reconciled to the income statement or its components disclosed (*sic*).
4 Cash equivalents may in some cases include receivables, inventories and even payables, when they are equivalent to cash.

Several respondents to the exposure draft said dividends do not fit well into any of the three main categories and so CICA allows it to be disclosed as a separate category (or as financing or as operating):

1 An SCF need not be presented at all when it would not provide

additional useful information (such as with some small businesses).

2 The SCF should include non-cash financing and investing activities because such activities affect an enterprise's capital and asset structure (this includes stock dividends).

No mention was made of cash flow per share figures so firms are free to disclose them or not as they prefer.

The provisions noted above distinguish the Canadian SCF from its American counterpart.

Britain

Adams (1988) expressed in *Accountancy* the opinion that SFAS 95 could influence UK accounting standard setters.

> Because of the relevance of US financial reporting standards to UK companies and the UK accounting profession generally – but enhanced recently by the 'British invasion' of the middle US corporate sector – it cannot be long before the statement of cash flows becomes a regular feature of the accounts of some UK based multinationals. From there to the ASC and thence to the educational curriculum is but a small step.
>
> (Adams 1988 p. 110)

Adams's prophecy was realized in less than two years with the publication of ED 54 which is detailed in the rest of this subsection.

In July 1990 the Accounting Standards Committee issued ED 54 whose main provisions are described here. It will be seen that the draft closely resembles the American SFAS 95.

ED 54's preface

SSAP 10's funds statement is to be replaced by a cash flow statement in either the direct or indirect formats. This proposal is in line with developments in the USA, Canada and the IASC (ED 54 1990, section 1.1).

SSAP 10 was reviewed in March 1989 'because the changing economic environment had led to increasing sophistication in the requirements of users of financial statements, particularly financial analysts'. Research revealed dissatisfaction in that some critics thought cash flows were more useful than changes in working capital; some thought increasingly complex decision making and forecasting models needed better information; some thought there was too much variety in the application of SSAP 10 for comparability or usefulness and too much ambiguity of definition in the standard (ED 54 1990, section 1.3).

There is general agreement in the frameworks developed on the conceptual basis of financial reporting that users of financial statements would find it useful to have information on the viability, liquidity and financial flexibility of the enterprises in which they were interested. This suggests the need for information on the amount, timing and certainty of cash flows. Historical cash flow can be a useful indicator of these factors. In addition, studies of investor decision making suggest that investors, formally or informally, develop a model to assess and compare the present value of the future cash flows of enterprises. Historical cash flow information could, therefore, be useful to check the accuracy of past assessments and indicate the relationship between the enterprise's activities and its receipts and payments. It also reveals the relationship between profitability and cash generation and expenditure, and thus the quality of the profit earned.

(ED 54 1990, section 1.5)

The information provided by a cash flow statement appears to have the following advantages over that provided by a working capital based funds statement.

1 Cash flows can be a direct input into a business valuation model and, therefore, historical cash flows may be directly relevant in a way not possible for funds flow data.
2 Funds flow data based on movements in working capital can obscure movements relevant to the viability and liquidity of an enterprise. For example, a potentially fatal decrease in cash available may be masked by an increase in stock or debtors. Enterprises may therefore run out of cash while reporting increases in working capital available. Similarly a decrease in working capital does not necessarily indicate a cash shortage and a danger of failure.
3 A funds flow statement is based largely on the difference between two balance sheets. It reorganizes such data, but does not provide any new data. A cash flow statement includes new data.
4 As cash flow monitoring is a normal feature of business life and not a specialized accounting concept, cash flow is a concept which

is easier to understand than changes in working capital (ED 54 1990, section 1.6).

The provision of cash flow information is new and the full advantages of it may not be immediately apparent to users and preparers. It may take time for them to develop the experience and tools necessary to appreciate fully the potential uses of the new statement (ED 54 1990, section 1.7).

Exemption is proposed for firms with turnover below £25,000 and which also do not have to report under the Companies Acts (ED 54 1990, section 1.8).

ED 54 imports the American distinction between operating, investing and financing cash flows into the statement and specifies that cash equivalents are to be treated as cash (ED 54 1990, section 1.9).

Cash equivalents should be defined as 'short-term, highly liquid investments which are both readily convertible into known amounts of cash and sufficiently near maturity that there is no significant risk that they will change in value in response to interest rate variations'. This includes short term bank borrowings held as an 'integral part of its treasury management'.

The firm should specify what it includes in cash equivalents and disclose changes in this definition in accordance with SSAP 6 (ED 54 1990, section 1.10).

Normally dividends should be treated as a financing activity (ED 54 1990, section 1.11).

The SCF should report every cash flow to and from the firm, except those that are merely changes in the form that cash is held, such as purchase and sale of cash equivalents. All flows must be reported gross. (ED 54 1990, section 1.15).

Non-cash transactions like debt redemption by way of new equity should be reported in the notes to the accounts (ED 54 1990, section 1.16).

'The reporting of historical cash flows helps the discharge of the stewardship function of management by making an enterprise's management accountable for its actions in terms of the enterprise's solvency and liquidity performance.' Also cash flows are argued to be less arbitrary and more easily verified than accrual-based items (ED 54 1990, section 8).

It is alleged that because interest is contractual, it is operational, unlike dividends which are a financing activity (ED 54 1990, section 15).

VAT should be apportioned between operating and investing flows to fit the transactions to which it is attached (ED 54 1990, section 19).

A firm using the direct method is NOT required to publish a profit reconciliation (ED 54 1990, section 35).

Forex flows should be translated at the rate applicable at the transaction date per SSAP 20 (ED 54 1990, section 43).

Translation differences between year start and year end forex balances should be SCF adjustments to opening balances (ED 54 1990, section 45).

ED 54 (1990) section 63 specifies that the indirect format must show the same information as the direct method except where 'this is impractical because the information is not available to make the relevant estimates and adjustments necessary to extract the information'.

ED 54 (1990) section 65 states tax and VAT refunds in respect of investing activities are themselves investing activities.

In conclusion and summary, ED 54 reads very much like SFAS 95 except for the VAT provisions, the tighter specifications in ED 54 for cash equivalence and the rather self-conscious irresolution concerning the classifications of dividend and interest, which resulted in FRS 1's separating of these items into a new classification called servicing of finance and returns on investment.

Taiwan

The stock exchange regulators in Taiwan reacted to the mounting international pressure to invest in its market in the mid 1980s. One consequence was a series of accounting standards closely modelled on the American FASBs. In 1990 came SSAP 17, a Taiwanese copy of SFAS 95.

Hong Kong

The exposure draft on cash flow statements issued in March 1992 justified its proposal to replace SSAP 4 on funds flow statements with SSAP 15 on cash flow statements, thus:

There is increasing dissatisfaction with the current standard in that:

a. The requirement of a funds flow statement tended to be inter-

preted as requiring the reporting of changes in working capital rather than the reporting of movements in cash flows.
b. There was a demand for information other than that provided by the usual form of funds statement. Better information was needed as input to the increasingly complex models used for forecasting and decision making.
c. The application of SSAP 4 varied widely in several areas, reducing comparability between statements and, therefore, their usefulness.
d. This lack of comparability was increased by the flexibility and ambiguity of definition of SSAP 4 which had been drafted to allow scope for innovation.

Advantages of an SCF over an SCFP were said to be:

a. Cash flows can be a direct input into a business valuation model and, therefore, historical cash flows may be directly relevant in a way not possible for funds flow data.
b. Funds flow data based on movements in working capital can obscure movements relevant to the viability and liquidity of an enterprise. For example, a potentially fatal decrease in cash available may be asked by an increase in stock or debtors. Enterprises may therefore run out of cash while reporting increases in working capital available. Similarly a decrease in working capital does not necessarily indicate a cash shortage and a danger of failure.
c. A funds flow statement is based largely on the difference between two balance sheets. It reorganises such data, but does not provide any new data. A cash flow statement includes new data.
d. As cash flow monitoring is a normal feature of business life and not a specialised accounting concept, cash flow is a concept which is easier to understand than changes in working capital.

Chapter 6 shows how closely Hong Kong's SSAP 15 follows the UK's FRS 1.

Brazil

The Brazilian securities regulators, the OVM, are at the time of writing considering a recommendation from the Brazilian Association of Capital Market Analysts to mandate the cash flow statement for public companies. The reasons given for the recommendation include international comparability, to enable performance indicators to be cash flow rather than earnings based and to use the same cash flow already used in more developed markets such as cash flow per share.

ACCOUNTING GEOGRAPHY AND THE SCFP

Introduction

The SCFP was adopted by most countries in the industrialized world with the notable exceptions of France, Switzerland, Germany and Japan. The SCF has been adopted only by the major English speaking economies as at end 1992. The purpose of this section is to explore whether the pattern of dispersion of the two statements corresponds with any cluster already known to the literature of accounting geography. It is particularly important to ascertain whether there is an English speaking cluster or a Commonwealth and US influenced one. If there is, then the dispersion of the SCF is following a track already laid down and one could therefore predict which countries will take up the SCF in future since one could simply ascertain which countries are on the same track as the adopters but have not yet adopted the SCF. Conversely, if the SCF/P dispersion patterns fit no already established clustering pattern, then the validity or reliability of previously established clusters comes into question and/or an explanation must be found for the dispersion that brings in factors hitherto untouched by the literature of accounting geography.

Clusters

The two approaches

Some writers have attempted to explain differences in accounting standards and their implementation across countries in terms of environmental characteristics – deductivism (Choi 1974, AAA 1976, Choi and Mueller 1984, Nobes and Parker 1981).

Others have clustered nations on the basis of their accounting behaviour and attempted to relate these clusters to environmental variables – inductivism (Goodrich 1982, Nobes 1983, Frank 1979, Nair and Frank 1980, Da Costa *et al.* 1978).

Deductivism

Mueller (1968) was one of the earliest to use the deductivist approach to accounting classification. He saw four patterns:

1 Macroeconomic – business accounting serves the purposes of national economic policies.
2 Microeconomic – accounting as a branch of business economics.
3 Independent discipline – accounting as a service function derived from business practice.
4 Uniform accounting – accounting as a means of administrative control.

Mueller (1968) thought similarities were as important as differences between various countries' GAAP. In his grouping of international practices, he aggregated together 'the developing nations of the Far East' which already excluded Japan. His article concluded that American GAAP should not be arbitrarily enforced in other countries but that complete international diversity of accounting principles was undesirable and unnecessary.

The AAA (1977) report asserted the existence of five international accounting zones: British, American, Franco-Latin, German-Dutch and Communist.

Nobes (1983, 1984) adopted and extended Mueller's approach, also ignoring culture but introducing hierarchy, and addressing the issue of what classification itself is for.

Nobes (1985 pp. 174–5) cites the AAA (1977 p. 77–8) as having laid down four necessary conditions of effective classification.

1 Consistency of application of classification criteria, which conversely implies different purposes, for a classification system leads to the use of different characteristics.
2 Thoroughness. An effective system will contain enough subsets to exhaust a given universe.
3 Exclusivity. No element can fall into more than one subset.
4 Preservation of hierarchical integrity, so that, for example in the Linnaean system, a species is a member of a genus in turn a member of a family *in all cases for all elements*.

Classifications of accounting are criticized for

1 Lack of precision in definition of what is to be classified,
2 Lack of a model with which to compare statistical results,
3 Lack of hierarchy to add subtlety to the portrayal of size differences between countries,

4 Lack of judgement in the choice of important discriminating features.

Nobes (1985) claims to attempt to solve the above in his post 1982 work, with its focus on measurement and valuation. His system divides developed Western countries into two classes; micro based and macro based, this being strongly supported by his factor analysis. The micro class has two subclasses: theoretical, whose only species is Holland, and pragmatic, which has two families – UK influenced (Australia, New Zealand, Ireland and the UK itself) and US influenced (USA and Canada). The three macro subclasses are continental (an empty set); economics driven comprising only Sweden; and government which has two families – tax based (Italy, France, Belgium and Spain) and law based (Germany and Japan).

Inductivism

Price Waterhouse (PW) conducted three surveys of international accounting practices in 1973 (38 countries), 1975 (46) and 1979 (64). The most important inductivist work was by Nair and Frank (1980). They used the PW survey data to generate five clusters of measurement practices and seven of disclosure practices. The hypotheses that (a) cultural and economic variables might be more closely associated with disclosure practices, and (b) trading variables might be more closely associated with measurement practices were not supported.

In three of their studies, Nair and Frank used the PW survey data as input into factor analysis to generate groups based on the single factor on which the country had the highest loading. They dichotomized the 1975 survey data between measurement and disclosure practices, clustering each separately. They found the two cluster patterns to be significantly unlike each other (Nair and Frank 1980 p. 436). Nair's (1982) update using the 1979 data found similar clusters.

Nair and Frank's (1980) disclosure groups based on the PW (1975) data disaggregated the 1973 continental European cluster to form a Scandinavian cluster (group 6), a French Belgian Latin American cluster including Zaire (group 1), a Dutch Canadian Irish cluster including the UK (group 4), an American German Filipino Japanese cluster (group 3) and a Swiss Italian cluster (group 7). There was also a Commonwealth cluster (2) and an Argentinean Indian one (5). The Commonwealth split between groups 2 and 4 may be the result of EEC entry, but South Africa stayed with group 2 while Rhodesia went with the UK to group 4. These disclosure groupings are quite different from the measurement groupings.

In each of their studies Nair and Frank rotated their initial factors orthogonally, a rotation which depends for its validity on the assumption that the underlying factors are uncorrelated. In this case that means that the countries have nothing in common. Doupnik (1987) therefore used oblique rotation (of the 1975 data and his own 1983 follow-up data) instead. Hong Kong was not listed in his groups but it would clearly have been in the UK group along with Singapore, Australia and South Africa. His factor analyses of the 1975 and 1983 data supported only the limited conclusion that during the eight-year period harmonization occurred on a noticeable scale only between the South American and Southern Europe country groups.

Goodrich (1986) factor analysed the political circumstances of 54 countries to see if the results displayed clustering significantly like the AAA (1977) morphology and his own earlier clustering (Goodrich 1980). Goodrich's 1980 clustering had five groups factor rotated to maximize the US–UK distance. The result is that his groupings are so unlike those of anyone else that the UK stands at the top of his group 3 followed by a list that embraces not only the expected cases of New Zealand, Hong Kong and Singapore but also the unexpected cases of France, Canada and the Philippines. Former French colonies on the other hand were in group 5 along with Jersey, Italy and the Netherlands.

There were strong positive correlations between centrist political systems and 'non-disclosure accounting types' and between polyarchic political systems and both the British and the inflation-focused accounting groupings.

Chang and Most (1981) looked in 1976 at the comparative information contexts of the UK, the USA and New Zealand for investment decisions. Their respondent groups all rated the annual report the most important source of information except the financial analysts groups in the UK and New Zealand who rated it second after newspapers and magazines. New Zealand institutional investors rated the SCFP second after the income statement.

Contingency frameworks

Introduction

Culture, in Hofstede's (1984 p. 13) often cited definition, is a 'collective programming of the mind which distinguishes the members of one human group from another'.

Examples of applied contingency theory per Thomas (1986) are Bailey (1975) who attributed UK–USSR differences in accounting to differences in ownership, Gray (1980) who attributed Franco-German accounting conservatism to the greater importance of bank-sourced funds over equity when compared with the UK situation, and Nair and Frank (1980) who tested the association of differences in measurement practices with differences in cultural and structural economic variables.

The market-based contingency explanations

Four studies which looked at the comprehensiveness of annual accounts found the USA, Canada and the UK the most comprehensive; Germany, France and Switzerland the least (Barrett 1976, Lafferty and Cairns 1980, Choi and Bavishi 1983, Cairns *et al.* 1984).

Choi (1974) reported empirical support for the competitive disclosure hypothesis: i.e. disclosure increases significantly up to the point of initial issue of a corporate share tranche in a sizeable capital market but stabilizes thereafter.

In a number of comparative empirical studies by Gray (1978a, b, c) support was obtained from European data for the hypothesis that the extent of financial disclosure is correlated with the development and efficiency of national equity markets. His study of 72 large company reports in the UK, France and Germany (Gray 1980) also concluded that regulatory and capital market differences directly affect the amount of profit disclosed. France and Germany were shown to be much more conservative in their reporting practices than the UK, reflecting the relative strength of equity compared with loan and government capital in the UK's case.

Gray (1980) suggested reasons why different countries have such different disclosure levels. Specifically, he attributed the greater conservatism of France and Germany than the UK to the dominance of loan financing over equity financing in those two countries. Loan creditors do not want generous measures of distributable profit relative to equity investors' preferences. Bankers have direct access to company records and do not wish to share the resultant information.

The main influences on French corporate reporting are the close relationship between tax accounting and financial accounting, the national accounting plan and the Commission des Operations de Bourse. The influence of the profession is growing but is nowhere near as strong as in the Anglo countries (Nobes and Parker 1985 p. 93).

German accounting reflects 'principles of orderly bookkeeping' which derive from company mercantile and tax law. Statements are more conservative, more tied to historical costs and more uniform than in the Anglo countries. Unpaid capital, losses and other negative liabilities are shown as assets, while some of the large number of types of reserves are treated as provisions (Nobes and Parker 1985 p. 123).

The ratio of German long term liabilities to shareholders' funds is 4:1. There is a very strong emphasis on solvency shown in very conservative methods of asset valuation and revenue recognition within a rigid legal framework (McComb 1979 pp. 13–14).

European companies listed on the London Stock Exchange not only comply with exchange disclosure requirements, but in many cases exceed them, probably because of the desire to make the most of international capital markets (Meek and Gray 1989).

Pratt and Behr (1987 p. 2) advance a transactions cost explanation of differential disclosure practices.

Market participants invest in external reporting systems because these systems reduce transaction costs by inducing managers to provide unbiased reports . . . Participants are essentially substituting the costs of the reporting system for the transaction costs associated with incomplete and asymmetric information.

Environmental factors which underlie the substitution attitudes between transaction costs and reporting costs include the number and complexity of capital market transactions, the dispersion of market participants, the ratio of managers to owners and the opportunism of market participants. It is suggested that capital markets characterized by a small number of relatively simple transactions, centralized, non-opportunistic participants and a low manager-to-owner ratio induce a smaller investment in the reporting system. The case of the USA as against Switzerland is held to lend support for this approach.

Any asymmetry in the distribution of information between the parties is a component of translation costs (Jensen and Meckling 1976).

Accounting standards can reduce transaction costs by inducing managers to provide reasonably uniform and unbiased reports. The optimum investment in building and maintaining standards of reporting occurs at the point where one dollar of marginal reporting cost reduces total transaction costs by exactly one dollar. Larger markets have both larger transaction and larger reporting costs than do smaller markets, so of course have higher optima. If the owner/manager ratio is low as in the USA, and if competitive pressures fail to induce managers to provide unbiased reports, a larger investment in the reporting system is required than in a country like Switzerland where a combination of competitive pressure and high owner/manager ratios mean the optimal investment in the reporting system is reached relatively more quickly. The turning point of the parabola will be lower for the USA. The competitive pressure to disclose effect is ascribed to Williamson (1975) who noted that as the number of new market participants increases, competitive pressures increased to cause more disclosure by participants.

In Switzerland the banks have access to firms' internal records as a result of their financial importance to their clients. 'Such an environment fosters little need for reporting standards, auditors or legally enforceable contracts' (Pratt and Behr 1987 p. 16). Capital owners in the USA cannot demand access to a firm's internal records and so must rely on an external reporting system.

Since individualism is more pronounced in the USA, opportunism is more prevalent. Income smoothing and the creation of undisclosed reserves through asset undervaluation are facilitated by enabling powers granted to directors by Article 663 of the Swiss Code of Obligations section of the Federal Articles. Only banks and insurance companies have to publish their accounts; other concerns may but need not.

Biddle and Saudagaran (1989) reported rather strong evidence to support the view that international firms are significantly deterred from listing on stock exchanges with extensive disclosure requirements. To explain the paucity of foreign listings on American exchanges relative to their copiousness on Swiss, Frankfurt's and Luxemburg's ones, this is plausible. It is somewhat less plausible as an explanation of the success of the London self-styled International

Stock Exchange in attracting more foreign listings than any other
stock exchange has done.

The culture-based contingency explanations

Values have been defined as 'a broad tendency to prefer certain
states of affairs over others' (Hofstede 1980 p. 19). Values at the
collective level represent culture; thus culture describes a system of
societal or collectively held values. The justifications assigning culture a major role in perceiving how social systems change proposed
by Harrison and McKinnon (1986 p. 239) were that culture influences the norms and values of such systems and the behaviour of
groups in their interactions within and across systems.

Hofstede induced four dimensions from very extensive cross cultural surveys his team conducted in over 50 countries (1980, 1983).
Their labels are Individualism, Power Distance, Uncertainty Avoidance and Masculinity. He defined these (1984 pp. 83–4) as condensed below.

Individualism denotes a loose social framework in which people
are supposed to take care only of themselves and immediate family.
It is opposite to collectivism where some social group, often bonded
by blood relatedness, is expected to look after its members in
exchange for unquestioning loyalty.

People in large power distance societies accept a hierarchical
order in which everybody has a place without need of justification,
whereas in small power distance societies people strive to reduce
inequalities and demand justification for any that persist.

Strong uncertainty avoidance societies maintain rigid codes of
belief and conduct, and are intolerant of deviations from the
norm. The opposite case has a more relaxed atmosphere where
'practice counts more than principles and deviance is more easily
tolerated'.

Masculinity denotes a society's preference for heroism, assertive-
ness, material success and achievement as opposed to the feminine
themes of relationships, modesty, caring for the weak and the quality of life.

Respectively the above dimensions address issues of social inter-
dependence, the handling of inequalities, the need to control an
uncertain future or instead to adapt to it, and the allocation of
social roles to the sexes.

Gray (1988) relates Hofstede's four dimensions to four 'values'
of accounting practice, thus:

Accounting values	Relationship with societal values	
	+ve	−ve
Professionalism	Individualism	Uncertainty avoidance
Uniformity	Uncertainty avoidance	Individualism
Conservatism	Uncertainty avoidance	Individualism
Secrecy	Uncertainty avoidance	Individualism

Four hypotheses are posited to link the polarities to the dimensions:

1 The higher a country ranks in terms of individualism and the lower it ranks in terms of uncertainty avoidance and power distance then the more likely it is to rank highly in terms of professionalism.
2 The higher a country ranks in terms of uncertainty avoidance and power distance and the lower it ranks in terms of individualism then the more likely it is to rank highly in terms of uniformity.
3 The higher a country ranks in terms of uncertainty avoidance and the lower it ranks in terms of individualism and masculinity then the more likely it is to rank highly in terms of conservatism.
4 The higher a country ranks in terms of uncertainty avoidance and power distance and the lower it ranks in terms of individualism and masculinity then the more likely it is to rank highly in terms of secrecy.

Empirical tests of those hypotheses are in the future awaiting further work to operationalize the link between accounting practices and values and to assemble the relevant cross cultural data coherently (Gray 1988 p. 14).

Perera (1989) represents the relationships in a different arrangement, thus:

Social dimensions	Accounting values	Accounting practice
Individualism/ collectivism	Professionalism	Authority
Strong/weak uncertainty avoidance	Conservatism	Measurement
Long/short power distance	Uniformity	Application
Masculinity/femininity	Secrecy	Disclosure

The difference between the Anglo and the European approach to accounting can be culturally explained because economic growth in the UK–USA coincided with classical liberalism and *laissez-faire*

Table 5.8 Hofstede's table

Country	Power dist.		Uncert. avoid.		Indivm		Masc.	
	X	R	X	R	X	R	X	R
Hong Kong	68	37/8	29	4/5	25	16	57	32/3
France	68	37/8	31	6/7	63	29/30	60	26/7
Sweden	86	36/41	29	4/5	86	36/41	5	1
Chile	71	40/1	71	40/1	23	15	35	22
Greece	43	17/8	5	1	28	8	57	32/3
UK	35	10/12	35	6/7	46	22	41	14/6
*UK/HK(X)(%)	58.33		120.69		184.0		71.93	
†ABS2(HK-UK)R	53		4		12		35	

Notes:
X is the index score; R the country rank
* Identical scores of HK to UK would give 100
† Identical rankings of HK and UK would give 0

attitudes to government. Individuals needed to be induced to invest with suitable reports and prospectuses. The French tradition is of government planning and economic intervention, with accounts serving macro planning ends; so the dominant French influence is the nationwide General Accounting Plan. The Anglos score high on individualism relative to the Europeans, and this is associated with expected positive professionalism and with negative uniformity, conservatism and secrecy.

Finally, it is instructive to note how far Hong Kong is from the UK on most of Hofstede's dimensions and which other nations are most like Hong Kong in each principal characteristic. Table 5.8 presents these data. It offers little cultural justification for the Hong Kong tradition of doing accounting the British way.

The two most dominant cultures and economies in East Asia belong to China and Japan. Hong Kong's colonial status has meant that its regulatory framework has been British. The colony's trading, banking and managerial personnel, however, are significantly affected by their Chinese background and by the consciousness that Japan has overtaken the USA in economic gravitational terms. In Chapter 1 we saw how different the history and structure of accountancy is in China and Japan from the UK and the USA.

Review

As stated by Nobes and Parker (1985 p. 3):

It is also possible to satisfy oneself that, where accounting methods do differ, the differences are justified by differences in the economic, legal and social environment and are not merely the accidents of history. Such accidents are unlikely seriously to impede harmonisation.

Also, in their view (Nobes and Parker 1985 p. 9):

Six countries can be identified as vital in any attempt at worldwide harmonization, that is, the USA, the UK, the GFR, France, the Netherlands and Japan. At present even these six have quite widely different financial reporting systems. These existing differences can be largely explained in terms of legal systems, types of business organization and sources of finance, the influence of taxation and the strength of the accountancy profession.

It is not at all obvious that British accounting would be more suitable for the bulk of German companies than German accounting is! It is quite possible that a standardized system like the French plan computable might be more suitable than Anglo-Saxon accounting for developing countries with few listed companies.

(Nobes 1985 p. 341)

A large difference exists between the Anglos and the Europeans on the role of the corporation in society (Samuels and Piper 1985 p. 95).

The general dichotomy between shareholder/fair-view presentation and creditor/tax/conservative presentation is an obstacle sufficiently difficult not to be overcome without major changes in attitudes and law.

(Nobes 1985 p. 334)

Bailey (1982) and Samuels and Oliga (1982) thought that there is no such thing as a conceptual framework applicable in all countries. Samuels and Piper (1985 p. 151) opined: 'Research in international accounting suffers from the lack of an appropriate perspective or frame of reference.' No accounting harmonization would be possible, though, without prior or at least concurrent harmonization of economic and social frameworks. For example, Bailey (1984) showed how the USSR withdrew from European accounting congresses once it committed itself to a unified system of national economic accounting.

The influence of FASB and IASC

The IASC

Cooper's Sir Henry Benson set up the Accountants' International Study Group in 1966 for the USA, the UK and Canada, to help him build an international practice. The Tenth International Congress of Accountants held in Sydney in 1972 accepted the need to set up a fully international body. The resultant IASC held its inaugural meeting of six nations on 29 June 1973. Benson (1976) predicted that this new body would be 'of dominating importance in the presentation of financial statements by about the year 2000'.

The original nine members of IASC were Australia, Canada, France, Japan, Mexico, the Netherlands, the UK with Ireland, the USA and West Germany (Benson 1976).

From 1 January 1984 all the member states' professional accounting bodies in IFAC (itself founded in 1977) automatically acquired membership of IASC.

Mintz (1978) compared and contrasted the USA with the international accounting standard setting process in the late 1970s. The principal similarities were:

1 the desire to narrow the areas of alternative accounting practice,
2 the solicitation of comments from interested parties during the process of establishing standards,
3 the need to balance the often conflicting interests of the parties affected.

The main differences were:

1 lack of international procedures to ensure viewpoints of all interested parties are adequately represented,
2 lack of adequate documentation detailing the analysis made in selecting alternative accounting standards,
3 lack of a clearly defined authority, enforcement mechanism or disclosure of recalcitrants internationally.

IASC Effectiveness

International standards do not derive from an internationally agreed conceptual framework, but rather from committee consensus susceptible to lobbying as shown by Watts and Zimmerman (1978). Laughlin and Puxty (1982) prefer to see a conflict between different groups' worldviews rather than different groups' narrow self-interests. This may be a distinction without a difference.

Walker (1978) argued that if IASC were merely a paper tiger, groups would not have wasted resources in lobbying it. He showed that for IAS 3 on group accounts IASC simply catalogued those technical procedures on which representatives of different national bodies could agree, irrespective of the conflict between the rationales underlying the various national practices. Stamp (1972) did not believe universal accounting standards could possibly be developed except at a ridiculous level of generalization, because of cultural, developmental and other international differences. Stamp (1972) said a conceptual framework needs general agreement on the overall objectives of financial reporting, general agreement on the needs and nature of various groups of users and the identification of a set of criteria to be used in choosing between alternative solutions to standard setting problems in either national or international standards.

Aitken and Wise (1984) in their eponymous paper asserted 'the real objective of the IASC' was to improve the decision making ability of multinational investors. Other promised objectives had not been achieved on account of low compliance, especially not the objective of greater comparability. Two other objectives mentioned by Wyatt (1989) in his review are developing a basis for LDCs to follow as the profession begins to emerge in these nations, and focusing on the accountability of multinational companies. It is not generally agreed that success has crowned the efforts made to realize these objectives.

> It is the countries influenced by the Anglo-American tradition which are most familiar with setting accounting standards and are most likely to adopt them professionally. It is not surprising, then, that the working language of the IASC is English, that its secretariat is in London, that all the Chairmen and Secretaries have been from countries using Anglo-Saxon or Dutch accounting, and that most standards closely follow or compromise between US and UK standards.
>
> (Nobes 1985 p. 340)

Those countries without pre-existing national standards who have adopted the IASC set include Kenya, Malaysia, Nigeria, Pakistan, Singapore and Zimbabwe, all of whom might sooner or later have followed British standards. Kenya also uses them but writes them in simpler English first before the KICPA promulgates them.

Canada is regarded as a world leader in its endeavours to support the objectives and activities of the IASC (Irvine 1988).

Bromwich and Hopwood (1983) argue: 'There is reason to believe that accounting standards and regulations often reflect the concerns of society with a lag. In other words, today's accounting reflects yesterday's concerns' (p. 7).

A lag is also thought to exist in setting standards subsequent to social and political change, while cultural factors may inhibit changes in accounting standards. In particular, the speed of change in the USA of accounting standard setting appears to be considerably greater than in other countries which may be partly attributable to cultural factors (Bloom and Naciri 1989). These reflections raise but do not answer the question of the relevance of standards to current economic decision making. They suggest implicitly a difference in the speed of adaptation to new conditions between the USA and Japan that is not apparent in areas other than accounting.

Differences between the UK and the USA have decreased since the IASC was founded, although not because of it to any great extent. For example, the US adoption of the current rate method of currency translation in SFAS 52 in 1981 and the UK move to capitalization of leases in SSAP 21 in 1984 were not caused mainly by a desire for transatlantic harmonization (Nobes 1985 p. 337).

Walker (1978) points out the contrast between the IASC members agreeing to use their best endeavours to ensure compliance with its standards and the US practice of only compelling compliance with an IAS that the FASB adopts, or the UK and Australian stances of not requiring compliance with any IAS in conflict with their own SSAPs. This is one reason why in 1978 the IASC aimed to harmonize the national accounting standards themselves.

In their fourth study Nair and Frank (1981) examined 131 practices for 37 countries reported in all 3 surveys. They found that the number of practices agreed on by a majority of countries increased from 8 in 1973 to 49 in 1979 and that the topics on which the IASC had pronounced were associated with the practices for which harmonization was detected.

Doupnik and Taylor (1985) found that Europe in 1979–83 had the lowest level of compliance with IASC standards of five broadly defined geographical areas. The UK, France and the Netherlands showed significantly greater compliance than the German speaking countries and Southern Europe. EC members showed greater compliance than non-members but this difference had narrowed by 1983.

Disclosure requirements attracted more conformity than measurement practices did.

Taylor *et al.* [1986] analysed returned questionnaires from accounting firms in 33 of the 93 then member countries of IASC about IASs 1,2,3,4 and 7 (respectively covering accounting policy disclosure, inventory, consolidations, depreciation and statements of charges in financial position). Respondents were asked to signify their agreement on a five-point Likert scale to four statements about accounting standards. 'Your nations's present financial reporting practices:

1 Were highly comparable before this IAS became effective?
2 Are highly comparable now?
3 Were highly consistent before this IAS became effective?
4 Are highly consistent now?'

In every case respondents deemed both comparability and consistency to be greater now than before the standard became effective. This is particularly marked for IAS 7 relative to the other standards but the international distribution of the improvement was a little harder to interpret as shown below.

EXTRACT FROM EXHIBIT 2 p. 7 of Taylor *et al.* (1986) for IAS 7

	National Standards comparability consistency		International Standards comparability consistency	
Anglo American				
Previous	3.9	3.9	3.3	3.6
Present	4.4	4.6	4.0	4.2
Difference	0.6	0.8	0.8	0.6
European				
Previous	1.7	2.7	2.8	3.1
Present	2.5	3.1	3.6	3.6
Difference	0.8	0.4	0.8	0.6
Other				
Previous	2.5	3.2	3.2	3.5
Present	3.4	3.9	4.3	4.3
Difference	0.8	0.7	1.1	0.7
Probability of F				
Previous	0.0072	0.1993	0.7404	0.6393
Present	0.0039	0.0182	0.1490	0.1542
Difference	0.9992	0.7413	0.7736	0.9198

These results suggest IASC has assisted the harmonization of SCFPs. Similar tables for other IASs are shown in Taylor *et al.* (1986) which provide clear, though slightly weaker, evidence of harmonization driven by the IASC.

IASC's plans

The main purposes of the IASC's new framework (IASC 1989 section 1) are to help develop future accounting standards, to promote harmonization of all aspects of accounting regulations and to assist national standard setting bodies in developing national standards.

> In those cases where there is a conflict, the requirements of the international accounting standard prevail over those of the framework (sec 3).
>
> While all the information of these users (listed in sec 9) cannot be met by financial statements, there are needs which are common to all investors. As investors are providers of risk capital to the enterprise, the provision of financial statements that meet their needs will also meet most of the needs of other users that financial statements can satisfy (sec 10).
>
> The objective of financial statements is to provide information . . . that is useful to a wide range of users in making economic decisions (sec 12).
>
> Those users who wish to assess the stewardship or accountability of management do so in order that they may make economic decisions. These decisions may include, for example, whether to hold or sell their investment in the enterprise or whether to reappoint or replace the management (sec 14).

Underlying assumptions of accounts are accrual basis (sec 22) and going concern (23) while report usefulness is said to derive from understandability (25), relevance (26–8), materiality (29 and 30), reliability (31 and 32), faithful representation of events (33 and 34), preferring substance over form (35), neutrality (36), prudence (37), completeness (38), comparability (39–42), timeliness (43) and the surplus of users' benefits over preparers' costs (44).

Just as the above shows clearly the Trueblood influence, so section 18 (with its identification of the need to specify separately operating, financing and investing funds) prejudges the funds flow question in favour of SFAS 95. The new IAS 7 indeed resembles SFAS 95 too closely for coincidence to be a plausible explanation. Thus, the foundation is laid for SFAS 95's own shortcomings to be copied round the world. This means arbitrary and confusing classification of interest and dividends, the persistence of the indirect format so that the SCF is scarcely distinguishable from a cash base SCFP, and as fuzzy a boundary around 'cash equivalence' as there was around 'funds'.

CONCLUSION

The 1988 Survey of the Use and Application of International Accounting Standards showed 50 countries had national requirements that conformed to the old IAS 7 while 4 did not. This suggests that the IASC's adoption of IAS 7 may prove influential in persuading major economies still using the SCFP to switch to the SCF, for example Singapore, Thailand and Korea. It is regrettable that it will be the SFAS 95 approach rather than the FRS 1 approach that will be copied in this way.

We can see that the earliest adopters of the SCF have been the major English speaking economies, and that accounting clusters have been shown to separate out such countries from the others. Usually the USA leads one cluster and the UK another. Thus the dispersion of the SCF to date is consistent with the main paradigms of accounting geography.

6 Cash flow statements

THE INTRODUCTION OF SFAS 95

Chapter overview

In this chapter I begin by going into greater depth than in Chapter 4 in reviewing the American process and rationale for replacing the SCFP by the SCF. Then I analyse the similarities and differences of the SCFs authorized by accounting standards in all the major jurisdictions that had mandated an SCF by the end of 1992. I also review the critiques and the empirical research that have been published in English on the ability of the SCF to deliver on its promises. In the concluding section I discuss whether the evidence to date enables us to form a judgement on the superiority of the SCF over the SCFP it replaced.

History of SFAS 95

Initial disquiet with APB 19

The American interest in radically reviewing the SCFP was traced by Seed (1984a) to concerns about liquidity and solvency caused by adverse economic conditions, deterioration of the credibility of the income statement caused by inflation, and the efforts of the FASB to establish a conceptual framework for financial statements (Seed 1984a).

FASB (1980) gave four reasons why a cash flow statement should replace the SCFP:

1 the difference between income and funds flows,
2 the need for information on liquidity and financial flexibility,
3 the inadequacy of prior practice, and

4 the further development of a conceptual framework for financial accounting and reporting.

This last reason is amplified in the next paragraph.

The Financial Accounting Standards Board (FASB) issued its Statement of Financial Accounting Concepts 5 (SFAC 5) in an attempt to develop a conceptual framework for business enterprises. The conclusions of SFAC 5 included the view that a full set of financial statements should disclose cash flows themselves, not a surrogate for them.

Emmanuel (1988) described the American disillusion with the income statement and SCFP in the following words:

> The International Harvester, Massey Ferguson, Penn Central and Chrysler Corporations of this world are only a few examples of how a mask of profitability can easily be superimposed upon a mass of insolvency.
>
> (Emmanuel 1988 p. 19)

> With proper analysis, the interpretation of profit results will show how well the company is performing at the business of making money, whilst cash flow information will tell how real that money is.
>
> (Emmanuel 1988 p. 21)

Against this background, FASB undertook its review of APB 19 and evolved its replacement, the statement of cash flow (hereafter SCF).

Zega (1988) asserted SFAS 95 was issued for two reasons:

1 To resolve disputes over definitions of funds and formats of the funds statement.
2 To improve the reliability and usefulness of financial reports.

Emmanuel (1988) viewed the SCFP as inadequate relative to the SCF in that the SCFP had failed to address

1 categories of related cash flows,
2 the capacity to service debt obligations, and
3 the need for external financing.

These concerns he thought SFAS 95 had broadly covered.

Using the APB 19 SCFP even on the cash basis, actual cash flowing from operations could only be indirectly and unreliably assessed, asserted Drtina and Largay (1985).

Cash flow from operations is not easily inferred and is not systematically related to its funds flow surrogates, was the conclusion of Thode *et al.* (1986) after processing the accounts of the companies in the Standard and Poors 400 Industrial Index during 1973–82. They concluded that there was a strong case for separate reporting of operating cash flows.

Maksy (1988) found systematic discrepancies between the SCFP and the balance sheet figures in respect of forex treatments, purchase and sale of business entities, and deferred taxes.

Thompson and Buttross (1988) commended the writers of SFAS 95 for allowing less format flexibility than in APB 3 and APB 19.

The justifications for introducing an SCF

Professional preferences

The 1980 Discussion Memorandum (FASB 1980) stated that SCFPs had been criticized for being too condensed, for lack of focus on one definition of funds and for failure to question whether working capital was the most useful definition. Sorter (1982) criticized this criticism as inadequately addressing the objectives of the funds statement.

The 1981 Exposure Draft (FASB 1981) provided concepts to guide the presentation of income, cash flow and financial position information. It stated that reporting cash flow components will generally be more useful than reporting changes in working capital, and Sarhan *et al.* (1987) reported that responses to the Exposure Draft were favourable. The Financial Executives' Institute encouraged firms to report cash flow in their 1982 statements (Golub and Hoffman 1984).

In 1982 the Auditing Standards Board stated that it would not breach the consistency principle if firms switched from a working capital to a cash basis SCFP. Of Braiotta's (1984) 66 company sample from 6 industries, 56 per cent were already using a cash basis. Gibson *et al.* (1986) surveyed 300 CPA practitioners and 278 accounting professors on the issues involved in the replacement of the SCFP by the SCF. They found the following:

1 CPAs underestimated both internal and external usage of the funds statement.
2 Support for the working capital definition was roughly as strong as support for a cash definition.
3 Educators preferred a cash focus.

4 CPAs preferred a sources and uses format.
5 Educators preferred the direct operating cash flow format.
6 CPAs, however, preferred the indirect format.

Ketz and Largay (1987) unsuccessfully tried to link SCFP numbers with their equivalents in the income and position statements. In particular, the income statement idea of operations differed from that of the SCFP. They recommended the FASB to fuse the two statements into one, or at least to impose a common definition of operations. They attributed the move from a working capital to a cash basis statement during the 1980s to 'strong encouragement provided by the Financial Executives' Institute and by publications of the FASB (p. 10). (The publications to which they refer are FASB (1980) and (1981).)

SFAS 95 draws heavily on SFAC 1 (*Objectives of Financial Reporting*) for its justification. Adams (1988) quoted two extracts from the latter:

> Since an enterprise's ability to generate favourable cash flows affects both its ability to pay dividends and interest and the market price of its securities, expected cash flows to investors and creditors are related to expected cash flows to the enterprise in which they have invested or to which they have loaned funds.
>
> Financial reporting should provide information about how an enterprise obtains and spends cash, about its borrowing and repayment of borrowing, about its capital transactions, including cash dividends and other distributions of an enterprise's resources to its owners, and about other factors that may affect an enterprise's liquidity or solvency.
>
> (Adams 1988 p. 113)

Commercial reasons

Seed's (1984b) survey of bankers', financial analysts' and investors' opinions found a majority in all groups favouring a cash definition of funds as being by far the easiest definition to understand and to apply.

Seed (1984b) reported the view of some respondents that cash flow was more objective than funds flow, especially when inflation drives up the value of inventory, and causes prudent management to minimize receivables and cash holdings. The working capital fund would be rising but its most liquid elements would be falling, and statement users may be confused as to which signal of managerial stewardship ability is the senior.

Sarhan *et al.* (1987) stated that five factors prompted firms to switch from working capital to cash-based funds statements:

1 inventory growth, especially when it begins to slow,
2 receivables growth,
3 industry financial reporting practices,
4 users' needs, and
5 efforts of standard setting and professional bodies.

Studying 20 years of SCFPs to 1985, Franz and Thies (1988) discovered that both operating income and operating working capital funds flow had recently diminished in significance as components of cash flow, due mostly to slower growth in inventory and receivables relative to cash flow. This suggested that funds flow had become an inadequate proxy for cash flow.

Increasingly normal practice

By the mid 1980s, Swanson (1986) could report a widespread move to a cash basis SCFP 'due to its clarity'. The use of the traditional sources and applications format had declined as more companies used an activity format for classifying transactions as financing, investing or operating activities.

Kochanek and Norgaard (1987) examined the SCFPs of the Fortune 100 largest companies for the years 1979–83. Only two firms in the sample used a cash basis in 1979 but by 1983 this had risen to 76 firms. Definitions of cash varied considerably and only 36 firms in 1983 identified cash flow rather than working capital funds flow from operations in their statements.

Gibson and Kruse (1984) reported that a majority of their 87 sample companies were already using a cash and equivalents basis SCFP as suggested in the 1981 FASB exposure draft. Four years later:

> A recent survey of Fortune 500 companies showed about 70 per cent adopted a cash based approach and about 50 per cent currently classify transactions according to operating, investing and financing activities.
>
> (Mahoney *et al.* 1988 p. 27)

The finding that inventory growth ratio is a significant variable in explaining the change from reporting working capital to cash flow in the funds statement indicates that companies tend to report cash flow rather than working capital in the funds statements when they succeed in reducing their inventory. Users of financial statements may interpret such reporting change as a message from management about the improved liquidity and financial flexibility of the company. Such interpretation may help improve the economic performance of the company.

The same effect was not found very strongly for receivables but it was there to a certain extent (Sarhan *et al.* 1987 p. 61).

The SCF prescribed by SFAS 95

Descriptions of the requirements of SFAS 95, and/or its preceding exposure drafts, appeared in virtually every US accounting and banking journal in 1988 (Mahoney *et al.* 1988, O'Leary 1988, Boze 1987, Kreuze 1987, Richman *et al.* 1988, Nixon 1988, Ketz 1985, Senatra 1988, Wasniewski 1988, Farragher and Reinstein 1988, Born 1988, Zega 1988, Giacomino and Mielke 1987). SFAS 95 made the SCF mandatory for firms with accounting years ending after 16 July 1989.

Mahoney *et al.* (1988) exemplified an SCF using both indirect and direct formats for the operating cash flows, thus:

STATEMENT OF CASH FLOWS USING THE INDIRECT METHOD

Operating activities

Net income	8,000
Adjustments	
Depreciation and amortization	8,600
Provision for losses on receivables	750
Provision for deferred income taxes	1,000
Undistributed earnings of affiliate	(2,100)
Gain on sale of equipment	(2,500)
Receipt of instalment sale payment	2,500
Changes in operating assets and liabilities net of effects from puchase of XYZ Inc	
Increase in receivables	(7,750)
Increase in inventories and prepayments	(4,000)
Increase in payables and accruals	3,850

Net cash provided by operating activities		8,350

Investing activities

Purchases of property, plant and equipment	(12,000)	
Purchase of XYZ net of cash acquired	(7,700)	
Proceeds from sale of equipment	6,500	
Receipt discharging note for sale of plant	4,500	
Net cash used in investing activities		(8,700)

Financing activities

Proceeds from revolving credit line and long term borrowings	14,500	
Principal payments on revolving credit line, long term debt and capital lease obligations	(11,700)	
Proceeds from sale of common stock	2,000	
Dividends paid	(2,950)	
Net cash provided by financing activities		<u>1,850</u>
Increase in cash and cash equivalents		1,500
Cash and cash equivalents at beginning of year		6,000
Cash and cash equivalents at end of year		<u>7,500</u>

Accounting policies note: The company considers all highly liquid investments with a maturity of three months or less when purchased to be 'cash equivalents'.

OPERATING CASH FLOWS USING THE DIRECT METHOD

Operating activities

Cash received from customers	144,750
Dividend received from equity investee	900
Other operating cash receipts	10,000
Cash paid to suppliers and employees	(137,600)
Interest paid	(5,200)
Income taxes paid	(4,500)
Net cash provided by operating activities	8,350

In their review of SFAS 95, Mahoney *et al.* (1988) drew attention to the following three other requirements:

1 An exception to the general rule that financing and investing cash flows must be presented gross is allowed for assets and liabilities of original maturities up to and including three months.
2 Flows of foreign currencies must be translated at the rate current at the date of the flow while closing balances are translatable at the closing rate.
3 Non-cash transactions must be disclosed in a separate schedule from the SCF.

The SFAS 95 definitions

In its definition of cash, SFAS 95 states that:

> For the purpose of this statement, cash equivalents are short term, highly liquid investments that are both readily convertible to known amounts of cash and so near their maturity that they present insignificant risk of changes in value because of changes in interest rates.

When a firm first complied with SFAS 95, it was obliged to reveal its policy on determining what items it regarded as being cash equivalents. Zega (1988 p. 55) amplified this:

> Short term, highly liquid investments that are readily convertible to cash and are not interest rate sensitive are known as cash equivalents. Money market funds and Treasury bills with original maturities of three months or less are common examples of cash equivalents. . . . Reporting gross amounts of cash receipts and payments is required if such reporting facilitates understanding of the firm's operating, investing and financing activities. For instance, a business that issues one-month commercial paper and rolls it over every month would be reporting financing cash inflows and cash outflows twice the size of those of a firm that issues two month commercial paper. Otherwise net amounts of cash receipts and payments may be used.

Zega (1988 p. 56) added:

> 'Dividend payments are classified as financing activities because dividends are a distribution of net income (i.e. dividend payments cause retained earnings to decline) . . . In contrast, the interest

cost paid on borrowed funds is a determinant of net income and is classified as an operating activity.

The same applies to interest received. Asset purchases financed in mixed modes are in the SCF only at the cash financed value, the balance being in a supplementary non cash financing schedule. Stock splits, bonus issues and appropriations to reserves are excluded both from the SCF and from the supplementary statement of financing and investing because they do not affect cash and 'they are not significant financing or investing activities'.

Zega (1988 p. 59) concluded:

> Currently, most financial statements are prepared using the indirect method to determine net cash provided by operating activities. . . . The reporting of cash flow per share is prohibited in the financial statements. The FASB concluded that reporting cash flow per share would falsely imply that cash flow is equivalent to earnings as an indicator of performance.

Thus the FASB explicitly dissociated itself from those who regard cash flow as a measure of overall corporate performance.

Carmichael (1988) believed that auditors should require restatement of the prior year's SCFP as an SCF in the 1989 accounts or else qualify the audit report on the grounds of inconsistency. This opinion was published in the *CPA Journal*.

In SFAS 95's paragraph 60 the FASB decided that interest is an operating activity, because it is reflected in income, whereas dividends distributed are financing outflows, because they are not reflected in income. Gains or losses on asset sales and debt redemptions are non-operating, however, despite being included in income. 'The reasons for this disparity', commented Ketz and Largay (1987 p. 13), 'are unknown'. Depreciation is uncontroversially a part of operations, but calculation of the gain or loss on disposal is a function partly of the depreciation accumulated to the point of sale. Foreign exchange gains and losses could be argued to be as much a matter of financing or of investing as of operations.

> Three members of the FASB dissented on the issue of how interest and dividends received and interest paid should be classified in the eventual cash flow statement. According to the above schema they rank as operating cash flows, but the dissenters argue that a more realistic approach would be to classify interest and dividends received as cash inflows from investing activities and interest paid as a financing activity cash outflow. These inter-

pretations would be consistent with the UK/European view which . . . computes operating profit before taking interest receivable (and similar income) and interest payable into account.
(Adams 1988 p. 112)

Most (1990) took these objections much further, arguing that the new SCF was at least as misleading, fuzzy and ambiguous as the SCFP had been, especially when the SCF was prepared on the indirect basis. He reviewed the SCFs of 40 of the largest industrials in the Fortune 500, and found that no firm used the direct method and that over half the firms avoided reporting forex rate effects altogether, in flagrant disregard of GAAP.

The direct:indirect choice

Farragher and Reinstein (1988) thought the indirect basis would be preferred by firms that do not want to disclose their major classes of gross operating cash flows.

Although the use of the indirect method predominates, commercial lending officers expressed a strong preference in comment letters to the FASB that the direct method be *required*. Whether this method catches on will depend strongly on these banking officials pushing corporate borrowers to use the direct approach.
(Mahoney *et al.* 1988 p. 28)

Mahoney *et al.* (1988) themselves, however, preferred the indirect approach for three reasons:

1 It provides a useful linkage between the SCF and the income statement and balance sheet.
2 Statement users are more familiar with it.
3 It is generally the less expensive approach.

On the other hand, supporters of the direct approach argue that its gross treatment of operating cash flows is consistent with the approach of the financing and investing sections of the SCF. O'Leary (1988 p. 22) wrote that Robert Morris Associates (RMA 1989) favoured the direct approach because:

By comparing the accrual based income statement with the direct method cash flow statement, a company's operating cycle could be better understood and more appropriately financed. After all, it is the gap between accrual earnings and the cash collection of those earnings that commercial lenders are called upon to finance.

This was strange, considering only the indirect method spells out depreciation and similar notional costs. 'By a 4:3 vote, the members of FASB defeated their staff's recommendation that only the direct method be permitted (p. 26).'

So there is not much more comparability between firms under SFAS 95 than there had been under APB 19.

Emmanuel (1988), following up O'Leary's article, pointed out that operating cash flows are direct sources of revenue, unlike financing or investment flows: and it was quite possible for the former to arise from the latter, as with income from an asset rented out to a lessee. Since the SCF is to explain the income/cash flow disparity, all payments on the income statement should appear on the SCF, in particular, dividends and taxes should (Emmanuel 1988 p. 34).

Farragher and Reinstein (1988) thought the indirect basis would be preferred by firms that do not want to disclose their major classes of gross operating cash flows.

Nurnberg (1989), however, pointed out the relevance of depreciation to the SCF, arising from using the absorption costing method instead of the marginal costing method of valuing inventory. He argued that it makes no difference whether the direct or indirect method is used; but this is wrong. With the indirect method, depreciation is clearly identified as one of the largest items comprising the earnings cash flow disparity. With the direct method, depreciation should not appear at all, least of all in inventory purchases.

The indirect method has been argued by Drtina and Largay (1985) not to equal actual cash flow from operations because of the many conceptual and practical problems intrinsic to the adjustment processes.

A direct basis for a prototype SCF in Allen's (1985) experiment resulted in the solvency judgments of professional analysts and portfolio managers outperforming their SCFP-based judgements.

COMPARATIVE ANALYSIS OF SCF STANDARDS AROUND THE WORLD

A selection of objectives of SCFs in the standards

The UK

To assist users of the financial statements in their assessment of the reporting entity's liquidity, viability and financial adaptability.

The objective of the standard headings is to ensure that cash flows are reported in a form that highlights the significant components of cash flow and facilitates comparison of the cash flow performance of different businesses.

(FRS 1, paragraph 1, page 4)

Hong Kong

Users of financial statements need information on the liquidity, viability and financial adaptability of the entity concerned. Deriving this information involves the user in making assessments of the future cash flows of the entity . . . long term provisions and other allocations associated with accruals accounting need to be eliminated in order to reveal the leads and lags in historical cash flows, thereby improving understanding of a reporting entity's cash generating or cash absorption mechanisms and providing a basis for the assessment of future cash flows.

(SSAP 15 paragraph 2, 1992)

In order to promote understanding and to help to achieve the objectives of cash flow reporting by securing the useful presentation of information, this Statement requires that individual cash flows should be classified under certain standard headings according to the activity that gave rise to them . . . [includes returns on investments and servicing of finance as a new class and taxation as a further separate new class]. . . . The objective of the standard headings is to ensure that cash flows are reported in a form that highlights the significant components of cash flow and facilitates comparison of the cash flow performance of different businesses.

(SSAP 15, paragraph 3, 1992)

The USA's SFAS 95

The main purposes of SFAS 95 are:

to help investors, creditors and others
(a) to assess a firm's ability to generate positive future net cash flows,
(b) to assess a firm's ability to meet its obligations,
(c) to assess a firm's ability to pay dividends,
(d) to assess a firm's need for external financing,
(e) to assess the reasons for differences between net income and its associated receipts and payments,

(f) to assess the effects on financial position of both cash and non cash investing and financing transactions (Mahoney *et al.* 1988).

Canada

to present information about the operating, financing and investing activities of an enterprise and the effects of those activities on cash resources . . . assists users of financial statements in evaluating the liquidity and solvency of an enterprise, and in assessing its ability to generate cash from internal sources, to repay debt obligations, to reinvest and make distributions to owners. This information is not provided or is only indirectly provided in the balance sheet, income statement and statement of retained earnings. Thus the SCFP [*sic*] complements, and presents information different from that provided in, the other financial statements.

> (Canadian Institute of Chartered Accountants Handbook,
> section 1540.01, page 281, August 1991)

Australia

Statement of Accounting Concepts SAC 2 'Objective of General Purpose Financial Reporting' states that general purpose financial reports shall provide information useful to users for making and evaluating decisions about the allocation of scarce resources. A statement of cash flows provides relevant information to users about the cash inflows and cash outflows of an entity during a reporting period.

The information provided in a statement of cash flows together with other information in the financial report may assist in assessing the ability of an entity to:

(a) generate cash flows in the future;

(b) meet its financial obligations as they fall due, including the servicing of borrowings and the payment of dividends;

(c) fund changes in the scope and/or nature of its activities; and

(d) obtain external finance where necessary.

> (Australian Accounting Standard AAS 28,
> paragraphs 8 and 9, pages 6 and 7, December 1991)

New Zealand

The objective of a SCF is to provide information about the operating, investing and financing activities of an entity and the effects of those activities on cash resources. The information in a SCF, if used with information in the other financial statements, should assist investors, creditors, and others to:

(a) estimate the entity's ability to generate positive future net cash flows;

(b) assess the entity's ability to meet its obligations and pay dividends and assess its needs for external financing;

(c) compare the net surplus reported on an accruals basis with the cash flows generated from operating activities; and

(d) construct significant ratios and make comparisons reflecting the entity's ability to generate cash, especially from operating activities.

Information on the liquidity of an entity is important to users of financial reports. Shortage of liquid resources can lead, and has led, to business failure and bankruptcy. Key liquidity indicators are cash provided by operations and cash absorbed by working capital requirements. Users also need information about financial flexibility which may be regarded as the ability to optimise cash resources and to respond to unexpected adversities and opportunities. Provision of cash flow information, in addition to the accrual based statement of financial performance and statement of financial position, ensures that users of financial reports are better informed as to liquidity and financial flexibility.

Income data supported only by a statement of financial position provides limited information for the estimation of the timing and uncertainty of future cash flows of an entity. Actual cash flow information disclosed in the financial reports may enable users to assess better the cash performance of the entity, to build up a better understanding of the variables which affect cash flows and hence be in a position to make projections of future cash flows.

Inflows and outflows of cash are not influenced by the subjective cost allocations which affect reported income. Thus cash flow information should improve comparability between financial reports of different entities.

A number of useful ratios may also be constructed from information on cash flows which, together with other ratios constructed from statement of financial performance and statement of financial position items, may give greater understanding of the financial position, results and trends of the reporting entity. Useful ratios may include:

(a) interest or dividend cover in cash flows from operating activities;

(b) ratio of current and long term debt to cash flows from operating activities;

(c) ratio of cash from customers to turnover; and

(d) ratio of cash flows from operating activities to reported net surplus.

(New Zealand Society of Accountants, Financial Reporting Standard No 10, 'Statement of Cash Flows and Guidance Notes', paragraphs 5.2 to 5.6, pages 4–5, March 1992)

The standards on SCFs to date: selected extracts

Canada

From the CICA Handbook, section 1540, February/March 1985, Toronto, Canada. (Note that in Canada the SCF is still called an SCFP.)

1540.02 The focus on cash and its equivalents 'provides a better indication of liquidity and solvency and the ability of an enterprise to generate cash resources than does a focus on working capital or other non-cash grouping'.

1540.03 'Cash and cash equivalents would normally include cash, net of short term borrowings, and temporary investments and may, in some cases, include certain other elements of working capital when they are equivalent to cash.'

12. The SCFP should include at least the following items:

(a) Cash from operations: the amount of cash from operations should be reconciled to the income statement or the components of cash from operations should be disclosed;

(b) cash flows resulting from discontinued operations;

(c) cash flows resulting from extraordinary items;

(d) outlays for acquisition and proceeds on disposal of assets, by major category, not included in a, b or c above;

(e) the issue, assumption, redemption and repayment of debt not included in a, b or c above;

(f) the issue, redemption and acquisition of share capital; and

(g) the payment of dividends, identifying separately dividends paid by subsidiaries to non controlling interests.

18. Flows should normally be classified by operating, financing and investing activities.

Other sections include:

Effective date 1 October 1985.

*The title of the statement may remain SCFP because of statutes already in place but a preferred title is Cash Flow Information,

Operating flows may be direct or indirect.

The USA, Mexico, Taiwan and Japan

SFAS 95 has been adequately elaborated in the previous subsections. It should be noted that SFAS 95 is the format preferred by Taiwanese and Japanese groups in their English language accounts, and their classification of dividends, interest and tax follows the SFAS 95 rules. Mexico became the first country in the world to adopt new style SCFs when it took the USA's 1981 Exposure Draft into its own accounting regulations.

South Africa

From *AC 118 Cash Flow Information*, South African Institute of Chartered Accountants, July 1988.

04. Cash includes such equivalents as money market instruments.

05. Investing means buying and selling fixed assets and investments including advances outside cash equivalents.

06. Financing activities change the size and composition of the debt and capital funding of the entity.

07. Operating activities are any other transactions.

12. Non-operating flows should be shown gross, e.g. with respect to loan repayments and new loans.

17. Cash generated by operations is normally calculated by adjusting operating income before tax for items not involving cash flows including depreciation, provisions and unrealized exchange differences.

18. Cash arising from or absorbed by the non-cash elements of working capital are disclosed as operating activities exclusive of amounts directly attributable to financing or investing activities.

23. 'The statement requires disclosure of cash flows and cash flow equivalents. For example, where an enterprise has issued its shares in order to acquire an interest in another enterprise, fair presentation requires that the issue of shares be disclosed under financing

activities and the acquisition of the interest in the other enterprise as an investing activity.'

27. Where practical, investing by way of maintenance of capacity should be differentiated from investing to expand it.

48. Implementation is for periods ending on or after 1 October 1988.

New Zealand

From FRS10, Statement of Cash Flows, replacing SSAP10 Statement of Cash Flows of October 1987, itself replacing SSAP10 on funds flows issued July 1979, New Zealand Society of Accountants, Wellington, March 1992.

4.1 'Cash means coins and notes, demand deposits and other highly liquid investments in which an entity invests as part of its day-to-day cash management. A highly liquid investment is one for which there is a recognised ready market enabling the unconditional conversion of the investment to coins and notes at the investor's option within no more than two working days. Cash includes borrowings from financial institutions, such as bank overdrafts, which are integral to the cash management function and which are at call.'

4.2 'The items identified as being part of the day-to-day cash management of an entity will vary, according to circumstances, from one entity to another.' Firms must therefore specify what they are including in the term cash.

4.3 Two working days is the absolute limit, however, for conversion into notes.

4.6 Financing activities comprise the change in equity and debt capital structure of the reporting entity and the cost of servicing the equity capital.

4.8 Interest is excluded.

4.9 Investing activities are those activities relating to the acquisition and disposal of non-current assets.

4.13 Operating activities include all transactions and other events that are not investing or financing activities. Interest and dividends received and interest paid are included in operating activities.

4.16 Operating flows include receipts from donations, grants, rates, levies and similar where such receipts are the main sources of revenue for carrying on the operating activities of the entity.

4.17 '. . . while a gain or loss on the disposal of an asset will appear as an operating surplus, the cash inflow in relation to that gain or loss is generally part of a cash inflow from investing activities'.

5.7 mandates the separation between operating, investing and financing activities.

5.11 mandates the direct method.

5.14 mandates the indirect reconciliation note.

5.16 classifies all interest and received dividends as operating flows, except capitalized interest is an investing flow, and dividends paid are financing except dividends on debt capital which is operating.

5.24 Income tax flows are operating.

5.30 mandates reconciliation of cash to opening and closing balance sheets.

5.32 Both abnormal and extraordinary items should be disclosed separately under one of the three classifications.

5.34 mandates disclosure in a note transactions of a financing or investing nature which do not result in cash flows in the period.

New Zealand Statement of Cash Flows (GST inclusive) for the year ended 30 June 19X1

	19X1 $000	19X0 $000
Cash flow from operating activities		
Cash was provided from:		
Receipts from customers	671,000	516,375
Net GST received from IRD	2,500	–
Interest received	6,000	3,000
Dividends received	4,000	4,500
	683,500	523,875
Cash was applied to:		
Payment to suppliers	630,000	377,438
Payments to employees	80,000	65,000
Other operating expenses	27,000	15,000
Net GST paid to IRD	–	8,770
Interest paid	13,000	14,000
Income tax	26,900	–
Net cash inflow (outflow) from	776,900	480,208
operating activities	(93,400)	43,667
Cash flows from investing activities		
Cash was provided from:		
Sale of fixed assets	54,000	–

Cash was applied to:

Purchase of fixed assets	(21,000)	–
Purchase of investments	(50,000)	
Net cash inflow (outflow) from investing activities	(17,000)	–

Cash flows from financing activities
Cash was provided from:

Issue of shares	30,000	
Term loan	45,000	
Cash was applied to:		
Repayment of loan	(60,000)	
Payment of dividends	(24,000)	(10,000)
Net cash inflow (outflow) from financing activities	(9,000)	(10,000)
Net increase (decrease) in cash held	(119,400)	33,667
Add cash at start of year (1 July)	38,165	4,498
Add effect of exchange rate change on foreign currency balance	100	–
Balance at end of year (30 June)	(81,135)	38,165

Australia

In June 1986 the Accounting Standards Review Board approved Australian Accounting Standard 12 as ASRB 1007 mandating the presentation of a statement of sources and applications of funds as a primary financial statement. In response to a number of comments on the exposure draft for that standard, a new exposure draft (ED 37 1986) was issued seeking to require in a note to the funds statement an analysis of cash flow from operations. In the same year, 1986, the Australian companies code and companies regulations were amended to mandate the cash flow statement, but the amendments were withdrawn in response to public accounting and corporate lobbying pressure, partly through satisfaction with AAS 12 but more through disapproval of the takeover of the standard setting process by the legislature (Sims and Cantrick-Brooks 1992). In November 1990 ED 37 was referred back to the Australian Accountants' Research Foundation who issued its replacement, ED 52 *Statement of Cash Flows*, in May 1991 and the draft became joint standard AAS 28/ASRB 1026 in December 1991 and came into effect for periods ending on or after 30 June 1992. It supersedes

AAS 12, issued in March 1983 and amended in June 1987, 'Statement of Sources and Applications of Funds'.

Selections from AAS 28:

7a. Requirement to present cash flow information replaces funds flow data required under AAS12/ASRB1007

13. definitions

A cash flow is a 'cash movement resulting from transactions with parties external to the entity'.

Cash equivalents are 'highly liquid investments which are readily convertible to cash on hand at the investor's option and which an entity uses in its cash management function on a day-to-day basis; and borrowings which are integral to the cash management function and which are not subject to a term facility'. The standard seeks consistency between periods but not between entities on the definitions of equivalents. Operating activities are 'those activities which relate to the provision of goods and services . . .'. Investing activities are 'those activities which relate to the acquisition and disposal of non-current assets . . . and investments such as securities not falling within the definition of cash'. Financing activities are 'those activities which relate to exchanging the size and composition of the financial structure of the entity, including equity, and borrowings not falling within the definition of cash'.

16. Money market funds and overdrafts repayable on demand would normally meet the definition of cash.

18. 'The guidance in paragraph 16 on whether an item such as a money market deposit can be regarded as cash is not expressed in terms of the period to maturity of the item. This is because such quantitative guidance will not always be an accurate indicator of the risk of changes in value of an item arising from changes in interest rates. Nevertheless, an entity may elect to adopt quantitative guidelines in establishing its policy for determining which highly liquid investments are used in its cash management function.'

24. The policy used by the firm to determine which items should be classified as cash must be disclosed.

34. However the following are classified by a firm, they must be separately disclosed:

'(a) interest and other items of a similar nature received;

(b) dividends received;

(c) interest and other costs of finance paid;

(d) dividends paid; and

(e) income taxes paid.

35. Cash flows for the following items may be reported on a net basis:

(a) items where the entity is, in substance, holding or disbursing cash on behalf of its customers; and

(b) investments, loans receivable and loans payable where turnover is rapid and the total volume of transactions is large.'

36. Any other flows must be reported gross.

38. 'Cash flows from operating activities shall be presented using the direct method whereby the relevant cash inflows and cash outflows are reported in gross terms' subject to the exemptions in paragraph 35.

39. A note should show the reconciliation of operating cash flow to profit after tax in the income statement.

41. The reasons for requiring the direct method are to ensure the SCF provides information not otherwise available and provides a method of estimating future cash flow more useful than the net presentation characteristic of the indirect method.

46. Forex flows are to be translated at actual wherever possible, but otherwise a period long weighted average rate may be used.

49. 'Information about transactions and other events which do not result in cash flows during the reporting period but affect assets and liabilities that have been recognized shall be disclosed in the financial report where the transactions and other events:

(a) involve parties external to the entity; and

(b) relate to the financing, investing and other non-operating activities of the entity.'

53. 'The financial report shall disclose separately the following information as at the reporting date:

(a) details of the entity's credit standby arrangements, including the nature of each arrangement and the total amount of credit unused; and

(b) a summary of the entity's used and unused loan facilities and the extent to which these can be continued or extended.'

The UK and Ireland

From FRS 1 CASH FLOW STATEMENTS, Financial Reporting Standard no 1, Accounting Standards Board Ltd, London 1991:

(Format below is Para,Page)

3,5 Cash equivalents

'Short-term, highly liquid investments which are readily convertible into known amounts of cash without notice and which were within three months of maturity when acquired; less advances from banks repayable within three months from the date of the advance. Cash equivalents include investments and advances denominated in foreign currencies provided that they fulfil the above criteria.'

12,7 Format

Standard headings are in this order: operating activities, returns on investments and servicing of finance, taxation, investing activities, and financing. Cash flows are to be totalled for each heading and overall before financing.

Operating activities
15,8 'Net cash flow from operating activities represents the net increase or decrease in cash and cash equivalents resulting from the operations shown in the profit and loss account in arriving at operating profit.'

16,8 They may be shown gross or net.

17,8 A note to the CFS should reconcile operating profit (normally for non-financial companies profit before interest) with operating cash flow so as to show movements in stock, debtors, creditors and other elements.

Servicing of finance
20 a,9 Interest paid includes capitalized interest and any tax deducted on behalf of a tax authority.

20 b,9 Dividends, however, are net of advance corporation tax.

20 c,9 The interest element of finance lease rental payments is a servicing cash outflow.

Taxation
21,9 Only includes direct taxes on revenue and capital profits but excludes all types of indirect tax.

22,9 Tax deposit certificate purchases and payments of advance corporation tax count as taxation cash flows.

Investing activities
25 d,10 Inflows include 'receipts from repayment or sales of loans made by the reporting entity or of other entities' debt (other than cash equivalents) which were purchased by the reporting entity'.

26 d,10 Outflows include 'payments to acquire debt of other entities (other than cash equivalents)'.

Financing

29,10 Financing cash outflows include:

a repayments of borrowings if not already in cash equivalents,

b the capital element of finance lease rental payments,

c payments to reacquire or redeem the entity's shares, and

d payments of expenses or commissions on any issue of financial paper.

30,10 Any finance flows to or from equity accounted entities should be separately disclosed.

37,12 Hedging flows should be shown under the heading applicable to the transaction being hedged.

39,12 Dividends paid to minorities are servicing cash flows.

43,13 'Material transactions not resulting in movements of cash or cash equivalents of the reporting entity should be disclosed in the notes to the cash flow statement if disclosure is necessary for an understanding of the underlying transactions.'

44,13 Movements of cash and equivalents in the financing section of the CFS should be reconciled to the corresponding balances in the opening and closing balance sheets.

46,13 FRS 1 is effective for accounting periods ending on or after 23 March 1992.

Hong Kong

From SSAP 15 September 1992 following the Exposure Draft Cash Flow Statements, Hong Kong Society of Accountants, 31 March 1992.

10. Cash equivalents defined as in FRS 1.

17. Classifications are: operating activities, returns on investments and servicing of finance, taxation, investing activities, and financing.

21. Operating flows may be reported net or gross.

22. Profit before tax and interest (after interest for finance companies) in the profit and loss account should be reconciled to the net operating cash flow and disclose movements in stocks, debtors and creditors related to operating activities.

23–25 define returns on investments and servicing of finance to include all gross interest receipts and payments, dividends net of tax credits and the interest element in any finance lease rental payment.

26–28 restricts taxation to profits taxation but allows it to include all cash transactions with the tax authority including purchase of tax reserve certificates. Explanatory note 77 explains why tax has a separate category. *'The taxation cash flows 'of a reporting entity in relation to revenue and capital profits may result from complex computations that are affected by the operating, investing and financing activities of an entity. It is not useful to divide taxation cash flows into constituent parts relating to the activities that gave rise to them because the apportionment will, in many cases, have to be made on an arbitrary basis. As taxation cash flows generally arise from activities in an earlier period, apportioning the taxation cash flows would not necessarily report the taxation cash flows along with the transactions that gave rise to them. In addition, a taxation cash flow is not normally a collection of individual cash inflows and outflows and thus analysing it in this manner would require preparers of financial statements to allocate individual cash flows over the standard headings and would not necessarily give information on the entity's underlying cash flows.'*

24–35 are very similar to FRS 1 on non-operating flows.

39 and 40 echo FRS 1 on indirect tax treatment.

41 for foreign currencies, 42 for hedging transactions, 45–7 for acquisitions and disposals, 48 for non-cash transactions, 49 for reconciliations with balance sheets all resemble FRS 1.

73. On the direct method: 'However, it is not believed at present that in all cases the benefits to users of this information outweigh the costs to the reporting entity of providing it and, therefore, the statement does not require the information to be given.'

81. Sales taxes are usually timing differences only so cash flows should be shown net of sales taxes and any payment thereof to the collecting authority should be within operating flows.

HK SSAP 15 Cash Flow Statements issued September 1992 effective for accounting periods commencing on or after 31 March 1992.

HONG KONG ILLUSTRATIVE EXAMPLE – SINGLE COMPANY

XYZ Ltd

Cash flow statement for the year ended 31 December 1992

	HK$000	HK$000
Net cash flow from operating activities		6,889

Returns on investments and servicing of finance

Interest received	3,011	
Interest paid	(12)	
Dividends paid	(2,417)	

Net cash inflow from returns on investments and servicing of finance | | | 582

Taxation

Profits tax paid	2,922	

Tax paid | | | (2,922)

Investing activities

Payments to acquire permanent textile quotas	(71)	
Payments to acquire fixed assets	(1,496)	
Receipts from sales of fixed assets	42	

Net cash outflow from investing activities | | | (1,525)

Net cash inflow before financing | | | 3,024

Financing

Issue of ordinary share capital	211	
Repurchase of debenture loan	(149)	
Expenses paid in connection with share issues	(5)	

Net cash inflow from financing | | | 57

Increase in cash and cash equivalents | | | 3,081

Cash and cash equivalents at 1 January 1992 | | | 21,373

Cash and cash equivalents at 31 December 1992 | | | 24,454

Analysis of the balances of cash and cash equivalents

Cash at bank and in hand	529
Short term investments	23,936
Bank overdrafts	(11)
	24,454

The IASC's IAS 7

The International Accounting Standards Committee Board approved a statement of principles (SOP) on cash flow statements in March 1990 which was strongly reflective of SFAS 95 rather than FRS 1; 23 member bodies sent in comments and 6 other bodies from altogether 19 countries, mostly supporting the proposal. The greatest diversity of opinion concerned whether equity or short term borrowings could be considered as cash equivalents, whether the direct method should be mandatory or not, and how interest and dividends should be classified.

'Virtually all the respondents to the SOP agreed with [the classification of flows between operating, financing and investing]. A minority argued that this distinction is arbitrary and that any explanation of the activities should be accompanied by a statement that the components for each of these activities could be different depending on the nature of an enterprise's business.'

Australia, Japan and New Zealand require the direct method while the USA encourages it. 'Approximately three-quarters of the respondents to the SOP stated that enterprises should be permitted to present a cash flow statement using either the direct or the indirect method. When asked if they preferred one method over the other, over one-third preferred the direct method while almost one-half had no preference.' E36 proposed to allow either but not to require direct method users also to present a reconciliation of cash flow to operating profit as 'the Board believes that the presentation of this reconciliation is a disincentive to enterprises considering using the direct method'.

'Approximately three-quarters of the respondents to the SOP argued that:

interest paid and interest and dividends received and paid [*sic*] should be classified as operating activities because they enter into the determination of net income; and

dividends paid should be classified as financing activities because they are a cost of obtaining financial resources.

However some respondents suggested that:

interest and dividends received should be classified as investing activities because they represent a return on investment; and

interest and dividends should be classified in a fourth category.'

E36 and IAS 7 stipulate interest and dividends should be separately disclosed under one of the three main headings and stay consistently under that heading from period to period, but do not mandate any particular classification.

E36 and IAS 7 require non-cash investing and financing activities to be disclosed in a note to the CFS. They require foreign currency to be translated at the rate applicable at the time of the cash flow.

Acquisitions and disposals must show under investing flows: the total price, the portion thereof discharged by cash and equivalents, the cash and equivalents in the business bought/sold, and the amounts of every other major asset and lability.

E36 and IAS 7 encourage distinguishing maintaining from expanding operating capacity, disclosing any unused borrowing facilities, disclosing any cash and equivalents not available for general use, and reporting segments and joint venture flows separately.

The SFAS 95 definition of cash is quoted with approval. Cash and cash equivalents which are short term highly liquid investments that are readily convertible to cash and so near to their maturity that they present insignificant risk of changes in value because of changes in interest rates. Generally, only investments with an original maturity to the enterprise of three months or less qualify as cash equivalents. 'Most respondents to the SOP preferred a definition that emphasized short term convertibility of cash equivalents to cash and low risk of changes in the value of investments considered to be cash equivalents. Five respondents argued that equity investments should be included in the definition because management intention should govern the selection of investments qualifying as a cash equivalent. Four respondents argued that short term borrowings should not be a component of cash and cash equivalents. The reasons given were that:

borrowings are a financing activity;

the determination of shortterm is likely to be arbitrary and therefore misleading; and

the inclusion of short term borrowings in cash could result in a negative cash balance in the cash flow statement which financial statement users would misunderstand and misinterpret.'

IAS 7 proposes that cash equivalents are short term highly liquid investments which are readily convertible into known amounts of cash and which are subject to an insignificant risk of changes in value. It is confined to investments with not more than three months' maturity at the date of acquisition. This will usually exclude equities except those subject to mandatory imminent redemption. Overdrafts repayable on demand which form an integral part of an enterprise's cash management are part of cash.

From E36 International Accounting Standard – Cash Flow Statements, IASC, July 1991. Approved as the replacement for IAS 7 in October 1992.

6. Definitions

Cash comprises cash on hand and deposits with banks.

Cash equivalents are short term liquid investments which are readily convertible to known amounts of cash and which are subject to an insignificant risk of changes in value; para 8 elaborates this. Equivalents are held only for the purpose of meeting short term cash commitments and normally include only those investments with three months or less maturity at acquisition date.

Investing is the acquisition and disposal of assets not included in cash equivalents.

Financing activities are 'those activities that result in changes in the size and composition of the equity share capital and borrowings of the enterprise'.

Anything else is an operating activity.

14. mandates the three way classification.

23. 'Enterprises are encouraged to report cash flows from operating activities using the direct method. However, many enterprises may not be able to report gross operating cash flows without incurring substantial costs that may outweigh the benefits of the information to external users. Therefore, this Statement also permits the presentation of cash flows from operating activities using the indirect method.'

24. Investing and financing flows should be reported gross, except as below.

27. Foreign exchange cash flows should be translated at actual rates at the time of the flow.

28. Cash flows of a foreign subsidiary should be translated actual rates as far as possible.

29. IAS 21 is to be applied to such translations.

30. Unrealized gains and losses are not cash flows, but rate change differences reconciling opening to closing cash have to be reported on the SCF – 'This amount is presented separately from cash flows from operating, investing and financing activities and includes the differences, if any, had those cash flows been reported at end of period exchange rates.'

33. 'Interest and dividends received and paid should be classified

in a consistent manner from period to period and each separately disclosed as one of operating, investing or financing activities.'

36. Income tax cash flows should be identified as operating.

40. Aggregate flows from acquiring and disposing of businesses should be presented separately classified as investing.

41. In the period of acquisition or disposal, aggregate disclosures are required of price, the portion of price discharged by cash equivalents, cash equivalents inside the business bought/sold, and other assets and liabilities therein.

43. Non-cash financing and investing transactions should be disclosed outside the SCF.

45. Cash and equivalents should be reconciled with their balance sheet amounts.

SAMPLE CASH FLOW STATEMENT UNDER IAS 7 USING THE DIRECT METHOD

Cash flows from operating activities

Cash receipts from customers	30,150
Cash paid to suppliers and employees	(27,600)
Cash generated from operations	2,550
Interest received	200
Dividends received	200
Interest paid	(270)
Income taxes paid	(900)
Net cash provided by operating activities before unusual item	1,780
Proceeds from litigation settlement	180
Net cash provided by operating activities	1,980

Cash flows from investing activities

Acquisition of subsidiary net of cash acquired	(550)
Purchase of fixed assets	(350)
Proceeds from sale of equipment	20
Net cash used in investing activities	(880)

Cash flows from financing activities

Proceeds from issuance of share capital	220
Proceeds from long term borrowings	250
Repayment of long term borrowings	(90)
Dividends paid on share capital	(1,200)

Net cash used in financing activities	(790)
Effects of exchange rate changes on cash and cash equivalents	(40)
Net increase in cash and cash equivalents	250
Cash and cash equivalents	
at beginning of period	160
at end of period	410

INTERNATIONAL SCF VARIATIONS

Classifications of interest and dividends

Country	Divs and int received	Interest paid	Divs paid
USA	Operating	Op	Fi
Australia	Operating	Fi	Fi
Canada	Not specified	n/s	Op or Fi
France	Operating	Op	Fi
Japan	Operating	Op	Op
New Zealand	Investing	Fi	Fi
South Africa	Operating	Op	Op
UK	Servicing	Svcg	Svcg
Hong Kong	Servicing	Svcg	Svcg

It is clear from the above table that although all adopters of the SCF use Heath's division of cash flows into operating, investing and financing, the boundary of operating flows varies from country to country, with the UK and Hong Kong having the narrowest view, Japan and South Africa the widest. It is also clear that the greatest diversity of classification occurs with regard to dividends paid which Canada, Japan and South Africa are prepared to regard as operating.

Corporate income tax

Tax is operating in Australia, France, Japan, New Zealand, South Africa and the USA, but the UK says tax should match the nature of the underlying activity and Canada provides no guidance on the matter. The UK and Hong Kong create a separate classification for tax on profits but IAS 7 follows SFAS 95 in making income tax flows operating.

Boundaries of cash

Five countries were reviewed by Wallace and Collier (1991) for their differences in definitions of cash and cash equivalents in their accounting standards on cash flow statements: Canada, New Zealand, the USA, South Africa, and the UK and Ireland. A review of existing standards and SCFs prepared in accordance with them reveals terminological confusion on what preparers and regulators understand by cash. The most important finding is that 'cash' is not always 'cash' in SCFs, whether viewed from the perspective of pronouncements in national accounting standards or the perspective of cash flow information published in financial statements from across the world.

National and global inter-company comparability of financial figures will not necessarily be improved by cash flow information.

Extract from table 2 in Wallace and Collier (1991):

Spectrum of definitions of cash in cash flow statements

1　Monetary assets – cash, demand deposits and highly liquid investments: USA, South Africa.
2　Monetary assets less bank overdrafts: UK and Eire.
3　Net monetary assets – as 1 above less short term borrowings: New Zealand, Canada, IASC.

1 is closest to lay meanings of cash, 3 to a corporate treasurer's view. Hendriksen's view (1977) is quoted favouring a net monetary assets definition; namely, many cash flows associated with short term debt are irrelevant to accounts users and since those flows' timing can be varied, netting of short term debt transactions allows a focus on more basic cash movements.

Cash is not an objective construct because its face and accounting values tend to diverge for two main reasons:

1　cash equivalents value varies with market conditions,
2　some equivalents lack a stable measure of value possibly as a result of the practice of marking to market and they are stated gross of the commissions etc. payable in liquidating them.

Twenty large firms were selected from each of the countries with SCF standards to see how they defined cash. A majority, 61 per cent, of the grand total followed a gross monetary assets definition and a third some form of net monetary assets, not necessarily in conformity with national standards. Canada and New Zealand specify a net monetary assets position yet over half the combined sample from those countries adopted a gross definition. Of the US sample 15 per cent used a net basis which is not provided for in SFAS 95.

Table 3 in Wallace and Collier (1991) shows the definitions of cash used in cash flow statements by country, as follows:

	Canada	New Zealand	USA	South Africa	Total
Cash		1			1
Cash and short term investments		8	5	4	17
Cash and cash equivalents	2	11	12	7	32
Cash, deposits, short term investments less overdrafts	11			4	15
Cash and equivalents less overdrafts, advances and notes payable	7		3	5	15
Country Totals	20	20	20	20	80

The narrower the definition of cash, the sharper the focus on liquidity.

OPINIONS ON THE SCF

Criticisms of the SCF

There were differences of opinion among FASB members regarding the classification of items, such as the treatment of interest and dividends received and interest paid as operating items rather than investment and financing activities. The issue was the classification of cash flows based on the underlying transaction rather than the cash flow itself (Richman *et al.* 1988).

Kistler and Hamer (1988) criticized SFAS 95 on four points:

1 the diversity of permitted formats,
2 the limited usefulness of the direct method,
3 the incorporation of non-cash transactions, and
4 the classification of interest and dividends.

Giacomino and Mielke (1988) thought SFAS 95 should have required more information than it did, namely:

1 long term financing distinguished from short term,
2 'other' operations sources and uses of cash, and
3 a classification for discretionary uses of cash.

Bierman (1988) reported a survey indicating the widespread availability prior to SFAS 95's start date of relevant software, but it would have been still more widespread if more than a third of the vendors surveyed had been aware of SFAS 95's provisions.

O'Leary (1988) reported that most credit officers and lenders would have liked to see more comprehensive details of the various types of cash flow than SFAS 95 mandated.

Arthur (1986) stated that controversy over the proposed SCF centred on three main issues. First, there was no agreement on cash flow format. Second, trend analysis is hard to develop from a cash flow statement. Third, cash flow statements are often used in long range planning (which seems at odds with the previous sentence's view).

Valenza (1989) pointed out that for financial institutions an SCF was really an inventory report so the FASB was considering specific disclosure requirements for them quite different from a mainstream SCF.

The Heath critique

A cash flow statement cannot by itself indicate a firm's performance but nor can the income statement do so, commented Heath (1987). Arguing which is more important is like arguing which shoe is. SFAS 95 is a step in the right direction but not far enough. It cuts and pastes the discredited SCFP instead of redesigning it *de novo*. Some financing activities do not affect working capital: borrowing/repaying of short term debt, issuance of loan stock for plant and equipment, and debt/equity swaps. Reporting these as sources and uses is necessary for activity reporting but is confusing, because these items are a source neither of working capital nor of cash. Although 'resources' are often used instead of 'funds' to get round that, the bottom line is still working capital or cash. Paragraph 20 of the exposure draft preceding SFAS 95 stipulated that all financing and investing activities have to be reported, not just those affecting cash. The secondary objective (all financial resources) is thus in conflict with the primary one (cash flows only). FASB took this point seriously because the final version of SFAS 95 excluded non-cash financing and investing activities from the prescribed SCF. Operating net cash flows by the direct method show cash receivable from customers, dividends etc. less cash paid for inventory, expenses, interest and tax; whereas the indirect method adjusts net income by depreciation, deferred tax and each component change in working capital.

> Cash flow is not the source of income, and income is not the source of cash; they are two different *effects* of buying and selling goods and services. . . . The indirect method is pernicious because it reinforces the widespread belief that both profit and depreciation are sources of cash.
>
> The direct method makes clear cash comes in from sales and out through expenses to which depreciation is irrelevant.
>
> (Heath 1987 p. 16)

Sondhi *et al.* (1988) praised SFAS 95 for requiring financing and investing cash flows to be stated gross, but decried the requirement to separate out non-cash financing and investing transactions. Acquiring assets for a mix of cash and securities would be fragmented in the reports and the cash flow effects of the transaction thereby be obscured.

RESEARCH ON THE SCF

Bankruptcy prediction

Amy Lau's (1982) finding that funds flows were more helpful than cash flows in enhancing the predictive accuracy of her MLA distress prediction model was mentioned in Chapter 4.

Casey and Bartczak (1985) examined 60 failed and 230 non-failed firms' reports for 1971–82 using multivariate discriminant analysis and conditional stepwise logit analysis. They found that operating cash flow data do not provide incremental predictive power over accrual-based ratios.

El Shamy's (1989) non-metric discriminant analysis study shows that cash flows measures have no information content beyond accrual earnings in predicting corporate failure. However, accrual earnings have information content over and above cash flow measures. On the other hand, neither cash flow measures nor accrual earnings improve the classification accuracy of bond ratings substantially.

Rujoub's (1989) evidence suggests that: (a) the new statement of cash flows (SFAS 95) data can be effectively used to discriminate between bankrupt and non-bankrupt firms; (b) the predictive accuracy of the new statement of cash flows (SFAS 95) data is greater than that of accrual accounting data; (c) the predictive power of SFAS 95 data is greater than that of APB Opinion No. 19 data, and (d) the predictive power of SFAS 95 data combined with accrual accounting data is greater than that of accrual accounting data alone.

The primary objective of the study by Mitchem (1990) was to determine whether a failure model derived from a working capital basis SCFP, converted to a cash basis, can classify and predict with reasonable accuracy firms that will fail. In this study, the amount of dividends, investments and changes in long term debt were found to discriminate between financially healthy and unhealthy firms. The inclusion of macroeconomic variables added only slightly to the ability of the models to discriminate between the financially distressed and non-distressed firms. In order to investigate each of the research hypotheses, models were formulated using six financial ratios based on the conventional accounting data, 24 financial ratios derived from SFAS 95 data and 16 financial ratios derived from APB Opinion No. 19 data. Stepwise procedures were used to reduce the number of financial ratios by selecting the best financial ratios that are useful for discriminating between bankrupt and non-bankrupt firms. The final models included the six financial ratios based on accrual accounting data, eight financial ratios derived from SFAS 95 data and eight financial ratios based on APB Opinion No. 19 data.

In conclusion, cash flow streams and SCFs have yet to be proven to be more useful than SCFPs and working capital flows in predicting corporate bankruptcy.

Association of cash flows, funds flows and earnings

Costigan (1985) found that working capital funds from operations had a marginally better predictive ability than cash flow from operations in predicting future cash flows.

FASB's SFAC (Statement of Financial Concepts) 1 pronounced the view that information based on accrual accounting provided a better indication of the ability to generate favourable cash flows than information about cash flows themselves (FASB 1978b p. ix). Greenberg *et al.* (1986) used 1963–82 COMPUSTAT data to test that assertion and found it well supported. Bowen *et al.* (1986, 1987), however, found that not to be true in that both funds flow and cash flow data had incremental information content.

Bracken and Volkan (1988) mentioned three reasons why the SCF will not necessarily improve forecasters' ability to predict cash flows:

1 Despite making formats more comparable, no new content of any importance appears in the statement.
2 Reports are still annual rather than quarterly.
3 The new rules do not mandate segmental cash flow reporting.

A study by Franz and Thies (1988) investigated the intertemporal stability of relationships among cash flow, working capital, and income from operations, in order to determine whether accrual income and working capital from operations have been diverging from cash flow from operations in recent years. Their study used two separate data sets for its analysis: (1) 13 years of data based upon APB Opinion No. 19 disclosures for the years 1972–85, and (2) a 19 year data series based upon less detailed disclosures from 1966 to 1985 that used approximated cash flow and working capital. It was shown that income and working capital from operations had diminished in the last few years as a percentage of cash flow, largely due to slower growth in accounts receivable and inventory relative to cash flow. This suggested that working capital from operations was no longer an adequate proxy measure for cash flow, even if it may once have been.

Two hypotheses of no differences between the income measures in predicting one-year or average three-year cash flows from operations were rejected at all levels of confidence by Schroeder (1988). Current operating profits plus specific holding gains and cash flows from operations were better predictors of future cash flows than the other measures, including historical cost income.

The results of tests by Gaharan (1988) indicated that working capital from operations is the best predictor of future cash flow. However, for the gas and oil industry, Waldron (1988) found that accrual basis accounting measures did not appear to be superior to cash basis measures for the prediction of cash flows from operations.

Financial theory assumes that cash flows should be positively associated with earnings. Previously, Wilson (1986, 1987) and Bowen *et al.* (1987) demonstrated incremental information content of cash flows given earnings; and Rayburn (1986) did the same given accruals. Bernard and Stober (1989) showed that disaggregating net income into cash from operations and accruals had no incremental information content beyond net income. These studies ignore financing and investing cash flows and ignore information about the components of cash flows. This study shows that there is incremental information content in disaggregating net income into accruals and cash flow components. Consistent with Lipe (1986) and Ou and Penman (1989), the study shows that financial statements contain more information than the earnings figure alone gives. Bernard and Stober (1989) showed, however, that Wilson's results are not obtained beyond his sample period while Bowen *et al.*'s results (1987) are driven by data from only two years and are not robust to statistical outliners. This adds up to an inconclusive picture.

Bowen *et al.* (1986) had found the best predictor of operating cash flow to be net income plus depreciation/amortization and working capital flow from operations. The British study by Arnold *et al.* (1991) supports such a finding: 'although accrual accounting appears to have some merit in relation to the prediction of future cash flows, accounting earnings were not found to display superior predictive properties in relation to any cash flow variable considered'.

Using COMPUSTAT data for 603 firms over the period 1966–85, support is found by Murdoch and Krause (1990) for the FASB's position that earnings are a better predictor of operating cash flow than the cash flow stream itself is. In addition, it was found that: (a) the primary predictive content of earnings is related to its current accruals component, and (b) utilizing more than one year of predictive data improves the accuracy of operating cash flow predictions.

Sommerville's (1991) study found that accrual variables have a stronger statistical relationship to cash flows, both aggregate and per share, than do cash basis variables. However, there is a significant statistical relationship with both accrual and cash basis variables. In addition, it was found that, while the results of the cash flow per share models exhibit a high degree of similarity to the aggregate cash flow models, the per share models are not identical to the aggregate ones. Therefore, there would appear to be information value in cash flow per share beyond its relationship to aggregate cash flows.

The results of a general cross industry test by Wenzel (1990) indicated that there were no differences between the predictive ability of accrual or cash flow variables. However, the results of an industry-by-industry test indicated that some industries' cash flows are more predictable than others.

Percy and Stokes's (1992) Australian study extends the Bowen *et al.* (1986) study through an industry analysis of the relationship of earnings to cash flows. Findings were these: low correlations between FFO and CFO (Funds From Operations and Cash From Operations); higher correlation between earnings and FFO than earnings, and CFO, both results being generalizable across Australian industry categories. FFO better predict future cash flows than do CFO or earnings models for the retail and building materials industries but do not systematically do so for developers, contractors and heavy engineers where large prediction errors were noted.

In sum, the balance of research evidence suggests that cash flows are not necessarily their own best predictors, although the cash flow stream has incremental information content over the funds flow stream precisely because CFO and earnings are not as closely associated as are earnings and FFO.

SCF information content for security returns

Andrew *et al.*'s (1986) study of Singaporean companies supported the American studies of Bowen *et al.* (1986) and Thode *et al.* (1986) that CFO is statistically different from earnings and not deducible therefrom, but WCFO (Working Capital From Operations) and earnings are closely associated. CFO may not be useful to equity shareholders as its series do not show associations with share price series.

In the 1986 Supplement to the *Journal of Accounting Research*, two papers reported on cash flow information content. Easton and O'Brien (1986) found that accrual elements of earnings and cash elements both have incremental information content for equity price movements beyond that possessed by the earnings figure alone. Non-current accruals, however, lacked such content. Rayburn and Jennings (1986) supported these findings from their own research but found inconsistency in the information content for the different accrual components, thereby casting doubt on Easton and O'Brien's failure to find content in the non-current accruals.

On a contrary note, Jacob (1987) found that in some years between 1971 and 1984 cash flow data for firms possessed incremental information content beyond that contained in earnings whereas working capital from operations did not. This supports the 1986 exposure draft preceding SFAS 95 in Jacob's view.

Ho (1988) found that neither annual cash flow nor working capital is as useful as annual accrual earnings in the valuation of securities.

Mooney's (1989) study confirmed the existence of an association between the market beta and all three sets of explanatory variables. Second, the findings suggest that earnings variables may be more useful in explaining market risk during times of high inflation than during times of low inflation. The cash flow measures possessed significant incremental information content beyond that provided by the earnings measures in the low inflation period but not in the high inflation period. Conversely, the earnings measures possessed significant incremental information content beyond that provided by the cash flow measures in both periods. The results of this study suggest that the ability of earnings measures to explain the variation in market risk is significantly affected by inflation. Inflation did not, however, significantly affect the ability of the cash flow measures to do so. Finally, this research supports the results of other incremental information studies in that while other funds definitions may be helpful in accomplishing some specific objective (e.g. assessing market risk), no definition is so clearly superior to earnings that the extent that earnings measures may be ignored.

Wilson (1987) had concluded that, for a given amount of earnings, the market reacts more favourably the larger (smaller) are cash flows (current accruals). This conclusion is based upon stock price behaviour around the release of annual reports in 1981 and 1982. The generality and robustness of Wilson's finding was assessed by Bernard and Stober (1989) whose sample consisted of all corporations that had filed quarterly and annual reports with the Securities & Exchange Commission from 1976 to 1985 for which required data were available. For the period of 1977–84, there was no evidence of the simple relation observed by Wilson in his two-quarter test period. Two conclusions are possible: (a) The security price reactions to the release of cash flow and accrual data in financial statements are too highly dependent on individual context to be modelled at all. (b) Important uncertainties about the contents of detailed financial statements are resolved prior to their public release.

Pressly (1989) in a protocol analysis found no evidence of significantly different usage between SCF and working capital information in stock price predictions encompassing two prediction periods by financial analysts, by portfolio managers or by MBA students.

Livnat and Zarowin (1990) find that operating cash inflows are positively associated, and outflows negatively associated, with stock returns, and this also applies to their individual components including tax payments. Debt issue is positively associated, stock issue weakly but positively associated, and dividends positively associated with stock returns. These results are robust to firm size, accumulation periods of abnormal returns and the kind of model used to predict cash flow components. Disaggregation of net income into operating cash flow and accruals does not significantly contribute to the association with security returns beyond the contribution of net income alone, according to the study by Livnat and Zarowin (1990). However, further disaggregation of financing and operating flows into their components significantly improves the degree of association, but no association was found with components of investing flows.

In the UK, Board *et al*. (1989) found security prices to be much more responsive to earnings than to funds flow or cash flow. This study was of 171 firms quoted on the London Stock Exchange for 20 years, 1965–84. Earnings and working capital flows were significantly correlated for a majority of firms, while no significant association was found between earnings and cash flow or net quick funds flow (working capital flow excluding stocks).

A cross-sectional equity valuation model was used by Charitou and Ketz (1991) who found the association of cash flows from operating, financing and investing activities with security prices to be strongly significant.

The evidence of research to date on the comparative information content of funds flow, cash flow and earnings to security returns is far from convergent, but there is some tendency for earnings to continue to display the strongest association of the three.

Other research

Shwarzbach and Higgins (1992) reported that, of nearly 4,000 companies in the October 1990 Wall Street Index database that had presidents' letters, only 31 emphasized operating cash flow as a performance measure while another 160 reported it as a measure of liquidity. Thus Raymond Lauver's fears in a dissenting note to SFAS 95 (1987 para 34) that CFO would be seen as a performance indicator seem unfounded. Firms generally are not emphasizing cash flow as a performance indicator and no significant evidence could be found of cash flow manipulation.

An experiment that investigated the comparative advantages of two cash flow statement formats was performed by Klammer and Reed (1990). Bank analysts were asked to: (1) study a set of financial statements, (2) answer a series of questions about the cash flows of an entity, and (3) make a decision whether to grant the company's loan request. The results show that there was less variability in the size of the loans than would be granted when analysts received the direct method, as opposed to the indirect method, statement of cash flows. These findings add to the evidence that the direct method of presenting cash flow information may be preferable to the more commonly used indirect format.

Finally, Most (1990) reported research showing the failure of many firms to apply the prescribed SFAS 95 treatments of cash equivalents and forex to their SCFs. There was a diversity of practices concerning the gauging of cash equivalence, the arranging of the cash flows into the financing-investing-operating classifications, the treatment of extraordinary items and the treatment of leases. Moreover, a quarter of the firms did not present cash flows on the gross basis in the financing or investing sections, and the balance sheet figures for opening and closing cash balances often failed to match the figures in the SCF. Most (1990 pp. 21–2) wrote in conclusion:

> According to the FASB, the SCF was intended to clarify information about liquidity and solvency that was obscured in the SCFP. However, the so-called direct method that was supposed to accomplish this objective has not been followed. Analysis of the text of SFAS 95 and my own research have shown that it has created its own problems of interpretation, preparation, and presentation that rival those of its predecessor. These include both practical and theoretical difficulties involving acquisitions and disposals of assets, noncash transactions such as monetary exchanges, and the effects on cash balances of foreign currency exchange rate changes. Finally, the information required by financial analysts – operating cash flow, free cash flow, and cash flow per share – are not more readily computed from the SCF than they were from the SCFP, leading inevitably to the conclusion that SFAS 95 should never have been promulgated.

CONCLUSION: IS THE SCF SIGNIFICANTLY MORE USEFUL THAN THE SCFP WAS?

If the SCF is more kinetically useful than the SCFP, the published research data might be expected to show broad general support for that view. It in fact does nothing of the kind. This could be because the indirect format for the SCF makes it scarcely distinguishable in any *important* respect from the SCFP. In Chapter 7 we move from kinetic usefulness to potential usefulness as we study a number of individual examples of SCFPs and SCFs to see if it is possible to say with any strong conviction that one tells a fuller and clearer story than the other.

7 Funds statement cases

INTRODUCTION

The purpose of this chapter is to present a set of final accounts from various countries and at various levels of difficulty so that the reader can make a personal judgement of the potential usefulness of the SCFP and SCF. Discussion notes are provided to guide the novice accounts analyst through the key patterns in the accounts.

BRITISH FUNDS STATEMENTS

Smith and Nephew

GROUP PROFIT AND LOSS ACCOUNT 1987

Note		1987 £m	1986 £m
1	Turnover	546.4	480.1
1,2	Operating profit	102.8	81.3
3	Net cost of borrowings	0.1	1.1
		102.7	80.2
4	Attributable profits of related companies	6.9	8.0
	Profit on ordinary activities before taxation	109.6	88.2
7	Tax on profit on ordinary activities	31.8	27.8
8	Profit on ordinary activities after taxation attributable to shareholders	77.8	60.4
9	Dividends	32.8	23.4
22	Retained profit for the year	45.0	37.0
10	Earnings per ordinary share	8.2p	

GROUP BALANCE SHEET At 2 January 1988

Note		1987 £m	1986 £m
	Fixed assets		
11	Tangible assets	159.7	157.8
12	Investments	33.0	26.1
		192.7	183.9
	Current assets		
13	Stocks	138.0	129.1
14	Debtors	132.9	125.9
15	Investments	56.5	37.0
16	Cash at bank and in hand	135.0	125.1
		462.4	417.1
	Creditors: Amounts falling due within one year		
16	Loans	125.5	125.2
	Taxation	22.5	17.7
	Dividend	19.3	18.7
17	Trade and other creditors	91.5	90.6
		258.8	252.2
	Net current assets	203.6	164.9
	Total assets less current liabilities	396.3	348.8
	Creditors: Amounts falling due after more than one year		
16	Loans	140.2	115.8
	Taxation	1.3	4.6
	Other creditors and government grants	4.9	5.8
		146.4	126.2
18	Provisions for liabilities and charges	8.7	12.0
		241.2	210.6
	Capital and reserves		
19	Called up share capital	96.4	94.4
21	Share premium account	28.2	13.5
22	Other reserves	25.4	24.0
22	Profit and loss account	91.2	78.7
		241.2	210.6

GROUP SOURCE AND APPLICATION OF FUNDS 1987

	1987 £m	1986 £m
Funds from operations		
Operating profit	102.8	81.3
Net cost of borrowings	(0.1)	(1.1)
Depreciation (less profit on asset sales)	14.4	16.1
Income from related companies	1.6	2.6
	118.7	98.9
Funds from other sources		
Proceeds of share issues	1.4	0.6
Sale of tangible fixed assets	7.1	4.5
Disposals of subsidiaries and fixed asset investments	23.7	1.0
	32.2	6.1
Total inflow of funds	150.9	105.0
Application of funds		
Increase in working capital stocks	19.6	10.8
Debtors	17.4	10.6
Creditors	0.3	(4.8)
	37.3	16.6
Purchase of tangible fixed assets	51.4	31.7
Acquisition of subsidiaries and fixed asset investments less shares issued in consideration	36.8	81.7
Taxation	24.9	19.2
Dividends	32.2	20.2
	182.5	169.4
Net outflow of funds	(31.7)	(64.4)
Exchange difference on foreign currency net borrowings	27.4	3.6
Net borrowings in new subsidiaries	(6.7)	(8.2)
Bond conversions less issue costs	15.7	10.5
Decrease/(increase) in net borrowings	4.7	(58.5)
Short term borrowings less cash and current asset investments	29.1	(36.5)
Borrowings repayable after one year	(24.4)	(22.0)
	4.7	(58.5)

The profit and loss account

Turnover and all levels of profits are up and no obscure or unusual narrative appears to confuse this simple picture.

The balance sheet

This balance sheet is probably the easiest to read in the entire set.

The asset base, current and liquidity ratios and the absolute level, but not the relative level, of long term creditors are all up. To decide whether there has been increased reliance on loan creditors, we need to take care to check the change in relative as well as absolute dependence; and for this the funds statement is needed.

The sources and applications of funds statement

Net borrowings are clearly shown as decreasing by 4.7 million and the fact that short term borrowings are included in the calculation of this figure is irrelevant to the question of increased reliance on *loan* creditors. This resolves the ambiguity in the balance sheet and we can now see clearly that reliance on loan creditors has decreased, not increased.

Internally generated funds clearly cover expansions and acquisitions though the latter were actually financed by shares.

The liquidity improvement already clear on the balance sheet is confirmed by the straightforward layout of the funds statement.

Rating – easy

GKN

CONSOLIDATED PROFIT AND LOSS ACCOUNT

	Notes	1987 £m	1986 £m
Sales	2	**1900.6**	2059.4
Surplus on trading	3	**138.4**	145.7
Income from investments and interest receivable	5	**4.8**	5.4
Interest payable	6	**(34.0)**	(42.5)
Share of profits less losses of related companies		**37.3**	23.8
Profit on ordinary activities before taxation		**146.5**	132.4
Taxation	7	**(49.8)**	(51.4)
Profit on ordinary activities after taxation		**96.7**	81.0
Profit attributable to outside shareholders' interests		**(12.4)**	(12.6)
Earnings of the year		**84.3**	68.4
Extraordinary items	8	**(22.4)**	(36.5)
Dividends	9	**(33.6)**	(30.6)
Transfer to reserves		**28.3**	1.3
Earnings per share	10	**34.7p**	28.5p

STATEMENT OF MOVEMENT ON RESERVES

	Notes	1987 £m	1986 £m
At 1 January 1987		**403.2**	397.1
Transfer from profit and loss account		**28.3**	1.3
Currency variations		**(29.6)**	17.5
Net premium on share issues		**1.8**	8.1
Subsidiaries acquired and sold	1	**(31.3)**	(18.4)
Change in policy	12	**(0.9)**	–
Other movements		**(3.6)**	(2.4)
At 31 December 1987	23	**367.9**	403.2

CONSOLIDATED BALANCE SHEET
At 31 December 1987

	Notes	£m	1987 £m	£m	1986 £m
Fixed assets					
Tangible assets	11		528.7		546.5
Investments	12		211.6		279.3
			740.3		825.8
Current assets					
Stocks	13	376.7		423.3	
Debtors	14	355.2		371.8	
Cash at bank and in hand	15	39.8		48.8	
		771.7		843.9	
Creditors: amounts falling due within one year					
Short term borrowings	16	(54.6)		(83.9)	
Creditors	17	(428.2)		(443.9)	
Taxation payable	18	(27.7)		(19.6)	
Dividend payable		(22.0)		(19.3)	
		(532.5)		(566.7)	
Net current assets			239.2		277.2
Total assets less current liabilities			979.5		1103.0
Creditors: amounts falling due after more than one year					
Term loans	19		(205.4)		(272.9)
Obligations under finance leases	20		(12.1)		(19.9)
Provisions for liabilities and charges	21		(83.9)		(83.3)
Net assets			678.1		726.9
Capital and reserves					
Called up share capital	22		244.8		241.9
Share premium account	23	118.2		117.4	
Revaluation reserve	23	26.8		33.7	
Other reserves	23	(74.5)		(22.7)	
Profit and loss account	23	297.4		274.8	
			367.9		403.2
Equity interest			612.7		645.1
Outside shareholders' interest in subsidiaries			65.4		81.8
			678.1		726.9

CONSOLIDATED SOURCE & APPLICATION OF FUNDS
For the year ended 31 December 1987

	1987 £m	1986 £m
Source of funds		
Profit before taxation, depreciation and share of profits		
less losses of related companies	**178.3**	176.5
Dividends from related companies	**4.2**	5.3
Sale of subsidiaries and other investments	**109.3**	58.6
Disposals of tangible fixed assets	**23.7**	24.1
Shares issued as part of the consideration for the acquisition of subsidiaries	**1.7**	10.9
Other sources (net)	**10.6**	8.3
	327.8	283.7
Application of funds		
Capital expenditure	**(107.6)**	(103.6)
Acquisition of subsidiaries and other investments	**(46.3)**	(45.9)
Stocks	**(15.6)**	(10.1)
Debtors less creditors	**(16.1)**	(70.6)
Dividends paid to:		
shareholders of parent company	**(30.9)**	(29.1)
outside shareholders in subsidiaries	**(5.4)**	(6.3)
Taxation paid	**(35.3)**	(52.7)
	(257.2)	(318.3)
Net inflow/(outflow) of funds	**70.6**	(34.6)
Movement in net borrowings		
Net borrowings at 1 January 1987	**(327.9)**	(294.7)
Net inflow/(outflow) of funds	**70.6**	(34.6)
Currency variations	**32.8**	(22.5)
Net funds of subsidiaries acquired and sold	**(7.8)**	23.9
Net borrowings at 31 December 1987	**(232.3)**	(327.9)

Net borrowings include obligations under finance leases of £12.1 million (1986 – £19.9 million).

The balance sheet movement on stocks and debtors less creditors is as follows:

	Stocks £m	Debtors less creditors £m
1 January 1987	423.3	(71.2)
Currency variations	(33.3)	8.8
Changes in the composition of the group and discontinued activities	(28.9)	(25.8)
Source and application of funds above	15.6	16.1
31 December 1987	376.7	(73.0)

Movements in funds of subsidiaries acquired and sold are included only from the date of acquisition or up to the date of disposal.
The sources and applications of funds of overseas subsidiaries are translated to sterling at average exchange rates.
The net borrowings at the beginning of the year are translated at year-end exchange rates and the difference is included in currency variations.

The profit and loss account

Sales are down but group profits and earnings are up.
This P&L is very easy to read and self-explanatory.

The balance sheet

The balance sheet is also easy to read with fixed assets clearly having fallen, but the overall asset structure has not changed much. Current ratios are over 1, but deteriorating, while liquid ratios are not large enough to ensure trade creditors, tax and dividends can get paid from liquid funds. Loan creditors fell by more than shareholders' funds, irrespective of whether minorities are included or excluded.

The statement of sources and applications of funds

Since assets have decreased, the firm can clearly finance growth from retentions, even if growth is seen as referring to the capital expenditure and acquisition of subsidiaries, both of which are exceeded by profit before depreciation, although not by profit after tax and dividends.

This statement is deceptively easy to read and care has to be taken over the following lines:

'Profit before taxation, depreciation and share of profits less losses of related items' (not the usual first line of a funds statement),

'Debtors less creditors' (this confounds two different fund streams).

The SSAF has a cash base and the movement on borrowings will probably be more readily understood than the more usual (in the UK) movement on working capital.

Rating – moderately difficult

AN AUSTRALIAN FUNDS STATEMENT

UNION CARBIDE
Profit and Loss Accounts
For the year ended 31 December 1987

	Notes	Consolidated 1987 $'000	1986 $'000	Holding Company 1987 $'000	1986 $'000
Operating Profit	3	**26,770**	22,546	**7,645**	4,814
Income tax attributable to operation profit	6	**13,185**	10,715	**66**	(27)
Operating Profit After Income Tax		**13,585**	11,831	7,579	**4,841**
Gain on inventory valuation after income tax	7		**1,488**		
Loss on extraordinary items		1,890	914	**350**	
Income tax attributable to loss		**30**	604		
Loss on extraordinary items after income tax	8	**1,860**	310	**350**	
Operating Profit and Extraordinary Items After Income Tax		**11,725**	132,009	**7,229**	4,841
Retained profits at the beginning of the financial year		**49,660**	39,109	**23,384**	21,001
Total available for appropriation		**61,385**	52,118	**30,613**	25,842
Dividends – interims paid		**5,409**	2,458	**5,409**	2,458
final proposed		2,950		2,950	
Retained Profits at the End of the Financial Year		**$53,026**	49,660	**$22,254**	23,384

UNION CARBIDE
Statement of financial position

	Notes	Consolidated		Holding Company	
		1987 $'000	1986 $'000	1987 $'000	1986 $'000
Funds have been provided from					
Shareholders' equity					
Paid capital of . . . shareholders	15	**1,552,095**	1,258,041	**1,552,095**	1,258,041
Share subscriptions receivable	15	**107,053**	–	**107,053**	–
Reserves and unappropriated profits	13	**5,756,729**	5,317,417	**2,262,187**	2,492,202
Total shareholders' equity		**7,415,877**	6,575,458		
Equity of other shareholders of subsidiary companies		**366,348**	144,483		
Total shareholders' equity		**7,782,225**	6,719,941	**3,921,335**	3,750,243
Non-current liabilities	17	**6,777,381**	**5,605,344**	**813,485**	944,339
Current liabilities					
Provisions	16	**702,936**	1,059,133	**983,396**	150,125
Borrowings repayable within 12 months	18	**905,413**	1,910,875	**51,929**	162,738
Credits	19	**1,291,739**	1,253,718	**3,964,916**	3,049,613
		2,960,088	4,223,726	**4,100,241**	3,362,476
Total funds provided		**1,7519,694**	1,6549,011	**8,835,061**	8,057,058
These funds are represented by					
Fixed assets	20	10,975,994	**10,657,068**	1,183,413	**1,088,694**
Investments	21	2,229,844	**2,029,566**	3,234,649	**2,771,765**
Other non-current assets	22	727,010	**539,336**	459,702	**33,302**
Current assets					
Inventories	23	**1,562,035**	1,407,275	**312,874**	271,128
Debtors	24	**1,479,599**	1,220,339	**2,623,491**	3,887,223
Cash and short term investments	25	**376,278**	567,718	**20,932**	4,946
		3,417,912	3,195,332	**3,957,297**	3,163,297
Intangibles	26	168,984	**137,709**		
Total assets employed		**17,519,694**	16,549,011	**8,835,061**	8,057,058

UNION CARBIDE
Consolidated Statement of Sources and Applications of Funds
For the year ended 31 December 1987

	Australia and New Zealand Limited and Subsidiary Companies			
	1987			*1986*
	$'000			*$'000*
SOURCES OF FUNDS				
Funds From Operations (1)				
Inflows of funds from operations	202,793		193,175	
Less outflows of funds from operations	171,639	**31,154**	167,360	25,815
Reduction in Assets				
Current Assets				
Investment	5,000			
Inventories			2,541	
Prepayments and deferred charges	317	**5,317**	–	2,541
Proceeds from Sales of Non-current Assets				
Real Estate	187			
Plant and Equipment (forming part of the loss arising from closing down chemicals operations)	–	**187**	262	262
Increase in Liabilities				
Current Liabilities				
Creditors and borrowings				1,431
		36,658		30,049

APPLICATIONS OF FUNDS
Increase in Assets
  Current Assets

Cash	5,011		6,739	
Receivables	1,290		1,572	
Investment			5,000	
Prepayments and deferred charges	–	9,254	43	13,354

  Non-current Assets

Property, plant and equipment		4,914	2,863

Reduction in Liabilities
  Current Liabilities

Creditors and borrowings		5,439

  Non-current Liabilities

Creditors and borrowings		140

Dividends paid		5,409		4,917
Income tax paid		10,717		7,565
Loss arising from closing down chemical operations	1,613		539	
Less amount set aside to provision	947	666	539	–
Costs associated with takeover responses		350		30,049

The profit and loss account

Turnover was not, in 1988, an obligatory disclosure on the profit and loss account in Australia and it is absent here. All levels of profit are clearly up, however, even after accounting for extraordinary items.

The balance sheet

The balance sheet follows the American format rather unusually for an Australian firm but it is clear and easy to read anyway.

Current and liquid ratios are both healthy for both years and 1987 is better than 1986 in this respect. Current borrowings are down, equity is up and no long term debt is disclosed, so the firm can be said to have become less reliant on its loan creditors over the year.

The asset base has risen and its structure has significantly changed with the selling off of all the non-current investments and the relative increase in the importance of both gross and net current assets.

The statement of sources and applications of funds

The funds statement follows a British sources and applications statement with the reconciliation of profit to operations funds flow shown as a note to the statement. It is quite easy to read and some readers will find its avoidance of brackets (in favour of spelling out whether an asset or liability group has increased or decreased) quite helpful.

Profit can easily finance expansion of facilities; the liquidity improvement is fairly easy to see as is the reduction in borrowings.

However, the 5 million reduction in investments is shown current on this statement whereas the balance sheet shows it non-current. This discrepancy does not affect substantive interpretation of the accounts by a sophisticated analyst but it will confuse the novice. In the full annual report, note 10 to the accounts explains the disposal as being of 'shares in unlisted non-related corporation' and explicitly deems it non-current. The same note shows current investments 'in unlisted non-related corporations' constant across the two year ends at 5 million – the coincidence in size is explicit. *It would seem the funds statement has misclassified this item*. The auditors, KMG Hungerfords, give the accounts their full support and the 'directors' statement' explicitly claims the funds statement gives a true and fair view.

Rating – moderately easy

AN AMERICAN SCFP

NEW JERSEY BELL
STATEMENTS OF INCOME AND REINVESTED EARNINGS FOR THE
YEARS ENDED DECEMBER 31

	1987	*1986**	*1985**
Dollars in Millions			
Operating Revenues			
Local service	**$942.5**	$947.8	$906.0
Network access	**802.9**	785.5	683.4
Toll service	**646.9**	618.6	622.0
Directory advertising and other	**395.2**	350.3	302.0
Provision for uncollectables	**(11.9)**	(8.4)	(9.5)
	2,775.6	2,693.8	2,503.9
Operating Expenses			
Employee costs, including benefits and taxes	**796.7**	803.4	784.6
Depreciation and amortization	**556.4**	435.2	394.6
Other	**565.5**	536.9	529.9
	1,918.6	1,775.5	1,709.1
Net operating revenues	**857.0**	918.3	794.8
Operating Taxes			
Federal income tax	**212.0**	283.6	214.1
Other	**169.4**	162.4	165.9
	381.4	446.0	380.0
Operating income	**475.6**	472.3	414.8
Other Income (Expense)			
Interest charged construction	**10.9**	9.4	15.5
Miscellaneous-net	**(3.4)**	(1.2)	(1.2)
	7.5	8.2	14.3
Interest Expense	**110.8**	106.9	128.9
Net Income	**372.3**	$373.6	$300.2
Reinvested Earnings			
At beginning of year	**824.2**	$710.0	$654.8
Add: Net income	**372.3**	**373.6**	300.2
	1,196.5	**1,083.6**	955.0
Deduct: Dividends declared and paid	302.0	**259.4**	245.0
At End of Year	894.5	**$824.2**	710.0

The accompanying notes are an integral part of these financial statements.
*Certain items have been reclassified to conform to the 1987 presentation.

NEW JERSEY BELL
BALANCE SHEETS AS OF DECEMBER 31

Assets	*1987*	*1986*
Dollars in Millions		
Telephone Plant – at cost		
In service	**$6,687.4**	$6,309.6
Under construction and other	**145.9**	130.0
	6,833.3	6,439.6
Accumulated depreciation	**(2,168.2)**	(1,802.2)
	4,665.1	**4,637.4**
Current Assets		
Cash	**6.7**	9.6
Accounts receivable (net of allowances for		
uncollectables of $15.8 and $14.0)	**436.6**	454.1
Material and supplies	**22.9**	20.5
Prepaid expenses	**27.4**	13.5
Deferred charges	**160.0**	146.0
	653.6	**643.7**
Deferred Charges and Other Assets	**104.2**	81.5
Total Assets	**$5,422.9**	**$5,362.6**
Shareowner's Investment and Liabilities		
Shareowner's Investment		
Common stock – one share, without par value,		
owned by parent	**$1,381.2**	**$1,381.2**
Reinvested earnings	894.5	**$824.2**
	2,275.7	2,205.4
Long-term Debt	1,216.5	**1,264.6**
Current Liabilities		
Debt maturing within one year	**171.8**	70.6
Account payable		
Parent and affiliates	**23.4**	20.1
Other	**370.3**	340.7
Advance billing and customer deposits	**134.8**	161.5
Accrued expenses		
Vacation pay	**56.7**	57.3
Interest	**27.7**	27.6
Taxes	**2.3**	55.7
	787.0	**733.5**
Deferred Creditors		
Deferred income taxes	**848.6**	833.5
Unamortized investment tax credits	**247.8**	273.9
Other	**47.3**	51.7
	1,143.7	**1,159.1**
Total Shareowner's Investment and Liabilities	**$5,422.9**	$5,362.6

NEW JERSEY BELL
STATEMENTS OF SOURCES OF FUNDS SUPPORTING
CONSTRUCTION ACTIVITY FOR THE YEARS ENDED DECEMBER 31

Dollars in Millions	1987	1986	1985
Funds from Operations:			
Net Income	**$372.3**	$373.6	$300.2
Items not affecting funds:			
Depreciation and amortization	**556.4**	435.2	394.6
Deferred income taxes, net	**22.7**	25.5	71.2
Investment tax credits, net	**(26.1)**	(8.2)	27.2
Amortization of discount and premium on long term debt, net	**1.4**	1.3	0.5
Interest charged construction	**(10.9)**	(9.4)	(15.5)
	915.8	818.0	778.2
Dividends	**(302.0)**	(259.4)	(245.0)
	613.8	558.6	533.2
Changes in Certain Components of Working Capital:			
Cash	**2.9**	3.6	0.1
Accounts receivable	**17.5**	(4.4)	57.9
Accounts payable	**32.9**	31.1	(85.5)
Accrued expenses	**(53.9)**	20.3	22.5
Other changes, net	**(64.6)**	64.6	6.7
	(65.2)	115.2	3.7
External Financing Activities			
Additions to long term debt	–	295.4	–
Increase (decrease) in debt maturing within one year and capital lease obligations, net of the current maturity of long term debt in 1987	**51.7**	(62.2)	(51.2)
Repayment of long term debt	–	(306.6)	–
	51.7	(73.4)	(51.2)
Other Changes, Net	**(20.1)**	(23.0)	18.0
Funds Supporting Construction Activity	**580.2**	577.4	503.7
Interest charged construction	**10.9**	9.4	15.5
Total Construction	**591.1**	$586.8	$519.2

The accompanying notes are an integral part of these financial statements.

The income statement

The very slight rise in net sales accompanied by a major rise in expensed depreciation has meant static profits where the fall in operating profit is compensated by a fall in tax to cause net income to stay virtually the same as it was in the previous year. The statement is informative and easy to read.

The balance sheet

The small rise in equity accompanies a small decline in long term debt, rendering the firm slightly less reliant on loan creditors.

The asset base has slightly risen but the asset structure has not materially altered.

Both year ends show that a deficiency of working capital and liquid assets will not be able to finance payment of payables plus maturing debt, a situation that has deteriorated over the year 1987.

'The statement of sources supporting construction activity'

The New Jersey Bell accounts have the most aberrant SCFP of all in that funds flows are tied not to working capital, cash or all assets but only to the special asset 'construction' which does not tie in with equivalent figures on the other accounts. Only some of the working capital changes are specified and the increase in debt maturing within one year is noted under external financing activities rather than under working capital. Internal funds are large enough to finance construction but profit alone is not. All in all, this statement is unhelpful. It is included in the accounts set to exemplify how a number of firms, especially in the USA, use the SCFP to conceal rather than reveal the deteriorating liquidity inferred from the balance sheet.

The full annual report avoids any discussion of liquidity problems, preferring to comment on sales and cost trends. The auditors, Coopers and Lybrand, give the accounts a clean report but tackle the problem of the SCFP's non-conformity with APB 19 in these words:

> In our opinion, the financial statements referred to above present fairly the financial position of New Jersey Bell Telephone Company as of December 31, 1987 and 1986, and the results of its operations and sources of funds supporting construction activity for each of the three years in the period ended December 31, 1987, in conformity with generally accepted accounting principles applied on a consistent basis.

There is no hint that a statement of funds supporting construction activity is not a generally accepted form of an SCFP.

Rating – difficult

HONG KONG

CHEUNG KONG GROUP
CONSOLIDATED PROFIT AND LOSS ACCOUNT
For the year ended 31 December 1991

	1991 $ Million	1990 $ Million
Turnover	9,990	4,413
Operating Profit	1,112	1,267
Share of results of associated companies	4,626	2,335
Profit before taxation	5,738	3,602
Taxation	844	349
Profit after taxation	4,894	3,253
Minority interests	8	2
Profit before extraordinary items	4,886	3,251
Extraordinary items	403	349
Profit attributable to shareholders	5,289	3,600
Dividends	1,494	1,055
Profit for the year retained	3,795	2,545
Profit for the year retained by:		
company and subsidiaries	1,610	1,023
associated companies	2,185	1,522
Earnings per share	$2.22	$1.48

CHEUNG KONG GROUP
CONSOLIDATED BALANCE SHEET
As at 31 December 1991

	1991	*1990*
	$ Million	*$ Million*
Fixed assets	1,944	1,751
Interest in associated companies	13,614	14,354
Other investments	3,488	879
Net current assets	6,395	5,234
	25,441	22,218
Deduct:		
Long-term bank loans	1,628	2,210
Bills payable	–	800
Deferred items	936	126
Minority interests	129	177
TOTAL NET ASSETS	22,748	18,905
REPRESENTING:		
Share capital	1,099	1,099
Share premium	2,752	2,752
Reserves	379	331
Retained profits	18,518	14,723
TOTAL SHAREHOLDERS' FUNDS	22,748	18,905

CHEUNG KONG GROUP
CONSOLIDATED STATEMENT OF CHANGES IN FINANCIAL
POSITION
For the year ended 31 December 1991

	1991 $ Million	1990 $ Million
SOURCE OF FUNDS		
Funds generated from operations		
Profit before taxation and extraordinary items	5,738	3,602
Extraordinary items	403	349
	6,141	3,951
Items not involving the movement of funds		
Amortization of deferred income	(33)	(31)
Depreciation	71	70
Share of results of listed associated companies less dividends received	(1,186)	(1,248)
Share of results of unlisted associated companies less dividends received	(1,797)	(530)
	3,196	2,212
Funds from other sources		
Disposal of fixed assets	7	49
Increase in long term bank loans	378	910
Net decrease in investment	326	556
Proceeds received on issue of warrants	839	–
	4,746	3,827
APPLICATION OF FUNDS		
Tax paid	154	219
Dividends paid	1,165	879
Purchase of fixed assets	144	114
Decrease in bills payable	400	–
Decrease in minority interests	62	41
	1,925	1,253
	2,821	2,574
INCREASE/(DECREASE) IN WORKING CAPITAL		
Stocks	(900)	199
Debtors, deposits and prepayments	63	(510)
Unlisted securities	957	190
Creditors and accrued expenses	426	(182)
Movement in net liquid funds		
Bank balances and deposits	1,045	7,716
Bank loans and overdrafts	(1,247)	437
Short term securities	2,477	774
	2,821	2,574

The profit and loss account

Sales have doubled over the previous year but operating profit has fallen. The associate companies, however, show nearly a doubling of profit so group profit both gross and net of tax shows an increase of 2.5 billion. Earnings attributable to parent company shareholders are up 47 per cent, representing a slight rise in the retention ratio from 71 per cent to 72 per cent.

The balance sheet

The nearly 4 billion increase in net assets includes a 1 billion increase in net working capital and over a 1 billion increase in investment in associate companies. Bank loans are down by 582 million and the 4 billion increase in retentions virtually matches the increase in net assets, so the group has become less leveraged in the year. This strengthening of the capital base owes much to the associate companies' good performance.

Statement of changes in financial position

Funds from operations are up 900 million and inventories are down by a similar amount, a healthy combination. Trade creditors less debtors are up 363 million and bank overdrafts are up by more than the increase in credit bank balances, so there is slightly greater reliance on short term creditors who are indirectly financing the large increase in short term securities of 2,477 million. There are new loans inwards of 378 million net. Proceeds from the exercise of warrants of 839 million partly finance the 957 million increase in trade investments – this year's trade investments could well be next year's investment in associates if the group continues its policy of expansion by gradual acquisition of interests in other companies. The whole picture suggests careful and detailed financial management with an aversion to assets lying idle.

Rating – moderately easy

CASH FLOW STATEMENTS

Goodyear Inc. (USA)

CONSOLIDATED STATEMENT OF INCOME
The Company and Subsidiaries

(Dollars in Millions, except per share)

| | Year Ended December 31, | | |
	1987	1986	1985
Net Sales	$9,905.2	$9,040.0	$8,341.1
Other Income	179.9	121.0	114.2
	10,085.1	9,161.0	8,455.3
Cost and Expenses:			
Cost of goods sold	7,374.6	6,941.5	6,550.4
Selling, adminstrative and general expense	1,634.9	1,596.6	1,380.9
Interest and amortization of debt discount and expense	282.5	121.9	101.5
Unusual items	(135.0)	10.1	21.3
Foreign currency exchange	38.9	19.1	33.8
Minority interest in net income	16.8	9.6	6.6
	9,212.7	8,698.8	8,094.5
Income from continuing operations before income taxes	872.4	462.2	360.8
United States and foreign taxes on income	358.5	245.4	133.7
Income form continuing operations	513.9	216.8	227.1
Discontinued operations	257.0	(92.7)	185.3
Net Income	$770.9	£124.1	$412.4
Per Share of Common Stock:			
Income from continuing operations	$8.49	$2.02	$2.11
Discontinued operations	4.25	(0.86)	1.73
Net income	$12.73	$1.16	$3.84

CONSOLIDATED BALANCE SHEET
The Company and Subsidiaries

(Dollars in Millions)

	December 31, 1987	December 31, 1986
ASSETS		
Current Assets:		
Cash and short term securities	$200.5	$130.5
Accounts and notes receivable	1,501.3	1,986.5
Inventories	1,501.4	1,352.2
Prepaid expenses	101.3	82.7
Net assets held for sale	–	107.8
Total Current Assets	3,304.5	3,659.7
Other Assets:		
Investments in non-consolidated subsidiaries and affiliates, at equity	107.6	32.9
Long term accounts and notes receivable	354.0	240.0
Investments and miscellaneous assets, at cost	53.8	34.4
Deferred charges	74.6	72.1
Deferred pension plan cost	373.1	320.2
Net assets held for sale	–	96.6
Properties and Plants	4,128.3	4,583.4
	$8,395.9	$9,039.3

LIABILITIES AND SHAREHOLDERS' EQUITY
Current Liabilities:

Accounts payable – trade	$821.9	$749.5
Accrued payrolls and other compensation	$322.9	337.1
Other current liabilities	375.9	406.9
United States and foreign taxes:		
Current	268.7	168.5
Deferred	16.0	–
Notes payable to banks and overdrafts	244.0	304.2
Long term debt due within one year	90.2	44.4
Deferred gain on sale of assets	–	134.7
Total Current Liabilities	2,139.6	2,145.3
Long Term Debt and Capital Leases	3,282.4	2,914.9
Other Long Term Liabilities	376.7	317.5
Deferred Income Taxes	679.3	586.4
Minority Equity in Subsidiaries	83.5	72.6
Shareholders' Equity:		
Preferred stock, no par value:		
Authorized, 50,000,000 shares		
Outstanding shares, none	–	–
Common stock, no par value:		
Authorized, 150,000,000 shares		
Outstanding shares, 56,986,579		
(97,080,482 in 1986)	57.0	97.1
Capital surplus	11.2	104.2
Retained earnings	1,922.6	3,122.2
	1,990.8	3,323.5
Foreign currency translation adjustment	(156.4)	(320.9)
Total Shareholders' Equity	1,834.4	3,002.6

CONSOLIDATED STATEMENT OF CHANGES IN FINANCIAL POSITION

(Dollars in Millions)

	Year Ended December 31,		
	1987	*1986*	*1985*
Funds provided from operations:	$513.9	$216.8	$227.1
Income from continuing operations			
Non-cash items:			
Depreciation	349.9	349.0	268.3
Unusual items	4.1	(45.5)	28.5
Accounts and notes receivable reduction (increase)	485.2	(295.2)	–
Inventories (increase) reduction	(149.2)	26.3	(45.1)
Long term accounts and notes receivable (increase)	(114.0)	(113.2)	(87.2)
United States and foreign taxes increase (reduction)	116.2	(64.2)	(59.3)
Deferred income taxes increase	92.9	111.1	26.4
Other items	118.7	170.7	138.6
Income (loss) from discontinued operations	$257.0	(92.7)	185.3
	1,674.7	263.1	682.6
Funds (used for) provided from financing:			
Notes payable to banks and overdrafts (reduction) increase	(60.2)	187.9	(41.1)
Long term debt and capital lease reduction	(2,846.2)	(109.6)	(234.7)
Long term debt and capital lease increase	3,259.5	1,455.7	982.4
Common stock issued	14.6	66.0	43.4
Common stock acquired	(2,027.2)	(614.2)	–
	(1,659.5)	985.8	750.0
Funds used for investment:			
Capital expenditures	(665.6)	(1,130.8)	(1,098.2)
Property and plant dispositions	925.0	254.3	405.6
Discontinued operations – capital expenditures	(92.2)	(256.8)	(577.7)
Other transactions	(185.9)	(43.4)	(47.0)
	(18.7)	(1,176.7)	(1.317.3)
Dividends paid	(91.0)	(174.1)	(171.3)
Foreign currency translation adjustment reduction	164.5	93.4	51.6
Cash and short term securities increase (reduction)	$70.0	$(8.5)	$(4.4)

The income statement

The clear and consistent picture is of rising sales and all levels of profits. An interesting aside is the line under the costs and expenses heading called 'unusual items' which, however, is too small to support suspicions of income smoothing.

The balance sheet

Current liabilities have gone down by only 5 million while current assets have gone down by 355 million and liquid assets are down by over 400 million, a story of deteriorating liquidity, but not a worrying one in the context of near unity liquid ratios and current ratios of over 1.5 in both years.

Long term debt is up by over 350 million while equity is down by over 1,100 million, so there is a marked increase in reliance on loan creditors.

The asset base has shrunk and the asset structure has changed not by very much but certainly by more than a little. Inventories, investments, long term accounts and deferred pension costs have all significantly risen against a background of other assets shrinking.

The statement of changes in financial position

The SCFP has a cash basis and *in fact is a simple cash flow statement per SFAS 95 in every respect bar the title.* (National Gypsum below is also an SCF but rather a difficult one.) The individual items are grouped by operating, financing and investing activities and with the sensible extra step of gathering dividends and forex adjustments outside of these three categories instead of arbitrarily assigning them to any one of them in the way the earlier SCF standards proposed.

Profit is too small to fund capital expenditure but profit plus depreciation is big enough.

Long term debt shows a clear net increase in the financing block, but the liquidity changes are not so clear, as the change in payables seems to be swallowed in the 'other items' figure in the operations block; while inventory and receivables changes are clearly stated. Nevertheless the SCFP is presenting a picture of enhanced liquidity in respect of all the items it does explicitly reveal.

All in all, most readers will find this format easier to handle than the older style formats, but it is regrettable that trade payables were obscured.

Rating – moderately easy

National Gypsum Company and subsidiaries

CONSOLIDATED STATEMENTS OF OPERATIONS AND RETAINED EARNINGS

Period from

	Year Ended December 31, 1987	May 1 through December 31, 1986*
	(Thousands)	
Net Sales	$1,379,786	$972,819
Cost of products sold	1,068,449	732,936
Gross Earnings	311,337	239,883
Selling, administrative and general expenses	152,678	99,764
	158,659	140,119
Other income (expense):		
Interest expense	(179,167)	(123,958)
Sundry expense	(21,455)	(13,120)
Sundry income	16,331	(6,772)
	(184,291)	(130,306)
Earnings (Loss) before taxes and extraordinary items	(25,632)	9,813
Income tax benefit	3,423	84,855
Earnings (Loss) before extraordinary items	(22,209)	94,668
Extraordinary items:		
Extraordinary loss on refinancing of debt (net of applicable income tax benefit of $5,582)	(8,373)	–
Extraordinary gain on early extinguishment of debt (net of applicable income tax expense of $5,448)	8,173	–
Net Earnings (Loss)	$(22,409)	$94,668
Retained Earnings		
Balance beginning of period	$91,668	$–
Net earnings (loss) for the period	(22,409)	94,669
Cash dividends	(3,000)	(3,000)
Balance End of Period	$66,259	$91,668

* Restated to reflect the adoption of SFAS No. 96, 'Accounting for Income Taxes'

CONSOLIDATED BALANCE SHEETS
LIABILITIES AND STOCKHOLDER'S EQUITY

	December 31,	
	1987	1986*
	(Thousands)	
Current Assets		
Cash and short-term investments	$22,973	$17,055
Trade and sundry receivables, less allowances		
(1987 – $24,054; 1986 – $24,596)	181,348	195,052
Inventories:		
Finished goods	65,217	77,379
Products in process	4,242	3,235
Materials and supplies	37,219	31,714
	106,678	112,328
Other	15,686	13,954
Total Current Assets	326,685	338,389
Property, Plant and Equipment – Based on Cost		
Mineral deposits	7,088	7,061
Plant sites	53,573	53,781
Buildings	252,932	254,225
Machinery and equipment	779,185	777,764
	1,092,778	1,092,831
Less allowances for depreciation and		
depletion	124,865	60,970
	967,913	1,031,861
Goodwill, net of accumulated amortization		
(1987 – $22,665; 1986 – $8,886)	529,914	527,243
Investment and Other Assets	149,524	156,832
	$1,974,036	$2,054,325
Current Liabilities		
Accounts and notes payable	$76,293	$71,739
Accrued liabilities	109,770	106,397
Income taxes	3,614	4,631
Current portion of long term debt	3,657	3,152
Total Current Liabilities	193,334	185,919
Long Term Debt	1,298,292	1,350,453
Deferred Items		
Income taxes	271,680	301,265
Other	55,473	36,278
Stockholder's Equity		
Common stock – $1 par value, 1,000 shares		
authorized and issued	1	1
Additional paid-in capital	89,999	89,999
Retained earnings	66,259	91,668
Equity adjustment from foreign currency		
translation	292	87
Notes receivable – management group	(1,294)	(1,345)
	155,257	180,410
	$1,974,036	$2,054,325

CONSOLIDATED STATEMENTS OF CHANGES IN FINANCIAL POSITION

	Year Ended December 31, 1987	Period from May 1 through December 31, 1986*
	(Thousands)	
Cash Provided:		
From operations:		
Net earnings (loss) before extraordinary items	$(22,209)	$94,668
Depreciation, depletion and amortization	76,516	52,292
Accretion of original issue discount	81,366	50,790
Amortization of intangible assets	18,015	11,939
Deferred income tax benefit	(7,841)	(100,999)
Total from Operations Before Extraordinary Items	145,847	108,690
Extraordinary Items:		
Extraordinary loss on refinancing of debt	(8,373)	–
Write-off of debt issuance costs	8,779	–
Extraordinary gain on early extinguishment of debt	8,173	–
Total from Extraordinary Items	8,579	–
Total from Operations	154,426	108,690
Changes in Non-cash Components of Working Capital (Excluding Financing Transactions):		
Increase in non-cash components of working capital related to merger	–	(225,857)
Accounts and notes receivable	13,704	15,140
Inventories	5,650	20,066
Other assets	(1,732)	7,538
Accounts payable and accrued liabilities	6,430	21,565
Income taxes	(1,017)	(8,847)
Net Changes in Non-cash Components	23,035	(170,395)

Investment Transactions:
  Increase in non-current assets related to
    merger:

Property, plant and equipment	–	(1,102,320)
Goodwill	(16,450)	(536,129)
Notes receivable – management group	–	(1,345)
Net pension asset	–	(53,576)
Organization costs	–	(25,769)
Other, net	–	(5,098)
Deferred income taxes	–	375,869
Property, plant and equipment purchases	(23,765)	(35,521)
Carrying value of properties sold or retired	10,528	28,983
Proceeds from sale of discontinued		
operations	–	64,192
Receipt of Lafarge Coppee stock	–	(39,269)
Sale of Compagnie du Platre stock	–	19,835
Other, net	4,157	–
Net Investment Transactions	(25,530)	(1,310,148)

Financing Transactions:

Increase in current portion of long term debt		
and notes payable	2,002	4,364
Issuance of long term debt	430,000	1,570,932
Reduction of long term debt	(575,015)	(273,388)
Issuance of common stock	–	90,000
Net Financing Transactions	(143,013)	1,391,908

Net cash provided before distribution of		
dividends	8,918	20,055
Cash dividends paid	(3,000)	(3,000)
Increase in Cash and Short Term		
Investments	$5,918	$17,055

The income statement

Sales are up, as are gross earnings, but the effect of the massive rise in interest expense is to turn all levels of net earnings from a 1986 profit into a 1987 loss that nonetheless is not allowed to prevent the dividend level being maintained. The extraordinary items both relate to refinancing of debt and do little to assuage concern that might be felt as a result of the huge rise in interest expense. It will require an unusually observant reader to spot the probable explanation for the interest rise in the 1986 heading, namely its eight-month duration instead of the expected full year. Nevertheless, interest has made a loss out of what would otherwise have been a profit.

The balance sheet

The asset base has declined slightly both gross and net of goodwill.

The structure of fixed assets has not materially changed but cash has risen and the raw materials inventory has grown while the other current assets have slightly shrunk, so one would be inclined to say that the asset structure has changed significantly over the year – just.

Current and liquid assets have declined while current liabilities have risen, so liquidity is declining and doing so from a satisfactory current ratio start but from a liquid ratio that is clearly too low in the first place.

Long term debt is down by 52 billion while equity is down by 25 billion as a result of this year's loss, a relative and absolute decrease in reliance on loan creditors.

The statement of changes in financial position

Here is an American SCFP that is laid out like the SFAS 95 SCF requirements, using the indirect method for operations flows and separating dividends from the main categories of flow. However, it contains some items which will be unclear to some readers: (a) 'accretion of original issue discount' in operations flows, and (b) the strange juxtaposition of the extraordinary loss on debt refinancing with the extraordinary gain on the early extinguishment of debt.

Moreover, the replacement of 575 billion old debt with 430 billion new debt in the financing flows block causes a net deduction of 145 billion which is far greater than the debt differences shown in the balance sheet. One has to subtract the 81 billion issue discount from the SCFP reduction to approach the 52 billion reduction on the balance sheet. *Here then is an example of the new SCF being just as able to confuse readers as the old SCFP was.*

Since the firm made a loss, there is no possibility of profit financing growth, although total operations cash flow is large and positive. Since the asset base has shrunk in the year, there has been no growth for operations to finance.

Receivables have *decreased* by twice the increase in payables and by more than twice the net cash inflow after dividends, reinforcing the balance sheet picture of deteriorating liquidity – albeit in a format whose use of brackets will confuse some readers of the SCFP.

This SCFP, really an SCF, will help few readers read the other accounts better or quicker, partly through its contrary use of bracketing logic, but more because it is concealing an in substance debt defeasance that gave rise to an extraordinary gain which in turn is matched by a refinancing loss. This is largely explained by the full annual report and its notes, which state that the new debt largely consists of junk bonds at 11.375% and credit lines for trade financing with Morgan Guaranty floating 'at approximately 9%' and linked to LIBOR. The debt already issued and still outstanding at end 1987 carried interest rates of 14.5% and 15.5% fixed. However, on page 6 of the report is stated the following:

> On April 29, 1986 the Company was acquired by Aancor Holdings Inc in a leveraged buy-out transaction. As a result of the merger, the Company's financial results, other than net sales, are not readily comparable to prior periods because of a substantial increase in interest expense and the depreciation and amortization of acquisition related items. For discussion purposes, eight month data ended December 31 1986 has been annualized, except net sales, for comparison with 1987 results.

The income statement, however, has kept the 1986 figures on an eight-month basis and this is the reason interest has increased.

Rating – moderately difficult

Toyota Group (Japan)

CONSOLIDATED BALANCE SHEETS
Toyota Motor Corporation and Consolidated Subsidiaries June 30, 1990 and 1989

ASSETS	*Millions of Yen*		*Thousands of US dollars*
	1990	*1989*	*1990*
Current Assets:			
Cash and cash equivalents	Y1,362,309	Y1,217,013	$8,903,982
Short term investments	842,271	718,874	5,505,036
Notes and accounts receivable	1,093,830	964,311	7,149,214
Inventories	337,985	334,226	2,209,051
Other	1,564,993	1,139,879	10,228,714
Less: allowance for doubtful receivables	(34,198)	(301,332)	(223,517)
Total Current Assets	5,167,190	4,343,971	33,772,480
Investments and Other Assets:			
Investments in securities	496,684	419,355	3,246,300
Investments in unconsolidated subsidiaries and affiliates	653,753	551,208	4,272,892
Long term loans	204,331	101,689	1,335,495
Other	358,409	358,427	2,342,546
Less: allowance for doubtful receivables	(4,763)	(4,144)	(31,128)
Total Investments and Other Assets	1,708,414	1,426,535	11,166,105
Property, Plant and Equipment:			
Land	366,566	331,694	2,395,858
Buildings and structures	815,869	741,161	5,332,474
Machinery and equipment	2,576,287	2,311,777	16,838,480
Construction in progress	101,677	52,629	664,555
Less: accumulated depreciation	(2,307,155)	(2,062,606)	(15,079,443)
Net property, plant and equipment	1,553,244	1,374,655	10,151,924
Translation Adjustments	2,247	7,725	14,687
Total Assets	**Y8,431,095**	**Y7,152,886**	**$55,105,196**

LIABILITIES AND SHAREHOLDERS' EQUITY	*Millions of Yen*		*Thousands of US dollars*
	1990	*1989*	*1990*
Current Liabilities:			
Short term debt	Y625,241	Y354,284	$4,086,541
Notes and accounts payable	680,528	585,843	4,447,897
Accrued expenses	555,805	429,761	3,632,711
Accrued income taxes	318,879	189,686	2,084,178
Deposits received	171,686	147,984	1,122,129
Other	339,121	251,025	2,216,478
Total Current Liabilities	2,691,260	1,958,583	17,589,934
Long Term Liabilities:			
Long term debt	1,221,274	1,219,463	7,982,182
Retirement and severance benefits	255,953	235,218	1,672,898
Other	9,604	14,614	62,771
Total Long Term Liabilities	1,486,831	1,469,295	9,717,851
Minority Interests in Consolidated Subsidiaries	17,135	15,431	111,994
Shareholders' Equity:			
Common stock, par value Y50:			
Authorized – 6,000,000,000 shares			
Issued – 3,061,294,959 shares in 1990	246,783	–	1,612,958
2,857,142,743 shares in 1989	–	187,317	–
Capital surplus	263,177	203,783	1,720,112
Legal reserve	49,561	36,061	323,930
Retained earnings	3,676,352	3,282,420	24,028,447
Less: treasury common stock	(4)	(4)	(30)
Total Shareholders' Equity	4,235,869	3,709,577	27,685,417
Total Liabilities and Shareholders' Equity	Y8,431,095	Y7,152,886	$55,105,196

CONSOLIDATED STATEMENTS OF INCOME
Toyota Motor Corporation and Consolidated Subsidiaries
Years ended June 30, 1990, 1989 and 1988

	Millions of Yen			Thousands of US dollars
	1990	1989	1988	1990
Net Sales	Y9,192,838	Y8,021,042	Y7,215,798	$60,083,910
Cost of Sales	7,479,054	6,704,924	5,989,300	48,882,707
Gross profit	1,713,784	1,316,118	1,226,498	11,201,203
Selling, General and Administrative Expenses	1,070,789	848,178	758,772	6,998,622
Operating income	642,995	467,940	467,726	4,202,581
Other Income (Expenses):				
Interest and dividend income	304,198	237,111	137,852	1,988,220
Interest expense	(119,162)	(84,130)	(22,296)	(778,833)
Other, net	9,778	4,734	26,973	63,909
Income before income taxes	837,809	625,655	610,255	5,475,877
Income Taxes:				
Current	410,410	300,147	320,042	2,682,418
Tax effect of timing differences	4,803	(2,668)	(5,015)	31,393
Minority Interests in Income of Consolidated Subsidiaries	1,461	979	1,477	9,551
Amortization of Consolidation Difference	(480)	359	(457)	(3,134)
Equity in Earnings of Unconsolidated Subsidiary and Affiliates	20,647	18,706	17,658	134,945
Net income	Y441,302	Y346,262	Y310,952	$2,884,326
Amounts per Share:				
Net income	Y138,20	Y109.45	Y102.28	$0,903
Dividends	19.00	17.69	16.78	0.124

CONSOLIDATED STATEMENTS OF SHAREHOLDERS' EQUITY
Toyota Motor Corporation and Consolidated Subsidiaries
Years ended June 30, 1990, 1989 and 1988 [Y millions]

	Number of shares stock	Common surplus	Capital reserve	Legal earnings	Retained	Treasury stock
Bal6/87	2,665,953,287	Y133,298	Y149,810	Y33,324	Y2,728,658	Y(3)
Net income					310,952	
Dividends paid					(49,321)	
Transfer to legal reserve				38	(38)	
Bonuses to directors and statutory auditors					(597)	
Conv c dbs	1,284,963	1,240	1,240			
Translation adjustments					(26,641)	
Other					3,303	
Bal6/88	2,667,238,250	Y134,538	Y151,050	Y33,362	Y2,966,316	Y(6)
Net income					346,262	
Dividends paid					(52,274)	
Transfer to legal reserve				2,699	(2,699)	
Bonuses to directors and statutory auditors					(679)	
Conv c dbs	45,133,494	42,806	42,760			
Ex of wars	9,946,597	9,973	9,973			
Free d/osh	134,824,402					
Translation adjustments					27,318	
Other					(1,824)	2

Bal6/89	2,857,142,743	Y187,317	Y203,783	Y36,061	Y3,282,420	Y(4)
Net income					441,302	
Dividends paid					(55,891)	
Transfer to legal reserve				13,500	(13,500)	
Bonuses to directors and statutory auditors					(683)	
Conv c dbs	56,214,001	54,837	54,765			
Ex of wars	5,081,078	4,629	4,629			
Free d/osh	142,857,137					
Translation adjustments					22,704	
Balance, June 30, 1990	3,061,294,959	Y246,783	Y263,177	Y49,561	Y3,676,352	Y(4)
Balance, June 30, 1989		$1,224,297	$1,331,915	$235,694	$21,453,725	$(30)
Net income					2,884,326	
Dividends paid					(365,301)	
Transfer to legal reserve				88,236	(88,236)	
Bonuses to directors and statutory auditors					(4,462)	
Conversion of convertible debts		358,403	357,939			
Exercise of warrants		30,258	30,258			
Translation adjustments					148,395	
Balance, June 30, 1990		$1,612,958	$1,720,112	$323,930	$24,028,447	$(30)

CONSOLIDATED STATEMENTS OF CASH FLOWS
Toyota Motor Corporation and Consolidated Subsidiaries
Years ended June 30, 1990, 1989 and 1988

| | Millions of Yen | | | US$000 |
	1990	1989	1988	1990
Cash Flows from Operating Activities:				
Net income	441,302	346,262	310,952	$2,884,326
Adjustments to reconcile net income to net cash provided by operating activities –				
Depreciation and amortization	339,413	295,043	258,378	2,218,386
Allowance for doubtful receivables, net	4,486	11,620	3,084	29,320
Loss on sales of fixed assets	8,198	2,769	29,586	53,582
Provision for retirement and severance benefits	20,735	9,959	16,870	135,523
Increase (dec) in minorities	1,704	2,357	(2,365)	11,137
Changes in current assets				
(Increase) in receivables	(129,519)	(141,291)	(107,670)	(846,529)
(Increase) in inventories	(3,759)	(72,507)	(2,672)	(24,568)
(Increase) in other current assets	(199,148)	(24,343)	(42,997)	(1,301,621)
Changes in current liabilities				
Increase in accounts payable	94,685	69,816	55,307	618,856
Increase in accrued expenses	126,044	121,400	15,684	823,817
Increase in accrued income tax	129,193	(70,620)	114,816	844,399
Increase in deposits received	23,702	(85,509)	45	154,915
Increase in other current liabs	193,400	12,476	6,836	1,264,052
Net cash from operating activities	1,050,436	477,432	655,854	6,865,595

Cash Flows from Investing Activities:

(Increase) in short term investments	(123,397)	(170,561)	213,464	(806,516)
(Increase) in trade investments	(179,874)	(49,500)	(153,940)	(1,175,647)
(Increase) in long term loans	(102,642)	(52,745)	48,437	(670,863)
Additions to fixed assets	(526,200)	(428,300)	(359,700)	(3,439,216)
Other	(331,253)	(576,134)	(130,288)	(2,165,052)
Net cash used in investing activities	(1,263,366)	(1,277,240)	(382,027)	(8,257,294)

Cash Flows from Financing Activities:

Increase in short term debt	270,957	190,289	21,449	1,770,961
Increase in long term debt	1,811	888,970	109,497	11,837
Proceeds from the exc of warrants	9,258	19,946	–	60,516
Dividends paid	(55,891)	(52,274)	(49,322)	(365,301)
Other	122,647	120,599	(8,802)	801,608
Net cash from financing activities	348,782	1,167,530	72,822	2,279,621
Effect of Exchange Rate Changes on Cash and Cash Equivalents	9,444	9,882	(7,622)	61,725
Net Increase in Cash and Cash Equivalents	145,296	377,604	339,027	949,647
Cash and Cash Equivalents at Beginning of Period	1,217,013	839,409	500,382	7,954,335
Cash and Cash Equivalents at End of Period	Y1,362,309	Y1,217,013	Y839,409	$8,903,982

The income statement

Toyota's English language accounts give more information than any one jurisdiction requires.

Its consolidated income statement gives comparative figures for the previous two years and gives the current year's figures both in millions of yen and thousands of US dollars. It also gives net income per share and dividends per share on the face of the income statement. On a separate page it reformats a conventional appropriation account as a statement of shareholders' equity over three years, showing how shareholders' funds have been augmented and how net income has been appropriated and how the number of shares has been changed year on year, all on the same statement – which is in consequence a rather formidable looking complex statement that the lay reader will be likely to bypass.

Sales increase by a trillion (a thousand billion) or so yen every year; gross profit increases by over 400 billion in the most recent year. Net profit before tax is up by just over 100 billion yen, net after tax by just under that sum. The statement of shareholders' equity shows dividends paid up by 3 billion yen. All in all this is a very rosy picture of good performance getting still better.

The balance sheet

The balance sheet gives only one year's comparative figures in contrast to the income statement's two. It shows total assets up 1.3 trillion yen, cash up 150 billion, inventories level with the previous year (despite the sales increase) and gross current increasing by around 50 billion more than the increase in current liabilities to show an improved net working capital position. Deferred liabilities are little changed from the previous year, issued shares are up 60 billion as is the capital surplus account, retentions are up 13 billion but total shareholders' funds are up by 500 billion. This is a picture of a strong capital base, improving liquidity and safe levels of leverage.

The cash flow statement

Cash flow from operations is up over 500 billion, investment cash outflow is down 15 billion and financing inflows are down 800 billion over the previous year. However, the net cash flow for the current year is a net inflow of 145 billion which is a respectable portion of the year's 441 billion net income. The largest cash outflow is investments in general of which about half is additions to property, plant and equipment. Net cash inflow from operations is some 200 billion less than the investment outflow but the financing inflow at nearly 350 billion more than bridges the gap. However, the major financing inflow is from a 270 billion increase in short term debt (maturity over one but under five years) which cannot really be considered a real increase in the business's capital base, especially when we notice the 102 billion increase in long term loans (outwards) classified under investments. There is a suspicion that the long term lending by the group has been indirectly financed by the short term borrowing. That is not very sensible financial management.

CONCLUDING REMARKS

We are told in the literature that SCFPs and SCFs are to help us get a clearer picture of liquidity and solvency than we would have without them. We are told that the SCF enables us to predict future cash flows with greater accuracy than we could without it. On this last point, Heath's (1982) comment on the necessity of the direct format for operations cash flow may seem persuasive to many readers. The indirect format leaves the SCF only marginally distinguishable from its predecessor, the SCFP. Grouping non-operating flows into financing and investment classes is easily done from the old SCFP, so in this respect the SCF is only presentationally better than the SCFP, but it claims to be substantively better. We have also seen that it is as easy for a firm to obscure the message of an SCF as it was to obscure the message of the allegedly already more obscure SCFP. On the other hand, this chapter has shown that the SCF and SCFP usually tell us news not always apparent in the other two final accounts. At best, the incremental information content of an SCF *can* be quite material. At worst, it obscures an otherwise clear set of signals from the other two final accounts. It is submitted that the principal determinant of whether the SCF helps or hinders accounts appreciation is the format of the operations cash flow presentation. In those jurisdictions which do not mandate the direct format, the indirect format will be used as it is so much cheaper and easier to prepare. In these cases, the SCF is really the cash basis SCFP in all material respects. The SCFP was widely seen as not very useful for investor and creditor decisions, even though there might be valuable information hidden within it. It was hidden too deeply for most commentators. The new SCF is vulnerable to all the criticisms of the old cash basis SCFPs when the indirect format is used. Nevertheless, it is hoped that most readers will have seen that the SCFP and SCF have potential usefulness in appraising corporate performance, even if the kinetic usefulness seems to fall rather short of its potential.

The next chapter addresses the view that cash flow statements do not go far enough towards full cash flow accounting and so do not realize the benefits of such accounting which chiefly concern objectivity and clarity.

8 Cash flow extremism

INTRODUCTION AND ORIGINS

The trigger for the emergence of cash flow accounting was the series of debates in the late 1960s and early 1970s over accounting standardization generally and accounting for inflation in particular. Conventional accounting was under widespread criticism. Income statements were widely agreed to be unable to disclose real operating profits as opposed to mere holding gains from inflation. Survey evidence (Lee and Tweedie 1977) was available to show that neither individual nor institutional investors widely understood or relied on published accounts. Balance sheets were criticized as disclosing costs rather than values and were hence of little use to investors. Accounting, it seemed, had lost its way. The American profession issued the Trueblood Report (1973) and the British issued the Corporate Report (1975) in an attempt to specify the kinds of statements modern companies should produce. Both of these were largely ignored at the time. The more limited question of correcting accounts for inflation-sourced distortions was, however, faced up to, and current cost accounting was forced through in many countries with varying degrees of resistance from the members of the accountancy profession. Nobody publicly expressed the views that CCA, CPP or any mixture of the two adopted as accounting standards were perfect. The strongest doubts concerned the subjectivity of some of the relevant adjustments such as that for backlog depreciation and the arbitrariness of such other adjustments as the notorious gearing adjustment in the UK. Against such a background it was only to be expected that nostalgia would be felt for a legendary golden age of accounting simplicity when cash was cash, prices were stable and owners controlled managers. The focus of this nostalgia was, and is, the cash book. In the cash book, payments and receipts are recorded without any subjective judgement being necessary. Posting to the ledgers to complete the double entry involves classification of cash flows but, as will be seen, even this is dispensed with by the extreme fundamentalists in the cash flow accounting ranks.

The earliest advocacy of cash flow accounting was by Lee (1972a), Lawson (1971) and Thomas (1969). Thomas's main argument was that cash flow accounting avoids the arbitrary allocation inherent in accrual accounting. Lawson's main argument, later echoed by Ijiri (1980), was that cash flow accounting would match the way firms did capital budgeting. Thus in Ijiri's words:

> Investment decisions are made on a cash flow basis but the results of those decisions are reported on the earnings basis and the two are often not reconcilable.

Lee's arguments included those mentioned above but to those he added the following:

1 'Cash flow accounting emphasizes the business's capability and potential to survive in terms of cash' (Lee 1972b).
2 Personal judgment involved in preparation of accounts is greatly reduced (Lee 1972a).
3 Since the business firm is only a vehicle for the individual consumer and since a company lacks human qualities, the proprietorial approach of conventional accounting is quite unsuitable, and so the allocation of transactions to categories to suit the proprietor is inappropriate (Lee 1979).
4 Scottish chartered accountants responding to a survey on the desirability of cash flow accounting were not opposed to it (49 per cent of respondents – 90 accountants – were opposed in fact) (Lee 1981b).
5 The conventional UK and Australian funds flow statement is almost valueless to users as a report on the firm's liquidity management, and its replacement by a cash flow statement would be a clear improvement in this respect (Lee 1984a).

Following on from argument 5 above, it is important to realize that cash flow accounting is not merely a reformulation of funds flow statements but a replacement of the income statement itself as a minimum, and of both it and the balance sheet in the later Lee writings. In his own words (Lee 1981c p. 63):

> CFA (cash flow accounting) is the term used to denote a system

of financial reporting which describes the financial performance of an entity in cash terms. It is based on a matching of periodic cash inflows and outflows, free of credit transactions and arbitrary accounting allocations. As such, it is a measurement and reporting system which avoids time lags and distortions.

PRESENTATION OF STATEMENTS

The presentation of cash flow accounts varies slightly between the two main advocates, Lee and Lawson. Lawson's approach has been consistent over time while Lee has developed his model somewhat.

Lawson's format (for which the glossary is given below) is $O - R - T - I + E + B - C = D$ and the distributable cash flow to shareholders is $D - E$, this being Lawson's main concern.

Lee's 1972 format was $O - R - I - T - D + E + B = C$ but by 1980 this had become $O - I - T - D + E + B - R = C$ and his focus remained the period end cash balance, C.

The complete key to the above formats is:

O – operations' net cash flow

R – replacement and growth investment cash outflows

T – tax cash outflows

I – interest paid

D – dividends and distributions paid in cash

E – cash proceeds of new equity issues

B – cash proceeds of new borrowings

C – cash resources (possibly including liquid paper beyond pure cash).

It can be seen that the presentation in the formats above attempts to replace both the funds statement and the income statement but not the financial position statement. Lee is the only cash flow advocate to have formulated a detailed presentation of a cash flow linked balance sheet so as to complete the replacement of conventional reports with cash flow ones. Lee (1984b) bases his balance sheet on immediately realizable values – what the assets would fetch if sold piecemeal without delay. For reasons that are not explained he denies that this violates the going concern assumption of accounting in that the firm can somehow continue even if each of its 'activities' is immediately terminated. This is rather like saying a car would continue to be a car even though it had been stripped of its wheels, engine, camshaft, bodywork and every other tangible component. It would be left with some memory or 'goodwill' but that can scarcely be identified with the car. Similarly a firm with no assets or activities is merely a name with an incorporation certificate. Chambers (1966), the originator and popularizer of exit value (realizable or sales value) accounting for assets, has always insisted on retaining the going concern basis for valuing assets. It is odd that Lee's adoption of Chambers's valuation philosophy should be rendered difficult to accept as fair by its unsolicited, and arguably unnecessary, insistence on forced sale values for its assets. It is as if Lee's preoccupation with cash over the last two decades has led him to distrust any valuation criterion other than liquidity. Indeed, his proposed balance sheet presentation reverses the traditional British marshalling order in favour of the American, thus:

Statement of Financial Position

Cash Asset
Bank accounts

Readily Realizable Assets
Debtors
Finished goods stocks
Motor vehicles
Property.'
Less short term liabilities (creditors, taxation and 'distribution')

Not Readily Realizable Assets
Work in progress
Plant and machinery
Total Net Assets
Less
Long Term Liabilities

Represent

Owners' Equity
Capital
Retained earnings

The last item above, retained earnings, is not to be understood as 'retained cash flow', nor is it quite the traditional 'retentions' of the traditional appropriation account. Rather it is the bottom line of Lee's income statement, which he renames the 'statement of realizable earnings'. This is exemplified below:

Statement of Realizable Earnings

Realized Earnings
Operating cash flow (cash flow from customers less cash outflow to suppliers and creditors)

Unrealized Earnings
(Increases in working capital and readily realizable fixed assets less decreases therein)

Total Earnings
Less tax provided
Less distribution provided
Plus retained earnings of prior periods equals

Gives

Retained Earnings
(which are carried forward in position statement)

There is no question here of recognizing *only* cash receipts already received. By acknowledging the role of working capital changes as 'unrealized earnings', Lee is acknowledging that there is a need for a concept called 'earnings' that goes beyond the simpler concept of 'net cash flow'. The statement of realizable earnings displaces only the traditional income statement.

Replacing the traditional funds flow statement, Lee (1984b pp. 66–9) has this:

Statement of Realized Cash Flow

Cash Inflows
Operating cash flow
Additional borrowing
Decrease in cash asset

Cash Outflows
Capital expenditure
Tax paid
Distribution paid
Increase in cash asset

The above statement of 'realized cash flow' is nothing more nor less than the familiar receipts and payments account. Many critics of traditional funds flow statements (e.g. Drtina and Largay 1985, Holmes 1976, Lau 1982, Clark 1983) have recommended such a format to replace the 'net liquid funds' layout of most published funds flow statements. Surveys by Lee and Tweedie (1977) in the UK and by Anderson (1981) in Australia discovered that readers of published accounts *both* used the funds statement less and appreciated the significance of fewer of its terms than the income or position statements. Rosen and De Coster (1969) showed that the historical justification for the introduction of funds flow statements was to shed light on a company's liquidity position. Lee (1984a) argues that this objective has not been achieved but his 'statement of realized cash flow' would achieve it. It is here that the cash flow accounting advocates are met with most support and fewest objections.

THE BRITISH CONTROVERSY

The two writers who have objected most cogently to the Lawson and Lee justification of cash flow accounting are Eggington (1984) and Rutherford (1982b). Rutherford, objecting to the assertion that cash flow accounting avoids arbitrary allocations, wrote (p. 47): 'Any cash flow which arises in connection with a transaction which affects at least one period other than that in which the flow occurs may be subject to interaction.' For example, debtors would have been cash at the period end but only if a big cash discount had been given. 'The advantage of not actually having to offer the cash discount in practice is an interactive effect attributable to the joint existence of the entity in both the period of sale and the period of collection.' So it is misleading to claim that liquidity is coterminous with cash. Moreover, (p. 48):

> Individual cash flows which are subject to interaction are uniquely determined by the economic events (real resource flows) with which they are associated. When interaction crosses the boundaries between categories in a disaggregated cash flow statement (whatever the basis for the disaggregation), some degree of discretion to make distributional allocations must inevitably reside with management.

In response to this, Lee (1982) conceded that no accounting system can be entirely allocation free, but insofar as allocation to various accounts follows from classification of various transactions, the accountant should not bias the user towards his particular model; for (p. 351), 'Who is to say what is capital, what is extraordinary and what is non recurrent?' Here we have the fundamentalist nature of the Lee position undisguised. He is saying that the statement user is *no less qualified*, willing or able than the accountant to make such classificatory distinctions as capital/revenue or ordinary/extraordinary.

Eggington (1984) argued that cash flow accounting cannot avoid either allocating or classifying. This is illustrated by the example of a firm paying once for a continuous supply of a resource such as electricity. The point of payment and the points of consumption of the resource paid for are different. The choice of one point to debit the books rather than another is itself an act of allocation. He goes on to attack the idea that cash flow accounting can avoid window dressing or payment-and-receipt year-end manipulation by presenting multi-year cash flow reports and forecasts, on the principle that the distortions of one year will be ironed out the following year.

> Such a view . . . Would ignore the fact that timeliness is crucial to accounting information; the interpretation of this year's figures cannot await next year's results. More seriously, cash flow is simply not a measure of corporate performance in the way that earnings or profit are.
>
> (Eggington 1984 p. 103)

Surprisingly perhaps, Lee (1985) agreed with this and asserted that his statements of realizable earnings and of financial position represent concessions to this view of earnings as central performance indicators. Lawson's (1985) response to Eggington is more obdurate. His system of cash flow accounting, he claimed, fully measures performance on a basis which would enable comparison to be made with previously forecasted present values of project cash flows. Ignoring Rutherford's arguments, he further asserted that cash flow accounting 'does not arbitrarily allocate because receipts and payments are empirically determined facts' (but their nominal ledger completions of the double entry are not, and Lawson may prefer returning to single entry bookkeeping if he follows his ideas to their natural conclusion).

Eggington (1985 p.109) expressed satisfaction that

> Lee is now more cautious about equating entity cash flows with distributability and avoids the phrase 'allocation free' but Lawson is not so inhibited.

In the balance sheet, Lawson prefers market values to Lee's forced sale values but Eggington objects that feeding asset market values back to the stock market is circular and conveys no new information.

There the debate rested. As far as the present review is concerned, the last word goes to Tweedie (1977) who questioned UK students attending their first accounting lecture on their 'intuitive' understanding of accounting concepts. Most students thought not of matching but rather of cash flow, not of replacement prices for assets but rather of exit values for them. Most students, in other words, in their uneducated state, are cash flow accounting thinkers on the Lee model. Lee and the cash flow accounting advocates would prefer the students to remain in that state. It is interesting that neither Lee nor Lawson have decided to quote Tweedie's uneducated students in support of their claims for the superiority of cash flow accounting over conventional accounting.

SUBSEQUENT DEVELOPMENTS

Hicks (1981) criticized the FASB for holding the position that in order to predict future cash flows, it was first necessary to predict future earnings which, in turn, requires a record of past earnings. This position, he said, was untenable because cash receipts and payments are the foundation of book entries which are then arbitrarily manipulated to produce final accounts: and such manipulations have to be reversed to extrude future cash flows from projections of future earnings. He then distinguished between a cash basis of accounting and a cash flow basis. The latter accounts not only for receipts and payments but also for 'future cash flows owed to or by the firm as a result of selling and transferring title to certain goods' (p. 30) *and* future cash flows represented by both future exit values of assets and future replacement values of assets (presumably one for inventory, the other for fixed assets). The result is accrual accounting without its allegedly arbitrary allocations and also without its historical cost-based balance sheet.

A very strongly worded attack on accrual accounting's arbitrariness of allocation is found in Thomas (1981) who compares the process to a futile attempt to apportion inputs to book between ink, paper, typewriter and brain in some spuriously precise way. He admitted that the cash-based input–output statement only tells where money came from and went to.

Since the adjustments (well known to preparers of funds statements) that convert a cash flow report into an income statement are exactly what introduce the arbitrarinesses described above, the cash flow statement is more informative than the income statement is. The reason is simple: however limited it may be, the cash flow statement at least is not larded with disinformation. Advocates of the status quo who criticize cash flow accounting for being insufficiently informative are like someone who would improve a thin chicken broth by adding mud,

declares Thomas.

Yet, replies the critic, cash flow statements abandon any effort to match effort with accomplishment. Unfortunately, received accounting doesn't match effort with accomplishment, either. Given the infinitely many ways to accomplish such matching, each as legitimate as any other, the odds against successful matching become vanishingly small. Moreover, as anyone who ever conducted a long research project or wrote a textbook knows, efforts and accomplishments often do not occur during the same time periods. Indeed, it is not their nature to do so, and an alien being (say, an intelligent puddle floating in the atmosphere of Jupiter) would marvel at our pretences to the contrary. Matching attempts to conjure up a childlike world in which good is not merely rewarded, but rewarded in exact proportion. The popularity of this gentle ideal is explicable only because, as we have seen, notional allocations are sheltered from the realities of life. In contrast, cash flow reporting is firmly based in economic events, not in sentimental fantasies. It reports effort when it occurs, and accomplishment when it occurs, without confounding the two in income.

(Thomas 1981 p. 129)

Staubus (1989) emphasizes the need that he perceives to distinguish between the concepts of liquidity and wealth when considering the relative merits of alternative prescriptions for external financial reporting. He concludes that cash flow accounting (CFA) external financial reports have potential value in enterprise liquidity assessment. However, in advocating such a restricted role for CFA, Staubus appears to have damaged his argument by two significant omissions. First, he defines the general prescription for CFA reporting strictly in terms of historical cash flow accounting (HCFA), rarely mentioning total cash flow accounting (TCFA). Second, he fails to critique either HCFA or TCFA in the context of an explicit statement of qualitative accounting criteria. The result is that the case of TCFA as a means of dealing with wealth and wealth changes has not been considered.

Finally, it is of interest to read Lee's (1992) response to the imminent coming into force of FRS 1. His comments were made when ED 54 had still to be adopted.

> I have spent over two decades arguing for and developing systems of cash flow reporting, and view the publication of the Accounting Standards Board's *Cash Flow Statements* as an important step to improve the relevance and reliability of financial reporting. However, it could prove as ineffective as the former SSAP 10 on funds statements unless guidance is given on its potential use, and unnecessary confusions over its meaning are eliminated.

Lee thinks that ED 54's working party of which he was a member, recommended omitting the reconciliation of profit to operating cash flow because there is no consistent pattern of good performance across both cash flow and accrual-based earnings. 'As every recent student is instructed when introduced to accounting – profit and cash flows are not synonymous except over the lifetime of the reporting entity.' Corporate cash flow is lumpy and cannot be related to immediate single period profitability. It is sensible to determine the extent to which profits are being translated into cash over a number of periods. The financial analyst should monitor over time the relationship between operating flows and financing flows

> to determine the relative dependence of the reporting entity on external funding and its potential effects through interest costs on future 'free' operating cash flows after deduction of debt interest; operating flow to investing (matching cash recovery from investment to investment); investment to distribution; and tax flow to operating minus investing flow (establishing a tax rate on a cash basis). And there is little point in complaining after the event about user misunderstanding if everything is left to market forces.

Lee is here implicitly recognizing the distinction between potential usefulness and kinetic usefulness of the new SCF.

HYPERINFLATION ACCOUNTING

Introduction

If Lee's and Lawson's claims for cash flow accounting are valid, then they may be especially persuasive to accountants in hyperinflationary economies such as those in Latin America. This is because hyperinflation divorces purchasing power of money from face value of cash and cash equivalents. If liquidity analysis is the main justification for the presentation of income statements SCFs, and SCFPs, as claimed by Lee and Lawson, then decision usefulness would incline hyperinflationary economies' accountants to employ cash-based statements. The arbitrariness of accrual accounting, per Lee and Lawson, is a further argument accountants might be swayed by in deciding to use actual cash rather than notional purchasing power as the basis of their financial statements. From our viewpoint, we would be somewhat impressed by the Lee and Lawson arguments if it turns out that at least one hyperinflationary economy has preferred the historical factuality of cash to the fuzzy abstraction of purchasing power.

Latin American practice

Brazil

Brazil allows the cruzado to devalue in line with inflation and introduces a new currency when the numbers get too large to handle, in the view of Australia's Norman Cain (1991). It has the largest foreign debt in the world.

In corporate annual accounts, opening balances are inflated by the official rate for the year and any net increase in assets is period profit. The revenue statements are ignored, although the monetary adjustment is disclosed on it to reconcile with the balance sheet profit. Local listing requirements demand accounts both in recorded New Cruzado format and in deflated OBD units deflated back to a common prior purchasing power. For management reporting to head office, NCz figures were translated to US dollars at the actual rate at the date of the transaction.

At the October 1991 annual congress of the Brazilian Association of Capital Market Analysts (Abamec), the members passed a recommendation to the national security regulators, that a cash flow statement should accompany or replace the funds statement currently shown in accounts:

1 to make Brazilian accounts compatible with international standards,
2 to enable company performance to be evaluated from the viewpoint of cash generation, and

3 to be able to calculate new indicators such as cash flow per share 'already used in more developed share markets' (Anon 1991).

Mexico in the 1960s

Although tangible assets may be revalued, Article 235 of the 1962 National Income Tax Law stipulates both that the revaluation must reflect real values and that movable fixed assets are subject to a 20 per cent tax on the holding gains irrespective of their unrealization (Elliot 1968). Mexico has adopted the SCF but it is not clear to the present writer how uniformly its accounting standards are promulgated or enforced.

Colombia in the 1960s

Land and buildings must be annually revalued in the books (Decreto 2521 of 1950 Articles 157–160). Excess profits tax is assessable on the increase in net worth. Further, 15 per cent of the historical costs of assets can be provided as a 'reserve for the protection and recoupment of assets'; 10 per cent of profits must be set aside every year to build up a non-distributable capital reserve for the protection of creditors (Decreto 2521).

Peru in the 1960s

Plant and machinery can be revalued whenever the exchange rate of the sol against the US$ fluctuates 75 per cent and the revaluation surplus cannot be distributed as dividends (Decreto 2521).

Chile in the 1960s

Law no. 15,564 allows annual revaluation of invested capital (i.e. net tangible assets) based on the variation between official cost of living index in the month preceding balance sheet date and that of the same month of the previous year. Unquoted investments can be revalued on the same basis (Decreto 2521).

Conclusion

Latin American countries typically permit CCA style revaluations but do not mandate any particular adjustments for inflation. Rather they are discouraged since some element of the monetary gain may be taxable. There certainly does not seem to be any obligation to produce a special purpose report on liquidity, and Brazil's possible adoption of the SCF is more a response to international trends than the formulation of a solution to any perception of the uselessness of currently presented accounts. In the next subsection we shall see that the International Accounting Standards Committee believes quite strongly in mandating certain adjustments in response to hyperinflation and has issued an uncharacteristically specific set of near instructions on the matter.

The IAS 29 provisions for hyperinflation accounting

Extracts from IAS 29 Financial Reporting in Hyperinflationary Economies IASC, London, July 1989:

Paragraph 2. *'In a hyperinflationary economy, reporting of operating results and financial position in the local currency without restatement is not useful. Money loses purchasing power at such a rate that comparison of amounts from transactions and other events that have occurred at different times, even within the same accounting period, is misleading.'*

3. Hyperinflation is indicated by characteristics of the economic environment of a country which include, but are not limited to, the following:

(a) The general population prefers to keep its wealth in non-monetary assets or in a relatively stable foreign currency. Amounts of local currency held are immediately invested to maintain purchasing power.
(b) The general population regards monetary amounts not in terms of the local currency but in terms of a relatively stable foreign currency. Prices may be quoted in that currency.
(c) Sales and purchases on credit take place at prices that compensate for the expected loss of purchasing power during the credit period, even if the period is short;
(d) Interest rates, wages and prices are linked to a price index.
(e) The cumulative inflation rate over three years is approaching, or exceeds, 100 per cent.

9–23 say that balance sheet items of a non-monetary nature must be presented at their purchasing power at balance sheet date using a general price index to effect the conversion. Same for the income statement by para 24.

25–6. Gain or loss on net monetary position may be estimated by applying the change in a general price index to the weighted average for the period of the difference between monetary assets and monetary liabilities, which is then included in the income statement. Index linked assets and liabilities' adjustments are offset against the gain/loss in net monetary position.

28. *Income statements drawn under CCA still have to be restated after CPP adjustment of the replacement prices.*

31. 'This Statement requires that all items in the statement of changes in financial position are expressed in terms of the measuring unit current at the balance sheet date. Therefore, the SCFP may be prepared using the opening and closing balance sheets and the income statement expressed in terms of the measuring unit current at the balance sheet date. *This Statement requires that the SCFP of an enterprise that reports in the currency of a hyperinflationary currency is presented in terms of cash or cash equivalents rather than in terms of working capital.*'

The importance of the IASC's views on hyperinflation lies in two main areas. First, its insistence on the superiority of purchasing power over historical cash for any statement of flows in the year is at variance with the Lee and Lawson position. Second, its demand that all accounts in hyperinflationary economies prepare an SCFP in closing cash equivalence terms is likely to lead to the SCF itself being adopted in Latin America, probably following the lead to be given by Brazil. It is not unlikely that it will be the SCF of IAS 7 rather than a cash-based SCFP that most Latin American companies will use to comply with IAS 29, since there is virtually no incremental cost in complying with both these standards rather than with IAS 29 alone.

However, Ugalde (1991) researched how SFAS 52 on forex translation and SFAS 95 itself have been applied by US companies operating in hyperinflationary economies. The main results of the research indicate that the SFAS requirements do not provide useful financial information since they fail to extract any implicit interest factor included in income statement and balance sheet items. Due to such failure, companies tend to modify their interpretation of the SFAS requirements. To present statements more economically realistic, companies offset part of the translation exchange gains or losses against interest income or expense and other items on the income statement. This is a practice that IAS 29 does not forbid.

CONCLUSION

Sorter (1982) had been research director for the Trueblood Committee and wrote to correct the misapprehension that the committee had been against accrual accounting. Nonetheless, the Trueblood principle of 'usefulness to decision makers' has become generally cited by the protagonists of cash flows replacing funds flows.

In Chapters 6 and 7 we have seen that the SCF is not the wholesale replacement for the SCFP that it promised to be. Firms still have to specify, albeit in a separate supplementary statement, their not-for-cash sources and applications of funds. Moreover, the indirect method of reporting operating cash flows results in a reconciliation of profit to cash flow very little different from the previous SCFP reconciliation of profit to funds flow. We have seen in Chapter 6 that a majority of US listed firms were already using a cash basis SCFP by the time SFAS 95 became operative in July 1988. We have seen that the ability of cash flows to predict their own future seems, on the whole, inferior to the ability of funds flows to predict the selfsame parameter. From all this we may conclude that the SCF can be regarded as a special form of the SCFP rather than an entirely new departure. Certainly it is not a form of cash flow accounting in the way Lee or Lawson envisaged.

Cash flow accounting, as advocated by Lee and Lawson, has been argued to be of little use as a performance measure. It may well be more transparently understandable than the conventional accrual-based statements, including the SCF prepared under the indirect method. However, what is understood by the receipts and payments account cannot be regarded as the same set of constructs as lie behind an income statement. Whether or not such an account can be regarded as equivalent to the SCF prepared under the direct method is also dubious. Critical to the SCF is the division of cash flows among the headings: operations, financing and investing. Such a division structures how the SCF is read and interpreted. It has no place, explicitly or by implication, in the Lee or Lawson scheme of things. Cash flow accounting is not sanctioned by Trueblood, far less by the Corporate Report (1975), as the Sorter (1982) citation explains. In sum, what is more easily understood by a pure cash flow account is something far less worth understanding in a Trueblood 'usefulness' perspective than what could be understood from a conventional set of accounts.

9 Information load and accounting statements

INTRODUCTION

Early discussion in the accounting literature of the relationship between financial data and their kinetic usefulness tended to focus on the merits of data expansion as a vehicle for the provision of decision useful information. Fertakis (1969 p. 681) questioned the process of increasing disclosure without research directed at an understanding of 'the problems and limitations inherent in the statement user . . . which influence his ability to act rationally on the basis of financial information'. His concern was with the individual's ability to locate and incorporate decision relevant information from financial reports. This hypothesized inability was attributed to various psychological and communication processes that possibly limit or impair an individual's search for, and use of, financial data.

In particular, Fertakis hypothesized the decision maker may be limited in his/her ability to perceive and organize data useful for a particular decision. Also, since accounting is a one-way feedback process (concrete events within the firm are reported to users in abstract financial terms), users may lack the mechanism necessary to relate fully the abstract communication with the real world event. Finally, the cognitive dissonance literature revealed to him a potential for financial information users to reject dissonant information in favour of more consonant elements in financial reports.

This chapter discusses studies of the way people search information sets, with special reference to studies of the effects of increasing information volume on information processing accuracy. The purpose of the material in this chapter is to provide methods and constructs that can be used to elucidate the results of funds flow experiments akin to those of Walker (1984), Bradbury and Newby (1989) and Donleavy (1991). In such experiments, accuracy in answering questions about accounts (with and without SCFPs) is measured for, *inter alia*, its association with the speed with which such questions are answered. The two earlier studies lacked a theoretical paradigm for explaining their results, except one provided by accounting itself Walker (1984) mentions the inverted U model which is adumbrated below, but he does not discuss it or use it as a possible explanation of his results. When experiments show that SCFPs do not significantly add to accuracy or speed, it is too easy to blame the statement for intrinsic uselessness, both kinetic and potential. The models and ideas discussed in this chapter provide the possibility of alternative explanations focusing on the nature of information overload. Essentially, these alternative explanations boil down to two:

Either,

1 SCF/Ps cause information overload wherever and however they are presented to accounts users, since it is impossible to prepare an SCF/P, in accordance with GAAP, devoid of overload.

Or,

2 SCF/Ps are no more overloaded than other final accounts, but may cause overload behaviour when they are presented on top of an accounts information set already at (or near) the point of overload.

ACCOUNTING DIMENSIONS

Dimensions and contexts

The accountant can vary information loads for decision makers by aggregation, summation, use of models, exception reporting, explanatory footnotes and multiple reports. Libby and Lewis (1977) and Schroder *et al.* (1967) caution that the effects of load on decision quality may vary with context, so it is important to specify the nature of the decision task. Iselin (1988 p. 148) commented on the importance of such specification being placed on Mason and Mitroff's (1973) structured/unstructured continuum. Iselin's own study was of a highly structured task.

Accounting load, decision speed and accuracy

A very few accounting studies addressed the question of the relationship between information load and decision making quality. Two of these studies involved bank loan officers' predictions of bankruptcy (Casey 1980a) and estimates of cash flows by subjects differing in accounting expertise (Snowball 1980b). In both these cases the information load manipulation may have failed (Libby and Lewis 1982 p. 271).

Casey (1980a) asked experienced loan officers to make predictions of bankruptcy for each of ten firms using one of three levels of information:

1 Group 1 used a three-year set of six financial ratios;
2 Group 2 used the same as group 1 plus balance sheets and income statements; and
3 Group 3 used the same as group 2 but were also given notes to the financial statements.

Loan officers in group 2 were more accurate than those in group 1 but spent no greater time doing the analysis, while those in group 3 spent more time than those in group 2 but were no more accurate. Casey noted that considering the time spent by subjects as well as predictive accuracy, there seemed to be (Casey p. 45) 'negative returns to processing the additional note information'. He wondered (p. 47) if the group 3 subjects perceived more information in the data as data supply increased even though its predictive content remained the same. Libby and Lewis (1982 p. 271) commented that the notes to the accounts 'may have merely lacked information content'. This is perhaps a tautology if information content is equated with information usage, i.e. kinetic usefulness. As Sterling and Harrison have pointed out, however, 'It can be observed that heroin is used but this does not permit one to validly conceive that it is useful' (in Gonedes and Dopuch 1974 p. 146). Potential usefulness is not a precondition of kinetic usefulness, as is exemplified in the accounting domain by the phenomenon of functional fixation that was reviewed in Chapters 2 and 3.

Snowball (1980b) addressed the effect of financial information user expertise in addition to information load in a cash flow prediction task. Five subjects were assigned to each of 18 conditions, comprising: three levels of expertise defined in terms of accounting education and experience, two levels of financial disclosure, and three levels of time restriction. The last two dimensions were researcher controlled and varied to test the effects of information load. The low disclosure condition consisted of a set of financial statements with outline notes; the high load condition had the same set but with very detailed footnotes. The time levels were 14 minutes, 25 minutes and unlimited. None of the three time variables had a significant effect on subject predictions. With respect to other dependent measures tested, variance of predictions and prediction confidence intervals, only the expertise level resulted in significant differences. The effect of varying disclosure level was negligible.

Subjects were asked to respond to several questions concerning their perceptions of the data and the task. No significant differences for the amount of relevant data, usefulness of data, or the complexity of the task were perceived by subjects across time and disclosure conditions. Perceived task prediction difficulty did differ significantly between high and low disclosure groups. This raises the possibility that the information load manipulations were not completely successful.

INFORMATION LOAD

Processing under pressure

There have been a number of studies of the effect of the amount of information available on judgement behaviour (Hayes 1964, Hendrick *et al*. 1968, Einhorn 1971, Jacoby *et al*. 1974). In general, the results from these studies seem to indicate that increasing the amount of information increases the variability of the responses and decreases the quality of the choices, but also increases the confidence of the decision maker in making judgements (Slovic and Lichtenstein, 1971).

Beach and Mitchell (1978) defined task complexity as not only the number of dimensions or alternatives in the decision problem *but also* the degree to which the outcome of the decision task influences how future decision problems are tackled. From a cost/benefit perspective, Onken *et al*. (1985) suggested that this increase in complexity results in an increase in the amount of cognitive strain, and an associated increase in the value of reducing that strain through simplifying strategies. This is a stress reduction explanation for the use of heuristics.

Beach and Mitchell (1978) built up a model which suggested that when decisions are irreversible, decision makers will tend to use more complex analytical strategies. A similar effect results from the decision maker perceiving him/herself as personally accountable for the result of the decision (MacAllister *et al.* 1979). This implies that experimental studies are likely to find simpler decision making strategies than the subjects would use in a real world situation where they felt themselves accountable for their decisions.

The SDS model

Nature of information load

The purpose of the SDS (Schroder, Driver and Streufert 1967) model is to show how judgement accuracy is affected by increases in the volume of available information. Volume of information in this particular situation is called information load. The controversy and scepticism surrounding theory building in this area of cognitive psychology is neatly expressed in the following quotation:

> Mental workload is a gyrating vector
> In multidimensional space.
> With an input detector and output selector
> One can fit any possible case.
>
> (Senders 1988)

The model

Brightness, saturation and hue are dimensions of light to human beings, but the amoeba recognizes only brightness. It cannot differentiate between different dimensions as fully as humans can. The larger the number of dimensions that exist, the more likely is the development of integratively complex rules or connections. Highly integrated structures have more connections between dimensions and between rules. They contain more degrees of freedom and are more subject to change as complex changes occur in the environment. The more integratively complex the information processing structure, the more the 'self' enters as a causal agent to generate new perspectives. Less integrated structures have categorical black and white thinking and avoid cognitive dissonance. Simple structures are adequate for coping only with simple environments. Environmental properties captured in the simple-complex continuum include information load, information diversity and the rate of information change. Properties affecting the degree to which a person explores his/her environment are noxity (severity of adverse consequences of behaviour), eucity (the opposite), degree of interest in the task environment, and the degree to which environment refutes or disorientates a person.

Hunt (1963) deduced from his observation that since novel situations are sometimes positive and sometimes negative, it can be inferred that (p. 73) 'there must be an optimal level of something involved somehow in the organism's relationship with the environment'. The 'something', according to Berlyne (1960), is arousal, optimized between boredom and panic. The earliest approach to the inverted U hypothesis was the Yerkes-Dobson law (1908) that performance at a task is optimized at moderate, rather than high or low, levels of motivation. SDS replaced motivation with task complexity and replaced optimal performance in general with conceptual performance in particular.

The SDS model, then, argues that information processing accuracy shows an inverted U curve with respect to load.

Miller (1986) asked 18 MBA students and 57 senior finance undergraduates to predict financial distress for 68 firms using sets of either 6 or 9 cues. Prediction accuracy decreased monotonically as load increased.

However, Miller's speculation was based upon the empirically unsupported differential peaking hypothesis. Wilson (1973) noted the lack of evidence supporting the differential peaking hypothesis, and so disagreed with Miller's speculation.

Cognitive style

Accounting studies of cognitive style largely have the purpose of designing information systems to fit more closely the decision maker's style and personality insofar as they are reflected in how he/she processes information. Lusk (1979) argued that only an interaction between cognitive characteristics and information stimuli can justify individualized information systems. However, Lusk's own study found no support for this phenomenon in that there was no interaction between cognitive style and information complexity.

Overload

Schneider (1987) defined organizational information overload as a condition in which the information processing requirements exceed the information processing mechanisms available so that the organization is unable to process information adequately. A similar definition would fit individual information overload. Overload can occur when the nature of the information is: (1) uncertain, (2) ambiguous, (3) novel, (4) complex, or (5) intense – in the perception of the user.

Keller and Staelin (1987) showed that too much information caused consumer assessments of alternatives to deteriorate.

Kim (1986) found that 'novel' information easily increased load to the point of overload but relevant 'old' information did not.

Craft (1984) looked at the interaction between cognitive style and the effects of information load. The decision style inventory was used to categorize subjects into four basic decision styles: analytic, behavioural, conceptual and decisive/directive (these styles behave as their names would suggest). Each style group was subclassified into high analytic (field independent) and low analytic (field dependent). Directive types receiving simple reports showed above average performance in below average time. The same group receiving complex reports did badly (with low analytics within the group doing worse in both accuracy and speed). Analytics and conceptuals did much better than directives across all levels of load, on both accuracy and speed.

Dolinsky (1984) studied the interaction between overload and the presentation of data in a second language in which subjects were proficient but not native. Cue sets of 16 to 256 data points were used on American and Hispanic students in a house buying simulation. Accuracy was gauged by the closeness with which their first choice matched their ideal specification, relative to other available house choices. The results indicated that individuals made worse choices as information increased from 16 up to 256 cues, and choices were better when data were presented in the native rather than the second language with significant overload effects occurring somewhat later.

Cook (1987) found that overload caused switching from compensatory to non-compensatory search strategies and from searching alternativewise to searching dimensionwise.

Pachella's Overview

Pachella's (1974 p. 59) idealized speed accuracy operating characteristic, after Pew (1969), is pictured (Figure 9.1) on next page.

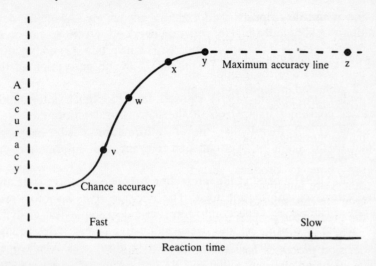

Figure 9.1 Pachella's Overview

Position glossary
v extreme speed emphasis
w moderate speed emphasis
x normal instructions
y theoretical definition point
z extreme accuracy emphasis

The theoretical definition point, y, is 'the fastest reaction time at which maximum accuracy is maintained'. Since even experienced performers show at least 3 per cent error rates in most speed tasks, this point is rarely achieved in practice. Some error is inevitable if time pressure exists as a result of the trial and error process people put in hand to optimize the speed-accuracy balance. Different experimental conditions can vary the subjects' view of where this optimum lies. Small differences (Pachella 1974 p. 60) in error rate can lead to large differences in reaction time, especially at the top end of the accuracy continuum. 'This means, of course, that what may look like relatively meaningless error differences might contaminate reaction time values extensively (Pachella 1974, p. 61).

Almost all tasks performed by individuals involve an error rate higher than zero. For example, Theios (1972) found that even such a simple task as naming a visually presented digit evoked a 3 per cent error rate.

Speed-accuracy models

There are three main models of the speed-accuracy relationship: the fast guess model (Yellott 1971), the accumulator model (Broadbent 1971) and the random walk model (Audley 1973). They are all explained in depth and compared in Pachella (1974) and are very briefly introduced below.

The fast guess model holds that the fall-off in accuracy produced by emphasizing speed is due to a failure of stimulus processing for some proportion of trials. While some responses will take the necessary time to produce accuracy (stimulus-controlled responses), others are much faster but have only a chance percentage of being accurate (fast guess responses). The greater the emphasis on speed, the greater the proportion of fast guess responses.

The accumulator model assumes that responses depend on central decision processes based on evidence acquired over time. All evidence on an alternative is stored till it reaches a critical value which triggers a response – high critical values mean long reaction times. Stress on speed lowers critical values which lowers accuracy.

The random walk model is similar to the accumulator model except that the decision to respond is based on a relative criterion rather than an absolute one; namely, the accumulated evidence favouring one alternative exceeds that favouring any others by some critical value. It is called random walk since the state of the evidence at any moment is a random walk among the alternatives.

All three models are macro trade-off models, dealing with totals and averages. Within them micro models are possible (Lappin and Disch 1972a, b, 1973). For example, in the studies Broadbent (1971 p. 276) surveyed, it was 'broadly true that the average speed of reaction was proportional to the average information per signal'.

Wright (1974, 1977), demonstrated that people under time pressure accentuate negative evidence and use less information in judgement situations involving personal investment. Ben Zur and Breznitz (1981) showed that subjects under time pressure make choices with lower risk, where lower risk is defined as gambles with lower variance, and spend more time viewing negative dimensions (amount of loss and probability of loss). Rothstein's (1986) study, using a task of predicting heights of lines on a computer screen, showed accuracy to be hardly affected by time pressure but consistency significantly deteriorated – though only markedly so for more complex tasks.

These studies are consistent with Pachella's overview which was depicted in the previous subsection, but do not provide sufficient evidence to decide which of the accumulator, fast guess or random walk models offers the most realistic explanation of that overview.

ISELIN, DONLEAVY AND OTHER LOAD STUDIES

Iselin's study

Information load has been most commonly measured in the literature (e.g. SDS 1967, Streufert 1973) in terms of the number of inputs or cues to the decision maker. Some cues may represent different dimensions, others repeat dimensions. For example, a simple specification of an NPV (Net Present Value) problem has the three dimensions of time, annual cash flow and cost of capital, but a five-year project will repeat the time and cash flow dimensions five times to make eleven cues altogether. Iselin (1988) hypothesized that repeated dimension cues like cash flow are digested far more easily by a decision maker than cues in any new dimension. The number of different dimensions in a cue set is that set's 'absolute diversity', while 'relative diversity' is the number of dimensions divided by the number of individual cues throughout all dimensions. The quantity of repeated dimensions is the number of total cues less the number of dimensions. He says that *n* different dimensions may be harder to process than *n* repeated dimensions. His is the first research to address the overload problem in this way.

Casey (1980a) had manipulated load over three levels. His dependent variables were bankruptcy-prediction accuracy and decision time. Iselin accused him of confounding four other variables with information load – irrelevant data, uncertainty, diversity and information value. It is probable that as load increases, irrelevant data would increase, uncertainty would change and so would diversity. Information value would increase in the particular circumstances of Casey's study where profit was the measure of information value. Casey's findings about the optimality of moderate loads were not supported by Iselin who found both accuracy and speed to be level initially, then to decline, instead of accuracy displaying an inverted U. Also, Iselin's subjects started to lose speed well before Casey's turning point of 15 cues. Iselin attributed the inconsistencies to Casey's confounding variables.

Based on Berlyne's (1960) model, Iselin hypothesized an inverted U for accuracy against volume of repeated dimension cues – a boredom effect. Conversely, he expected a U curve for time against repeated dimension cue volume. These were his first two hypotheses. The remainder were as follows:

3 both curves in the first two hypotheses will show turning points between 9 and 15 cues (partly derived from SDS and partly from Streufert (1973));
4 information of higher diversity will result in lower accuracy and
5 will take longer to process;
6 higher experience should result in greater accuracy; and
7 shorter processing time; .
8 higher task learning should result in higher accuracy; and
9 shorter processing time.

Decision accuracy was measured by grading each decision as correct or incorrect. A correct answer not only correctly calculated NPV but also correctly specified accept/reject in consequence. Decision time was measured with a stop-watch in full view of the subjects, and this created a certain amount of pressure. In the analysis, reliability was gauged with Cronbach's (1970) alpha and found to be satisfactory (from 0.62 for accuracy under low diversity to 0.93 for accuracy under high diversity). Face validity was measured by having subjects rate on a seven-point scale the degree to which they believed the experimental task represented structured practical decision making. The mean result of 4.86 'is regarded here as satisfactory' (Iselin 1988 p. 157).

Confirmed effects were the following. There were repeated dimensions effects at only the lowest learning level and without any accompanying boredom effects. There were diversity effects, experience effects and learning effects at the two lowest levels. The turning points of the accuracy curve and the time curve were as expected. Unpredicted results were that both time and accuracy failed to display any boredom effects.

The conclusions drawn were that learning and experience greatly increased the ability to digest repeated dimension cues but they have a much weaker effect on the ability to absorb increases in the number of dimensions. This has considerable bearing on the question of the incremental information content and kinetic usefulness of SCF/Ps. If the SCF/P merely juggles information already present in the other two final accounts, then it does not provide any new dimensions of information. The SCF/P would then not increase information load, and should not cause any symptoms of information overload. Iselin (p. 162) counselled the accountant to limit the number of dimensions in any one report, and:

Also greater concern should be held if the use of explanatory footnotes or multiple reports results in a considerable *increase* in information diversity.

He further recommended that learning effects should always be gauged in overload research because of its importance on the speed and accuracy involved in processing repeat dimension cues. Finally, he pointed out that inexperienced decision makers have been shown to be poor substitutes for experienced ones in this type of research.

Other empirical studies

San Miguel (1976) investigated the relationship between the level of environmental complexity and the level of information processing. The focus was on information processing rather than on predictions. In his study, the subjects were asked to make decisions about the level of operations of a plant, prior to the actual outcome of a large government contract bid by the firm on behalf of this plant. The results were consistent with the SDS model. Information purchases graphically exhibited the inverted U shape. It is not clear, however, how rigorous a test this was of the SDS model, in that the experimental manipulation may not have been neutral with respect to purchase behaviour since subjects were first told the quantitative probability of losing the government contract, then they purchased information, then they decided by how much (if at all) to scale the plant operations. Environmental complexity, surrogated by the probability of losing the contract, may be interpreted as first increasing then decreasing, as the possibility of losing increases. Greatest uncertainty exists when the probability of winning and losing are equal. As the probability of loss increases beyond 0.5, the uncertainty connected with the contract diminishes. It is plausible to expect information needs to be greatest at the point (equiprobability) where uncertainty is greatest.

If the environmental complexity measure is accepted as appropriate, then it still remains unclear how well the process of information integration in the SDS model is represented by information purchase. The content, criterion and construct validities all seem shaky.

Dermer (1973) studied the information preferences of managers differing in tolerance for ambiguity. The findings indicated that individuals intolerant of ambiguity preferred a greater volume of information than individuals tolerant of ambiguity. Dermer suggested that these results supported the findings of Schroder *et al.*

(1967) that conceptually concrete subjects preferred more information than conceptually abstract subjects.

Chervany and Dickson (1974) studied the effects of data aggregation on subject performance, decision confidence and decision speed. Student surrogates were asked to make operating decisions for a simulated manufacturing operation. One group received raw data, process reports and status reports similar to a typical managerial report. Another group received the information statistically summarized. The results indicated that those receiving summarised data performed slightly better, were slightly less confident, and took significantly more time in reaching decisions than those receiving raw data. However, it could readily be argued that both load conditions represented data overload. For the ten decisions made by each subject, the raw data users received a total of 1,040 data items, while the summarized data users received 449 data items.

In another simulated production environment experiment, Benbasat and Schroeder (1977) varied the number of reports available for selection by decision makers (who also happened to be students). One group received a 'necessary' set of eight reports, the other group received an overload set of the necessary eight and also a further eleven reports. Those with the overload set selected significantly more reports than those with the necessary set but failed to demonstrate any difference in performance. The researchers interpreted this to indicate that subjects did not know what reports were needed but instead relied on what was available. They fell short of interpreting the additional information requests by the overload group as additional information incorporated into decisions.

Donleavy's work

Introduction

Finally, Donleavy (1991) tested the null hypothesis that measures of information load show no systematic relationship to either speed or accuracy results for any set of final accounts. Regression was performed of speed and of accuracy on every reasonable operationalization of Iselin's information load constructs, using accounts sets like those reviewed in Chapter 7.

No significant correlations at 5 per cent alpha were found for any set or combination of accounts. This fails to support the Pachella (1974) overview described above where speed increases were said to be associated with accuracy decreases, especially when speed was

Table 9.1 Types of accounts sets

Statistic	Type F only		Type N only	
	Speed	*Accuracy*	*Speed*	*Accuracy*
N	341	341	341	341
Mean	6.866	2.263	5.813	3.402
Std dev.	2.263	1.050	1.764	1.101
Minimum	2.583	0.0	1.433	0.0
Maximum	16.133	5.0	13.350	5.0
Pearson's rho	plus 0.09894		plus 0.07724	
H_o Prob. > rho	0.0680		0.1547	

emphasized as in these experiments. The next subsection quantifies Donleavy's (1991) overall results.

Correlation analysis by type of account

In Table 9.1, type F accounts included SCF/Ps, type N excluded them.

Although there was some insignificant positive correlation between speed and accuracy within both types (N and F) of accounts set, the hypothesized correlation was *negative* and there was no instance of any such correlation. None of the models relating accuracy to processing speed is supported in these results. Either accuracy in accounts processing is independent of speed for accounts users, even under the explicit and deliberate time pressure that subjects endured in Donleavy's (1991) experiments; or else any such relationship as may exist was muffled by stronger effects from other sources of variation, not least from the differences in ability between subject samples.

Information load regressions on all cues

This subsection presents the results of Donleavy's (1991) test of Iselin's dimensions and their effects on speed and accuracy of accounts analysis:

Regression of speed on accuracy

Constant		2.223342
R^2		0.002511
R	0.050111	
X coefficient(s)	0.045817	

Regression of speed on all cues

Constant		5.139780
R^2		0.065548
R	0.256024*	
X coefficient(s)	0.007766	

Regression of accuracy on all cues

Constant		155.4398
R^2		0.000125
X coefficient(s)	−0.40361	

Note:
* Significance of between 0.1% and 1%

Conclusion

Speed is affected by the number of cues, since speed has been measured as the time taken to process one set of accounts. If instead speed had been measured, with more construct validity, as the time taken to process one cue, then speed would have probably been constant, whilst the time taken to process one accounts set would have increased in proportion to the increase in the number of cues in the set.

Absolute information diversity

Iselin (1988) renamed the number of dimensions or classifications in a data set 'absolute diversity'. Three alternative operationalizations of 'dimension' in this sense are possible with a set of final accounts:

1 the number of columns used for different years, or for parent as opposed to group results,
2 the number of rows, since every row of numbers fits a common narrative alongside and to the left of the numbers, or,
3 the number of times rows are totalled or subtotalled, on the basis that every such event should create a meaningful summary and integration of the aggregated figures, into such meaningful dimensions as 'current assets', 'funds arising from operations', and so forth.

Intuitively, this operationalization of the construct 'dimension' seemed most promising to test the Iselin view that absolute diversity is the primary factor operative in producing information load effects on processing accuracy.

However, the results below do not support such a view.

Regression of speed on columns

Constant		2.344269
R^2		0.004423
R	0.066512	
X coefficient(s)	0.019868	

Regression of speed on totalled blocks

Constant		15.68429
R^2		0.004948
R	0.070344	
X coefficient(s)	0.134228	

Regression of accuracy on totalled blocks

Constant		16.90991
R^2		0.004072
R	0.063813	
X coefficient(s)	−0.13473	

Regression of speed on 1/number of columns

Constant		0.455119
R^2		0.007047
R	0.083949	
X coefficient(s)	−0.00405	

Regression of accuracy on 1/number of columns

Constant		0.427915
R^2		0.000126
R	0.011263	
X coefficient(s)	0.000595	

Regression of speed on 1/number of rows

Constant		0.022868
R^2		0.073423
R	0.270968*	
X coefficient(s)	−0.00077	

Regression of accuracy on 1/number of rows

Constant		0.017820
R^2		0.000364
R	0.019087	
X coefficient(s)	0.000059	

Regression of accuracy on columns

Constant		2.484778
R^2		0.000314
R	0.017727	
X coefficient(s)	-0.00579	

Note:
* Significance of between 0.1% and 1%

Conclusion

Absolute diversity has no significant effect on accuracy and the Iselin view is not supported.

Relative Information Diversity

Iselin divided total cues by number of dimensions to obtain what he termed the relative diversity of an information set:

Regression of speed on rows/cues

Constant		0.146330
R^2		0.060006
R	0.244963*	
X coefficient(s)	-0.00414	

Regression of accuracy on row/cues

Constant		0.120037
R^2		0.000000
R	0.000380	
X coefficient(s)	0.000007	

Note:
* Significance of between 1% and 2%

Conclusion

Again, there is no effect on the accuracy of variations in relative diversity and another Iselin view is not supported.

Repeated dimensions

By the term 'quantity of repeated dimensions', Iselin means the number of times a dimension is manifested in various data points after the first such manifestation. It is the total cues less the number of dimensions in a data set.

Regression of speed on cues less rows

Constant		54.75859
Std err of Y est.		51.15550
R^2		0.055586
No. of observations		682
Degrees of freedom		680
R	0.235768*	
X coefficient(s)	5.921573	
Std err of coeff.	0.936004	

Regression of accuracy on cues less rows

Constant		92.92116
R^2		0.000081
R	0.009050	
X coefficient(s)	−0.24861	

Note:
* Significance of between 1% and 2% but with such a large standard error for the Y estimate, the significance is trivial

Yet again, accuracy scores are unmoved by the Iselin constructs.

Donleavy's information load conclusions

Regression of speed on cues less rows, regression of speed on rows/cues, regression of speed on 1/rows, and regression of speed on all cues are the only significant information load results. This study, therefore, lends no support to any of the main information load paradigms that relate speed to accuracy. The tendency for more data (cues) to take more processing time, and thus to show slower processing speeds per accounts set, is scarcely surprising. That the number of rows in an accounting statement seems to carry more significance as an information dimension than the number of totalled blocks (such as the current assets block) or than the number of columns (comparative figures) is of rather more interest. It suggests accounts are read line by line with no systematic skipping between block totals, and raises the possibility that present block totalling and block heading patterns are **not seen by users** as simplifying the task of accounts interpretation. 'Funds' represent a rather clear illustration of just such a failure of arithmetic aggregation to represent the outward manifestation of conceptual integration.

CONCLUSION

No information load model was supported in Donleavy's (1991) SCF/P study, since speed failed to vary with accuracy, and none of Iselin's measures of information load showed that the effects on accuracy and the effects on speed were not really effects but rather tautologies.

Many SCFPs used both a sources and applications format and presented working capital changes in a confusing way that only distinguished current asset changes from current liability changes by the use of brackets rather than subheadings. Many SCFs confuse by mixing inflows with outflows under each of the three headings: operating, financing and investing. Sometimes brackets round the numbers are the only way of knowing whether an inflow rather than an outflow is involved, unless the reader were conscientious enough to check the arithmetic on the face of the statement. This variation in numerical presentation could interact with information load in many subjects. Processing accuracy, in such instances, would only be partially explained by any of the main effects of information load even if the Pachella (1974) or Iselin (1988) explanations had been otherwise adequate. As it is, however, we are almost forced to infer from the evidence that each and every figure on the SCF/P adds to information load, with none of them serving to lighten the load. This suggests that the failure of accuracy of accounts analysis to relate to time taken in that analysis is stochastically affected by information overload, but in a way not well captured by Pachella (1974), Iselin (1988) or any other model operationalized so far. This, in turn, suggests that *we are still a very long way indeed from understanding what are the necessary conditions for kinetic usefulness of accounting statements and what kind of training is needed to convert potential usefulness into kinetic usefulness.* We assume that the process of obtaining accounting, finance and business qualifications includes such training *per se*, but this belief is not yet substantiated by rigorous and well-replicated research evidence. It is possible to claim that we are far better informed about what sort of accounting is *not* useful than about what is. This reflects a long tradition in the accounting literature, especially the professional literature, of confounding descriptions of what *is* with prescriptions of what *ought* to pertain – the Naturalistic Fallacy. 'Usefulness' is a construct peculiarly vulnerable to the Naturalistic Fallacy, and the distinction made in this book between kinetic and potential usefulness is only a first small step in trying to discover how to make accounts useful in some sense, especially the SCF.

10 Conclusion

IMPLICATIONS OF DONLEAVY'S REPLICATION OF WALKER

The most important of Walker's (1984) findings were replicated by Donleavy (1991) in the very different context of Hong Kong; namely, that any incremental information content SCFPs may possess is not demonstrated consistently at the level of the individual credit analyst. This is easily taken as support for the replacement of the statement by something that more accounts users will be able correctly to understand more readily. It is very far from clear that the SCF is going to turn out to be that something, especially under the indirect format. However, it may well also be the case that any new statement will only yield up its expected benefits if accompanied or preceded by an effective campaign of user training in the purpose and implicit messages of the new statement. The relatively poor accuracy performance of analysts even with the type N sets (containing only the presumably familiar balance sheets and profit and loss accounts) suggests that the problem resides not exclusively in formats, measurements and disclosures, but that user education represents a hitherto strongly underestimated element. After administering the experimental session to a particularly badly performing group, Donleavy (1991) exposed the participants to a two-hour seminar on the messages intrinsic to SCF/Ps, their potential usefulness in fact. It was only too evident that most of what was presented was new (and also, fortunately, interesting) to most of the subjects. In short the hidden contaminant of much usefulness research, possibly applicable to Walker's and certainly to Bradbury and Newby's (1989) research in this field, was user ignorance of how to assemble accounting report lines and paragraphs into a coherent story. Many analysts rely mechanistically on ratios and spreadsheet outputs, so the wood is not detected subsuming the trees. Perhaps as a result, functional fixation on earnings and reliance on the chairman's cheer-leading essays in the annual report have become rather prevalent.

Another major implication of the results of this research is the importance of clear presentation. While accounting standards theorists and practitioners have spent many person-years standardizing and trying to harmonize disclosures and measurement policies for virtually all the items on the final accounts of business enterprises, **the presentation of the numbers themselves has not been addressed. It would seem feasible and reasonable, however, that agreement could more readily be obtained on when numbers should be bracketed than on how fictitious assets should be expensed.** It would certainly be more fruitful on the evidence of this present study. Accountancy centres on numbers, but the accounting standard on their acceptable, desirable or even generally accepted mode of presentation has yet to appear anywhere in the world, according to published evidence as at end 1992. This issue is particularly serious for statements of changes, irrespective of what is purportedly changing. If we take as an example a 5 million increase in receivables accompanied by a 3 million increase in payables, we will find in real world accounts examples of all the following presentations and more besides:

1 Increase in receivables 5
  less
  Decrease in payables 3
  Increase in working capital 2
2 Increase in receivables 5
  Add
  Decrease in payables (3)
  Change in working capital 2
3 Change in receivables less payables 2
4 Decrease in payables less receivables (2)
5 Increase(decrease) inreceivables 5
  Increase(decrease) in payables (3)
  Increase(decrease) in working capital 2
6 (Increase)/decrease in receivables (5)
  (Decrease)/increase in payables 3
  (Increase)/decrease in working capital (2).

It is suggested that the above variations may well be a more significant barrier between the preparers and users of accounts than most variations in disclosure or measurement practice so far addressed in the literature of accounting standards. It is not clear when or why accounts preparers first decided or assumed that readers should be capable of algebraic addition, but such is the necessary assumption behind the judgement that the above variations are not a problem. They were for Hong Kong bank analysts, as evidenced both by performance in the experiments and by clear testimony in the post session debriefings (Donleavy 1991).

The final major implication of the results of the studies referred to in this book is that information load or overload is not yet well understood, nor yet operationalized into accounting-based measures that could provide rigorous tests of the principal models in the field, especially those consonant with or developed from the Pachella overview. SCFP studies have shown no significant association between processing time and processing accuracy. A subsequent administration of the experiment using Donleavy's (1991) study could well show an association of information load effects with some particular dimension of cognitive style. There is clearly a need to look more closely at user characteristics, *before* venturing any generalizations about accounts usefulness. In that sense, I can be said to have supported the specific accounts for specific users school of accounting rather than the general purpose statement school. To some extent, however, such support is an artefact of the research design used by Walker and Donleavy, which implicitly assumed lenders looked for different things in accounts from what equity investors would seek. The equity-lender difference need not have the slightest association with some cognitive style difference and it would be astonishing if a systematic association were found. It would be fascinating to search for such an association, however, and it is quite important for designers of accounting formats to have available considerably more information about the cognitive styles of their users than they have currently. We accounting academics and professional practitioners have not lost the tendency to design and discuss accounts prescriptively, implicitly seeing accounts readers as patients rather than as customers, but we have not done a particularly effective job in convincing them that we know what's good for them.

POSSIBILITIES FOR FUTURE RESEARCH

The most important accounting nations in the English speaking world have decided to replace funds statements by cash flow statements. Nobody used published experimental findings in making that decision. Walker's Australians, Bradbury and Newby's New Zealanders and Donleavy's Hong Kong Chinese and expatriates may not necessarily triangulate the funds statement processing behaviour of their equivalents elsewhere in the world. In particular, it is probable that Anglo-American bank credit officers have more extensive accounting training and a greater regard for the role of accounts in making loan decisions than any of the subject groups so far examined. Therefore, it is important that Walker (1984) and Donleavy (1991) be replicated in equivalent British and American banking settings.

It is also important to conduct speed and accuracy tests of the SCF against its predecessor SCFP using common source final accounts data, to discover whether the SCF has significant incremental information content. It would have been even better to do so before FRS 1 and SFAS 95, even at the cost of sacrificing external validity through inventing fictitious results for fictitious companies. The present writer has begun a series of such tests in Asia.

It is important to research the most effective means of presentation of numerical information without preconceptions as to what readers can and cannot do arithmetically; and to do this research as a precondition of standardizing such presentation.

There is much work still to be done around the world by way of surveying user confidence in locally produced and audited accounts. The users' perception of accounts may well be less trusting than the efficient market academics and the accounting practitioners assume, but may be less cynical than Watts and Zimmerman or the 'critical perspectives' school seem to advise.

The pioneering work of Iselin on information load and dimensionality has strong cautionary implications for increments in accounting disclosures, as did the earlier musings of Fertakis and others. This field is right for strictly controlled experimental settings where accounting students are a not unreasonable proxy for older decision makers in the real world. As things presently stand, we simply do not know what a generally acceptable definition of accounting information overload would be for the principal user groups in the principal industrial countries. If we are genuinely concerned with capital market efficiency, then we should encourage research on the overload question. Donleavy's (1991) results *tentatively suggest* that difficult accounts and most instances of SCFPs – and even SCFs – may represent such overload, but that overload is more a matter of the subject's cognitive style than it is of the document's inherent clarity or volume of signals.

ACCOUNTING AND MEANINGFULNESS

As Chapter 1 reminded us, accounting dates back far beyond the invention of writing. Yet archaeologists have been less than delighted when they dig up inventory lists of wealth rather than accounts of epic battles. We use all the techniques of modern computer-aided graphics to make annual reports as visually interesting as possible, but we do not generally produce the accounts themselves with communicative clarity as a primary explicit concern. If accounting is the 'language' of business, then the evidence fails to suggest it is a language widely spoken or understood. Instead, users use non-accounting cues like insider tips or they become fixated on one overloaded figure, usually earnings. It is like getting by in a foreign language with a few stock phrases and implicitly assuming we can handle novels and newspapers. Creditor and investor appraisal of companies uses accounts but does not rely on them for anything like a full picture of the firm's risk profile and expected returns. This suggests that accounts in present day circulation are to decision useful information as Pidgin English is to the Queen's English. After 14,000 years of accounting activity, the so-called language of accounting has yet to produce even a Chaucer, let alone a Shakespeare. If this is because the language metaphor is itself misconceived, then what is accounting for? If it is a kind of science, then where are its falsifiable propositions? If it is a kind of mathematics of economic measurement, where are its explicit links with econometrics? As a set of measurements of business wealth and income, where are its equivalents of the constant length central to the metric measurements of physical space? Monetary units of constant purchasing power are not yet central to generally accepted accounting principles, although IAS 29 may have made a small contribution to bringing this about. It is obvious that there can be no reliable measurement system while the basic measuring unit, money, refuses to stay a constant size. The only other purpose often ascribed to accounting activity is stewardship, with its roots in medieval legal history. It requires little reflection to acknowledge that most financial accounting activity takes place in order to comply with the laws of a jurisdiction in which a firm's business is carried out. This might well suggest to some readers that accounting by an entity to its external stakeholders is a subset of jurisprudence, the philosophy of law. It is submitted that this represents the next important field of academic accounting activity. International accounting studies already acknowledge the role of comparative legal systems in shedding light on comparative accounting activity. It is a logical next step to examine comparative jurisprudence for the insight it may give in understanding why accounting is the way it is and what could be done to improve both its kinetic and its potential usefulness.

Bibliography

AAA, see under American Accounting Association.

ABDEL-KHALIK, A. R. and K. EL-SHESHAI, 'Information Choice and Utilization in an Experiment on Default Prediction', *Journal of Accounting Research*, 325–42, Autumn 1980.

ABDEL-KHALIK, A. R. and T. F. KELLER, 'Earnings or Cash Flows: An Experiment on Functional Fixation and the Valuation of The Firm', *Studies in Accounting Research* 16, American Accounting Association, 1979.

ABDEL-KHALIK, A. R. and J. C. McKEOWN, 'Understanding Accounting Changes in an Efficient Market: Evidence of Differential Reaction', *Accounting Review*, 851–68, October 1978.

ABELSON, R. P. and A. LEVI, 'Decision Making and Decision Theory', in G. Lindzey and E. Aronson, eds, *Handbook of Social Psychology*, Hillsdale, NJ: Erlbaum, 1985.

ACCOUNTANTS INTERNATIONAL STUDY GROUP, The Funds Statement – Current Practices in Canada, the United Kingdom and the United States, March 1973.

ACCOUNTING STANDARDS STEERING COMMITTEE, *SSAP 9 Stocks and Work in Progress*, ICAEW 1975.

——, *SSAP 13, Accounting for Research and Development*, ICAEW 1978.

ADAMS, ROGER, 'Cash Flow Statements: The Transatlantic Effect', *Accountancy* 102:1143, 110–13, November 1988.

AG of Ontario, Report of the Attorney General's Committee on Securities Legislation, Ottawa: Queen's Printer, 1965.

AICPA, *Report of the Study on Establishing Financial Accounting Standards*, Francis A. Wheat Chairman, New York: AICPA, March 1972.

——, *Objectives of Financial Statements*, aka the Trueblood Report, New York: AICPA, 71, 1973.

AITKEN, M. J. and T. D. WISE, 'The Real Objective of the IASC', *International Journal of Accounting* 20:1, 171–7, Fall 1984.

ALLEN, G. L., An Empirical Investigation of the Complementary Value of a Statement of Cash Flows in a Set of Published Financial Statements, PhD Dissertation, University of North Texas, 1985.

AMERICAN ACCOUNTING ASSOCIATION, *A Tentative Statement of Accounting Principles Underlying Corporate Financial Statements*, AAA, 1936.

——, *Accounting Review*, p. 174, January 1971.

——, *Report of the Committee on International Accounting*, New York: AAA, 1976.

——, 'Report of the AAA Committee on International Accounting Operations and Education 1975–76', *Accounting Review Supplement* 52: 65–101, 1977.

ANDERSON, MATTHEW J., 'Some Evidence on the Effect of Verbalization: A Methodological Note', *Journal of Accounting Research* 23:2, 843–52, Autumn 1985.

ANDERSON, N. H., *Cognitive Psychology and Implications*, New York: W. H. Freeman, 1980.

ANDERSON, N. S. and P. M. FITTS, 'Amount of Information Gained during Brief Exposure of Numerals and Colours', *Journal of Experimental Psychology* 56:4, 362–9, 1958.

ANDERSON, R., 'The Usefulness of Accounting and Other Information Disclosure in Corporate Annual Reports to Institutional Investors in Australia', *Accounting and Business Research* 11:44, 259–66, Autumn 1981.

ANDREW, B. H., L. AUSTIN and A. CHEW, 'On the Relationship Between Profit, Funds and Cash Flows', working paper, National University of Singapore Dept of Accounting, 1985.

——, 'A Study of the Relationship Between Three Business Flows: Some Evidence from Singapore, *International Journal of Accounting*, 57–70, 1986.

ANDREWS, F. C., 'Asymptotic Behavior of Some Rank Tests for Analysis of Variance', *Annals of Mathematical Statistics* 25: 724–36, 1954.

ANG, J. S. and R. A. POHLMAN, 'A Note on the Price Behavior of Far Eastern Stocks', *Journal of International Business Studies*, 103–7, Spring/Summer 1978.

ANON, 'Brazil:- Analysts Press for Cashflow Accounting', *World Accounting Report*, Lafferty Press, Dublin, December 1991, p. 9.

ANTON, H., *Accounting for the Flow of Funds*, Boston: Houghton Mifflin, 1962.

ARBEL, A. and B. JAGGI, 'Impact of Replacement Cost Disclosures on Investors' Decisions in the United States', *International Journal of Accounting*, 71–82, Fall 1978.

ARNOLD, A. J., C. D. B. CLUBB, S. MANSON and R. T. WEARING, 'The Relationship Between Earnings, Funds Flows and Cash Flows: Evidence for the UK', *Accounting and Business Research* 22:85, 13–19, 1991.

AROWOLO, EDWARD A., 'The Development of Capital Markets in Africa, with Particular Reference to Kenya and Nigeria', International Monetary Fund Staff Papers, 420–69, July 1971.

ARTHUR ANDERSEN & CO, *A Management Guide to Better Financial Reporting*, Arthur Andersen & Co, 81/2, 1976.

ARTHUR, W. J., 'Cash Flow Yardstick: Here's One Way to Make the Cash Flow Statement More Useful', *FE: The Magazine for Financial Executives* 2:10, 35–40, October 1986.

ASHTON, ALISON HUBBARD, 'A Field Test of Implications of Laboratory Studies of Decision Making', *Accounting Review* 59:3, 361–75, July 1984.

ASHTON, R. H., 'Cue Utilization and Expert Judgments: A Comparison of Auditors with Other Judges', *Journal of Applied Psychology*, 437–44, August 1974.

——, 'Cognitive Changes Induced by Accounting Changes: Experimental Evidence on the Functional Fixation Hypothesis', *Studies on Human Information Processing in Accounting: Supplement to Journal of Accounting Research* 1–17, 1976.

ASHTON, ROBERT H., 'Human Information Processing In Accounting', *Studies in Accounting Research* 17, Florida: American Accounting Association, 1982.

ASHTON, ROBERT H. and P. R. BROWN, 'Descriptive Modelling of Auditors' Internal Control Judgments: Replication and Extension, *Journal of Accounting Research*, 269–77, Spring 1980.

AUDLEY, R. J., 'Some Observations on Theories of Choice Reaction Time: Tutorial Review', in S. Kornblum, ed., *Attention and Performance IV*, New York: Academic Press, 1973.

BACHELIER, LOUIS, *Theorie de la Speculation*, Paris: Gautier Villars, 1900, but translated and reprinted pp. 17–78 in *The Random Character of Stock Market Prices* ed. Paul Cootner, Cambridge, MA: MIT Press, 1964.

BACKER, MORTON and MARTIN L. GOSMAN, *Financial Reporting and Business Liquidity*, New York: National Association of Accountants, 1978.

BAILEY, D. T. 'The Business of Accounting East and West', *Journal of Management Studies*, 28–44, February 1975.

——, 'Accounting in Russia: The European Connection,' *International Journal of Accounting*, Fall 1982.

——, 'European Accounting History', in H. P. Holzer, ed., *International Accounting*, New York: Harper and Row, 1984.

BAKER, WILLIAM MAURICE, 'The Effects of Accounting Reports on Loan Officers: An Experiment', PhD Dissertation, Virginia Polytechnic Institute and State University, 1987.

BALL, R. J., 'Changes In Accounting Techniques and Stock Prices', *Journal of Accounting Research Supplement: Empirical Research in Accounting* 10: 1–38, 1972.

——, 'Filter Rules Interpretation of Market Efficiency: Experimental Problems and Australian Evidence', *Accounting Education* 18: 1–17, November 1978.

BALL, R. J. and P. BROWN, 'An Empirical Evaluation of Accounting Income Numbers', *Journal of Accounting Research* 6: 2, 159–78, Autumn 1968.

BALL, R. J., P. BROWN and F. J. FINN, 'Published Investment Recommendations and Share Prices: Are There Free Lunches In Security Analysis?', *Journal of the Australian Society of Accountants* 2: 5–10, 1978.

BALL, R. J., and R. WATTS, 'Some Time Series Properties of Accounting Income', *Journal of Finance*, 663–81, June 1972.

BAMBER, LINDA SMITH, 'The Information Content of Annual Earnings

Releases: A Trading Volume Approach', PhD Dissertation, Ohio State University, 1983.

BANZ, R. W., 'The Relationship between Return and Market Value of Common Stocks', *Journal of Financial Economics* 9: 1, 3–18, March 1981.

BARBER, J. P., 'The Funds Statement Redesigned to Fulfil the Objectives of Financial Reporting by Business Enterprises', PhD Dissertation, University of Texas at Austin, 1981.

BARK, HEE-KYUNG K., 'Risk, Return, and Equilibrium in the Emerging Markets: Evidence from the Korean Stock Market', *Journal of Economics & Business* 43:4, 353–62, November 1991.

BARLEV, BENZION and JOSHUA LIVNAT, 'The Information Content of Funds Statement Ratios', *Journal of Accounting, Auditing and Finance* 5:3, 411–31, Summer 1986.

BARNETT, VIC and TOBY LEWIS, *Outliners in Statistical Data*, London: John Wiley and Sons, 1984.

BARRETT, M. E., 'Financial Reporting Practices: Disclosure and Comprehensiveness in an International Setting', *Journal of Accounting Research*, 10–26, Spring 1976.

BARTON, A. D., *The Anatomy of Accounting*, University of Queensland, 263, 1975.

BARTON, THOMAS MICHAEL, 'On the Prediction of Mergers and Bankruptcies with Ratios from the SCFP and Different Funds Flow Measures', PhD Dissertation, Georgia State University, 1986.

BASU, S., 'Investment Performance of Common Stocks in relation to their Price Earnings Ratios: A Test of the Efficient Markets Hypothesis', *Journal of Finance*, 663–82, June 1977.

BEACH, L. R. and T. R. MITCHELL, 'A Contingency Model for The Selection of Decision Strategies', *Academy of Management Review*, 439–49, 1978.

BEAVER, W. 'The Behavior of Security Prices and its Implications for Accounting Research', *Accounting Review* Supplement to Vol. 47 Committee Reports, 407–37, 1972.

BEAVER, W. H., 'The Information Content of Annual Earnings Announcements', *Journal of Accounting Research Supplement; Empirical Research in Accounting* 6: 87–92, 1968.

——, 'The Information Content of the Magnitude of Unexpected Earnings', paper presented to the 1974 Stanford University Research Seminar.

BEAVER, W. H., A. A. CHRISTIE and P. A. GRIFFIN, 'The Information Content of SEC Accounting Series Release 190', *Journal of Accounting and Economics*, 127–57, August 1980.

BEAVER, W. H. and R. E. DUKES, 'Interperiod Tax Allocation, Earnings Expectations and the Behavior of Security Prices', *Accounting Review* 320–32, April 1972.

BEAVER, W. H., PAUL KETTLER and MYRON SCHOLES, 'The Association Between Market-Determined and Accounting-Determined Risk Measures', *Accounting Review*, 654–82, October 1970.

BEAVER, W. H. and JAMES MANEGOLD, 'The Association Between Market Determined and Accounting Determined Measures of Systematic Risk', *Journal of Financial and Quantitative Analysis*, 232–84, June 1975.

BECKHART, B. H., *Business Loans of American Commercial Banks*, New York: Ronald Press, 1959.

BECKMAN, T. N., and R. S. FOSTER, *Credits and Collections*, 8th edition, New York: McGraw-Hill, 1969.

BELKAOUI, AHMED, 'Accounting Determinants of Systematic Risk in Canadian Common Stocks: A Multivariate Approach', *Accounting and Business Research*, 3–10, Winter 1978.

BEN ZUR, H. and S. J. BREZNITZ, 'The Effects of Time Pressure on Risky Choice Behavior', *Acta Psychologica* 47: 89–104, 1981.

BENBASAT, I., and A. DEXTER, 'Value and Events Approaches to Accounting: An Experimental Evaluation', *Accounting Review*, 735–49, October 1979.

BENBASAT, I., and R. G. SCHROEDER, 'An Experimental Investigation of Some MIS Design Variables', *MIS Quarterly*, 37–49, March 1977.

BENJAMIN, J. J. and K. G. STANGA, 'Differences in Disclosure Needs of Major Financial Statements', *Accounting and Business Research*, 187–92, Summer 1977.

BENSON, H., 'The Story of International Accounting Standards', *Accountancy*, July 1976.

BENSTON, GEORGE J., 'Published Corporate Accounting Data and Stock Prices', *Journal of Accounting Research Supplement: Empirical Research in Accounting* 5: 27/28, 1967.

BENSTON, G. J. AND M. A. KRASNEY, 'Demand for Alternative Accounting Measurements', *Journal of Accounting Research Supplement to Vol. 16; Studies on Accounting for Changes in General and Specific Prices*, 1–30, 1978.

BERESFORD, DENNIS R. and ROBERT D. NEARY, 'FASB Explores Options of Cash Flow Reporting', *FE: The Magazine for Financial Executives* 1:12, 5/6, December 1985.

BERLE, A. and G. C. MEANS, *The Modern Corporation and Private Property*, New York: Macmillan, 1933.

BERLYNE, D. E., *Conflict, Arousal and Curiosity*, New York: McGraw-Hill, 1960.

BERNARD, V. L. and T. L. STOBER, 'The Nature and Amount of Information Reflected in Cash Flows and Accruals', *Accounting Review* 64: 624–52, 1989.

BERRY, AIDAN, DAVID CITRON, ROBIN JARVIS and JOHN ROSS, 'Most Corporate Loan Decisions Ignore CCA', *Accountancy* 96:1100, 81/2, April 1985.

BERTHOLDT, R. M., 'Discussion' (of the impact of uncertainty reporting on the loan decision), *Journal of Accounting Research*, 325–42, Autumn 1979.

BIDDLE, GARY and S. SAUDAGARAN, 'The Effects of Financial Disclosure Levels on Firms' Choices Among Alternative Foreign Stock Exchange Listings', *Journal of International Financial Management and Accounting* 1:1, 55–87, Spring 1989.

BIERMAN, HOWARD, 'Survey Shows Accounting Software Vendors Are Ready for FASB No 95', *Computers in Accounting* 4:3, 62–7, April/May 1988.

BIGGS, S. F., 'An Empirical Investigation of the Information Processes Underlying Four Models of Choice Behavior', in T. J. Burns, ed., *Behavioral Experiments in Accounting II*, Columbus, Ohio: College of Administrative Science, Ohio State University, 1979.

BIGGS, S. F., J. C. BEDARD, B. G. GABER and T. J. LINSMEIER, 'The Effects of Task Size and Similarity on the Decision Behavior of Bank Loan Officers', *Management Science* 31: 970–87, 1985.

BINKLEY, M. A., 'Components of the Report of Financial Changes', *Accounting Review*, 304–7, July 1949.

BIRD, PETER, *Understanding Company Accounts*, London: Pitman, 13–16, 1979.

BLACK, FISCHER, 'Yes Virginia, There Is Hope: Tests of The Value Line Ranking System', *Financial Analysts Journal*, 10–14, September/October 1973.

BLALOCK, H. M. JR, *Social Statistics*, New York: McGraw-Hill, 1984.

BLISS, J. H., *Management Through Accounts*, New York: Ronald Press, 1924.

BLOOM, R and M. A. NACIRI, 'Accounting Standard Setting and Culture', *International Journal of Accounting* 24:1, 91, 1989.

BOARD, J. L. G., J. F. S. DAY and M. WALKER, *The Information Contentment of Unexpected Accounting Income, Funds Flow and Cash Flow: Comparative Evidence for the US and UK Economies*, London: Institute of Chartered Accountants in England and Wales, 1989.

BOATSMAN, J. R., 'Why Are There Tigers and Things?', *Abacus*, 156–67, 1977.

BORN, BERNICE DREWYER, 'The Statement of Cash Flows: A Step-by-Step Guide', *National Public Accountant* 33:8, 18–23, August 1988.

BOUWMAN, M. J., 'The Use of Accounting Information: Expert versus Novice Behavior', Working Paper, University of Oregon, April 1980.

BOUWMAN, MARINUS J., 'The Use of Protocol Analysis in Accounting', *Accounting and Finance*, 61–84, May 1985.

BOWEN, R. M., D. BURGSTAHLER and L. A. DALEY, 'Empirical Evidence on the Relationship Between Earnings, Cash Flows and Cash Flow Surrogates', working paper 1984–6, School of Management, University of Minnesota, July 1984.

——, 'Evidence on the Relationships Between Earnings and Various Measures of Cash Flow', *Accounting Review*, 713–26, October 1986.

——, 'The Incremental Information Content of Accrual Versus Cash Flows', *Accounting Review* 62:723–47, 1987.

BOZE, KEN M., 'Cash Flow Statements: Converting from Accrual Basis Financial Statements', *National Public Accountant* 32:6, 35–41, June 1987.

BRACKEN, ROBERT M. and ARA G. VOLKAN, 'Forecasting Cash Flows – Will The New Reporting Rules Help?', *Journal of Business Forecasting* 7:1, 8–10, Spring 1988.

BRADBURY, MICHAEL and SONJA NEWBY, 'The Use of Changes in Financial Position to Interpret Financial Data: An Empirical Investigation', *Abacus* 25:1, 31–8, 1989.

BRAIOTTA, LOUIS JR, 'Cash Basis Statement of Changes', *CPA Journal* 54:8, 34–40, August 1984.

BREALEY, R. A., *An Introduction to Risk and Return From Common Stocks*, Cambridge, MA: MIT Press, 1969.

——, 'The Distribution and Independence of the Successive Rates of Return from the British Equity Market', *Journal of Business Finance*, 29–40, Summer 1970.

BRENNER, MENAHEM, 'The Effect of Model Misspecification on Tests of the EMH', *Journal of Finance* 32:1, 57–66, March 1977.

BRISTON, R. J., 'The Evolution of Accounting in Developing Countries', *International Journal of Accounting*, 105–20, 1978.

——, *Introduction to Accountancy & Finance*, London: Macmillan, pp. 148–50, 1981.

BROADBENT, D. E., *Decisions and Stress*, London: Academic Press, 1971.

BROMWICH, M. and A. G. HOPWOOD, eds, *Accounting Standard Setting: An International Perspective*, London: Pitman, 1983.

BROWN, P., 'The Impact of the Annual Profit Report on the Stock Market', *Australian Accountant*, 277–83, July 1970.

BROWN, P. and P. HANCOCK, 'Profit Reports and The Share Market', in I. Tilley and P. Jubb, eds, *Capital, Income and Decision Making*, Sydney: Holt, Rinehart and Winston, 1977.

BROWN, PHILIP and JOHN KENNELLY, 'The Information Content of Quarterly Earnings: An Extension and Further Evidence', *Journal of Business*, 403–15, July 1972.

BROWN, S. L., 'Earnings Changes, Stock Prices and Market Efficiency', *Journal of Finance*, 17–28, March 1978.

BROWNLEE, E. RICHARD, 'What Bankers Think About the Funds Statements', *Magazine of Bank Administration* 54:1, 32–3, 37–41, January 1978.

BRUNING, J. L. and B. L., KINTZ *Computational Handbook of Statistics*, Glenview, Illinois: Scott Foresman, 1977.

BRUNSWIK, E., *The Conceptual Framework of Psychology*, University of Chicago, 1952.

——, *Perception and the Representative Design of Psychological Experiments*, University of California, 1956.

BRYANT, J. V., 'Proposed: A New Statement of Changes', *Management Accounting*, 49–52, April 1984.

BULL, J., *Accounting in Business*, London: Butterworths, 451–69, 1980.

BYRD, DAVID B. and SANDRA D. BYRD, 'Using the SCFP', *Journal of Small Business Management* 24:2, 31–8, April 1986.

BYRNE, R., 'Planning Meals: Problem Solving on a Real Data Base', *Cognition*, 287–332, December 1977.

CAIN, NORMAN, 'Accounting in a Banana Republic', *Australian Accountant*, 32–5, September 1991.

CAIRD, K. G., and D. M. EMANUEL, 'Some Time Series Properties of Accounting Income Numbers', *Australian Journal of Management*, 7–15, December 1981.

CAIRNS, D., M. LAFFERTY and P. MANTLE, *Survey of Accounts and Accountants*, London: Lafferty Publications, 1984.

CALLEN, E., and D. SHAPERO, 'A Theory of Social Imitation', *Physics Today* 27:7, 1974.

CAMPBELL, JANE E., 'An Application of Protocol Analysis to the Little GAAP Controversy', *Accounting Organizations and Society* 9:3/4, 329–42, 1984.

CAMPBELL, LES G., 'Financial Reporting in Japan', in C. W. Nobes and R. H. Parker, eds, *Comparative International Accounting*, Oxford: Philip Allan, 152–69, 2nd edition, 1985.

CANNING, JOHN B., *The Economics of Accountancy: A Critical Analysis of Accounting Theory*, Ronald Press, 1929, New York: Arno reprint in 1978.

CARMICHAEL, D. R., 'Audit Reporting Considerations for the New Statement of Cash Flows', *CPA Journal* 58:6, 72–3, June 1988.

CASEY, C. J., 'Variation in Accounting Information Load: The Effect on Loan Officers' Predictions of Bankruptcy', *Accounting Review*, 36–49, January 1980a.

——, 'The Usefulness of Accounting Ratios for Subjects' Predictions of Corporate Failure: Replication and Extensions', *Journal of Accounting Research*, 603–13, Autumn 1980b.

CASEY C. J. and N. J., BARTCZAK 'Cash Flow: It's Not The Bottom Line', *Harvard Business Review*, 61–6, July/August 1984.

CASEY, CORNELIUS J. and NORMAN J. BARTCZAK, 'Using Operating Cash Flow Data to Predict Financial Distress: Some Extensions', *Journal of Accounting Research* 23:1, 384–401, Spring 1985.

CASSINO, MICHAEL, 'Cash Flow Analysis: Its Relevance to the Credit and Investment Decision Making Process', *Australian Accountant*, 19–26, July 1987.

CHAMBERS, R. J., *Accounting, Evaluation and Economic Behaviour*, Englewood Cliffs, NJ: Prentice Hall 1966.

——, 'Stock Market Prices and Accounting Research', *Abacus*, 39–54, June 1974.

CHAN, S. Y., J. P. DICKINSON and G. D. DONLEAVY, 'Economic Efficiency and Stock Market Unification', *Securities Bulletin No. 37*, Hong Kong, 30–4, May 1989.

CHAN, W., *Merchants, Mandarins and Modern Enterprise in Late Ching China*, Cambridge, MA: Harvard University Press, 97–102, 1977.

CHANDRA, GYAN, 'A Study of the Consensus on Disclosure Among Public Accountants and Security Analysts', *Accounting Review*, 733–42, October 1974.

CHANG, L. S. and K. S. MOST, 'An International Comparison of Investor Uses of Financial Statements', *International Journal of Accounting*, Fall 1981.

CHARITOU, A. and J. E. KETZ, 'An Empirical Examination of Cash Flow Measures', *Abacus* 27:1, 51–64, March 1991.

CHERNOFF, H., and M. H. RIZVI, 'Effect of Classification Errors on Random Permutations of Features in Representing Multivariate Data by Faces', *Journal of the American Statistical Association*, 584–54, September 1975.

CHERVANY, N. L., and G. W. DICKSON, 'An Experimental Evaluation of Information Overload in a Production Environment', *Management Science*, 1335–44, June 1974.

CHESLEY, G. R. and J. H. SCHEINER, 'The Statement of Changes in Financial Position: An Empirical Investigation of Canadian and US Users in Nonpublic Companies', *International Journal of Accounting* 17:2, 49–58, Summer 1982.

CHEWNING, EUGENE G. JR, 'Information Load and Decision Makers' Cue Utilization Levels', PhD Dissertation, University of South Carolina, 1984.

CHI, MICHELENE T. H., MIRIAM BASSOK, MATTHEW W. LEWIS, PETER REIMANN and ROBERT GLASER, 'Self-Explanations: How Students Study and Use Examples in Learning to Solve Problems', *Cognitive Science* 13:145–82, 1989.

CHIU, ERIC, 'Joint Venture Accounting In China', MBA Dissertation, Hong Kong University, 1992.

CHOI, DANIEL F. S., MANFRED C. HO and ILEX K. K. LAM, 'The Efficiency of the Hong Kong Hang Seng Index Futures Market', working paper MS 89024, Hong Kong Baptist College, October 1989.

CHOI, F. D. S., 'Financial Disclosure and Entry to the European Capital Market', *Journal of Accounting Research*, Autumn 1973.

——, 'European Disclosure: The Competitive Disclosure Hypothesis', *Journal of International Business Studies*, Fall 1974.

——, 'Primary Secondary Reporting: A Cross Cultural Analysis', *International Journal of Accounting*, 83–104, Fall 1980.

——, *Accounting and Financial Reporting in Japan: Current Issues and Future Prospects in a World Economy*, New York: Van Nostrand Reinhold, 1987.

CHOI, F. D. S. and V. BAVISHI, 'International Accounting Standards: Issues Needing Attention', *Journal of Accountancy*, 62–8, March 1983.

CHOI, F. D. S. and G. G. MUELLER, *International Accounting*, Englewood Cliffs, NJ: Prentice Hall, 2nd edition, 1984.

CHOI, F. D. S. and A. SONDHI, 'SFAS No 52 and the Funds Statement', *Corporate Accounting* 2:2, 46–56, Spring 1984.

CHOI SUNG KYU, 'Differential Information Content of Publicly Announced Earnings: Theoretical and Empirical Analysis', PhD Dissertation, University of Iowa, 1985.

CHOW, CHEE W., 'Empirical Studies of the Economic Impacts of Accounting Regulations: Findings, Problems, Prospects', *Journal of Accounting Literature* 2: 73–109, 1983.

CLARK, R. S., 'Statement of Changes in Need of a Change', *CA Magazine*, 26–30, February 1983.

CLARKSON, GEOFFREY P. E., *Portfolio Selection: A Simulation of Trust Investment*, Englewood Cliffs, NJ: Prentice Hall, 1962.

CLEMENS, J. H. and L. S. DYER, *Balance Sheets and the Lending Banker*, London: Europa, 5th edition, 1982.

CLEMENTE, H. A., 'The Funds Flow Statement: Striving for Greater Accuracy', *Financial Executive* 540:12, 27–32, December 1982.

CLIFT, R. C., *The Funds Statement*, Australian Accountants Foundation, Melbourne 1979.

CLOWES, MICHAEL J., 'Study Puts Beta on Back Shelf', *Pensions and Investments* 20:5, 3 and 35, 2 March 1992.

COHEN, J. K., T. C. GILMORE and F. A. SINGER, 'Bank Procedures for Analyzing Business Loan Applications', in K. J. Cohen and F. S. Hammer, eds, *Analytical Methods in Banking*, Homewood, IL: Irwin, 1966.

COHEN, K. C., W. L. NESS, H. OKUDA, R. A. SCHWARTZ and D. K. WHITCOMB, 'The Determinants of Common Stock Returns Volatility: An International Comparison', *Journal of Finance*, 733–52, May 1976.

COKER, JOHN L., 'What Balance Sheets Actually Tell You', *Credit and Financial Management* 88:8, 22–4, September 1986.

COLE, R. H., *Consumer and Commercial Credit Management*, Homewood IL: Irwin, 1984.

COLE, W. M., *Accounts – Their Construction and Interpretation*, Houghton Mifflin, 1908 and 1915 editions.

——, *Accounting and Auditing*, Cree Publishing, 1910.

——, *The Fundamentals of Accounting*, Houghton Mifflin, 1921.

COLEMAN, ALMAND R., 'Restructuring the Statement of Changes in Financial Position', *Financial Executive* 47:1, 34–42, January 1979.

COLLINS, DANIEL W., 'SEC Product Line Reporting and Market Efficiency', *Journal of Financial Economics*, 125–64, June 1975.

COLLINS, D. W., and R. SIMMONDS, 'SEC Line of Business Disclosures and Market Risk Adjustment', *Journal of Accounting Research*, 352–83, Autumn 1989.

COLLINS, N. J., 'Credit Analysis: Concepts and Objectives', in W. H. Baughn and C. E. Walker, eds, *The Bankers Handbook*, Homewood, IL: Dow Jones Irwin, 1966.

COMMITTEE ON CONCEPTS AND STANDARDS FOR EXTERNAL FINANCIAL REPORTS, *Statement on Accounting Theory and Theory Acceptance*, American Accounting Association, 1977.

COOK, GARY JOE, 'An Analysis of Information Search Strategies for Decision Making', PhD Dissertation, Arizona State University, 1987.

COOK, THOMAS and MICHAEL ROZEFF, 'Size and Earnings/Price Ratio Anomalies: One Effect or Two?', *Journal of Financial and Quantitative Analysis* 19: 449–66, December 1984.

COOPER, D., 'Tidiness, Muddle and Things: Commonalities and Divergences in Two Approaches to Management Accounting Research', *Accounting Organizations and Society*, 269–86, 1983.

COOPER, D., D. HAYES and F. WOLF, 'Accounting in Organized Anarchies: Understanding and Designing Accounting Systems in Ambiguous Situations', *Accounting Organizations and Society*, 119–32, 1981.

CORPORATE REPORT (The), *Accounting Standards Steering Committee*, London, through the Institute of Chartered Accountants in England and Wales, August 1975.

COSTIGAN, M. L., 'The Marginal Predictive Ability of Accrual Accounting Information with respect to Future Cash Flows from Operations', PhD Dissertation, St Louis University, 1985.

COURTIS, J. K., 'The Flow of Resources Statement', *Accountants Journal*, 269–73, September 1976.

COWAN, T. K., 'The Statement of Sources and Applications of Funds', *Research Bulletin R-103*, New Zealand Society of Accountants, 3, July 1971.

CRAFT, CLIFFORD JUSTIN, III, 'An Examination of the Decisive Decision Style in Tasks Using Accounting Information', PhD Dissertation, University of Southern California, 1984.

CRONBACH, L. J., *Essentials of Psychological Testing*, London: Harper and Row, 3rd edition, 1970.

DA COSTA, R., J. BOURGEOIS and W. LAWSON, 'A Classification of International Financial Accounting Practices', *International Journal of Accounting*, 73–85, Spring 1978.

DANN, L., 'Common Stock Repurchases: An Analysis of Returns to Common Stockholders and Bondholders', *Journal of Financial Economics* 9:113–38, 1981.

DANOS, PAUL, DORIS L. HOLT and EUGENE A. IMHOFF JR, 'Bondraters' Use of Management Financial Forecasts: An Experiment in Expert Judgement', *Accounting Review*, 547–73, October 1984.

——, 'The Use of Accounting Information in Bank Lending Decisions', *Accounting Organizations and Society* 14:3, 235–46, 1989.

DAWES, R. M., and B. CORRIGAN, 'Linear Models in Decision Making', *Psychological Bulletin*, 95–106, January 1974.

DAWSON, S. M., 'Secondary Stock Market Performance of Initial Public Offers, Hong Kong, Singapore and Malaysia: 1978–1984', *Journal of Business Finance and Accounting* 14:1, 65–76, Spring 1982.

DAY, JUDITH F. S., 'The Use of Annual Reports by UK Investment Analysts', *Accounting and Business Research* 16:64, 295–307, Autumn 1986.

DE RIDDER, JEROME J., 'Comparison of Seven Fundamental Features of the Statement of Changes in Financial Position in the United States, Canada, the United Kingdom, New Zealand and Australia', PhD Dissertation, University of Nebraska-Lincoln, 1980.

DEAKIN, EDWARD B. and SMITH, CHARLES H., 'The Impact of Earnings Information on Selected Foreign Securities Markets', *Journal of International Business Studies*, 43–50, Fall 1978.

DEAKIN, EDWARD B., GYLES R. NORWOOD, and CHARLES H. SMITH, 'The Effect of Published Earnings Information on Tokyo Stock Exchange Trading', *International Journal of Accounting, Education, and Research*, 123–36, Fall 1974.

DEINZER, HARVEY T., *Development of Accounting Thought*, New York: Holt, Rinehart and Winston, 1965.

DELAPORTE, RENE, *Méthode Rationelle de la Tenue des Comptes*, Paris: Encyclopaedie Roret, 1936.

DERMER, J. D., 'Cognitive Characteristics and the Perceived Importance of Information', *Accounting Review*, 511–19, July 1973.

DEWING, A. S., *The Financial Policy of Corporations*, Vol. 1, 5th edition, 708–9, New York: Ronald Press, 1953.

DOLINSKY, CLAUDIA, 'Cultural and Linguistic Barriers to Consumer

Information Processing: Information Overload in a Hispanic Population in the United States', PhD Dissertation, Purdue University, 1984.

DONLEAVY, G. D., 'The Usefulness of Funds Flow Statements', PhD Dissertation, Glasgow University, 1991.

DOUGHTERTY, W. H., 'Financial Reporting: A Banker Looks at the Scene', *Financial Executive* 46:12, 47–53, December 1978.

DOUPNIK, TIMOTHY S., 'Evidence of International Harmonization of Financial Reporting', *International Journal of Accounting* 23:1, 47–57, 1987.

DOUPNIK, TIMOTHY S. and MARTIN E. TAYLOR, 'An Empirical Investigation of the Observance of IASC Standards in Western Europe', *Management International Review* 25:1, 27–33, First Quarter 1985.

DOWNES, DAVID and THOMAS DYCKMAN, 'A Critical Look at the Efficient Market Empirical Research Literature as it Relates to Accounting Information', *Accounting Review*, 300–17, April 1973.

DREMAN, DAVID, 'Bye-Bye to Beta', *Forbes* 149:7, 148, 30 March 1992.

DRIVER, M. J., 'The Relationship between Abstractness of Conceptual Functioning and Group Performance in a Complex Decision Making Environment', Masters Thesis, Princeton University, 1960.

DRTINA, R. E. and J. A. LARGAY III, 'Pitfalls in Calculating Cash Flow from Operations', *Accounting Review* 60:2, 314–26, April 1985.

DRURY, D. H., 'Effects of Accounting Practice Divergence: Canada and the United States', *Journal of International Business Studies* 75–87, Fall 1979.

DYCKMAN, T. R., M. GIBBINS and R. J. SWIERINGA, 'Experimental and Survey Research in Financial Accounting: A Review and Evaluation in the Impact of Accounting Research on Practice and Disclosure', ed. A. R. ABDEL KHALIK and T. F. KELLER, 48–105, Durham, NC: Duke University Press, 1978.

EASTON, P. D., 'Empirical Aspects of an Information Perspective on Accounting', PhD Dissertation, University of California-Berkeley, 1984.

EASTON, G. PETER and PATRICIA C. O'BRIEN, 'The Relative Information Content of Accruals and Cash Flows: Combined Evidence at the Earnings Announcement and Annual Report Release Date/Discussion', *Journal of Accounting Research Supplement* 24, 165–203, 1986.

EBBESEN, E. and V. KONECNI, 'Decision Making and Information Integration in the Courts; The Setting of Bail', *Journal of Personality and Social Psychology*, 805–21, 1975.

ED 37/RELEASE 410, 'Proposed Amendment to Statement of Accounting Standards AAS 12 and Approved Accounting Standard ASRB 1007 to require Disclosure of Cash Flow from Operations', Caulfield Victoria, AARF: and Sydney, ASRB: July 1986.

ED 54, *Cash Flow Statements*, London: Accounting Standards Committee of the CCAB, July 1990.

EDWARDS, JAMES DON, 'Some Significant Developments of Public Accounting in the United States', *Business History Review* 30: 211–25, June 1956.

EDWARDS, J. R. and H. J. MELLETT, *Introduction to Accountancy for Banking Students*, London: Institute of Bankers, 1985.

EGGINGTON, D. A., 'In Defence of Profit Measurement: Some Limitations of Cash Flow and Value Added as Performance Measures for External Reporting', *Accounting and Business Research* 15:54, 99–112, Spring 1984.

——, 'Cash Flow, Profit and Performance Measures for External Reports: A Rejoinder', *Accounting and Business Research* 15:58, 108–12, Spring 1985.

EINHORN, H. J., 'Use of Nonlinear, Noncompensatory Models as a Function of Task and Amount of Information', *Organization Behavior and Human Performance* 6: 1–27, 1971.

EINHORN, H. and R. A. HOGARTH, 'Confidence in Judgment: Persistence in the Illusion of Validity', *Psychological Review*, 394–416, September 1978.

——, 'Unit Weighting Schemes in Decision Making', *Organization Behavior and Human Performance* 85: 14, 1979.

EINHORN, H. J., D. N. KLEINMUNTZ and B. KLEINMUNTZ, 'Linear Regression and Process Tracing Models of Judgment', *Psychological Review* 86: 465–85, 1979.

EL SHAMY, MOSTAFA AHMED, 'The Predictive Ability of Financial Ratios: A Test of Alternative Models', PhD Dissertation, New York University, Graduate School of Business Administration, 1989.

ELLIOT, EDWARD L., *The Nature and Stages of Accounting Development in Latin America*, Urbana-Champaign, IL: Center for International Education and Research in Accounting, 1968.

ELSTEIN, A. S., L. E. SHULMAN and S. A. SPRAFKA, *Medical Problem Solving: An Analysis of Clinical Reasoning*, Harvard University Press, 1978.

EMANUEL, D. M., 'Asset Revaluations and Share Price Revisions', *Journal of Business Finance and Accounting* 16:2 213–27, Spring 1989.

EMMANUEL, CHRISTINE B., 'Cash Flow Reporting Part 2: Importance of Cash Flow Data in Credit Analysis', *Journal of Commercial Bank Lending* 70:10, 16–28, June 1988.

ENGLARD, BARUCH and PHILLIP GOODMAN, 'The Statement of Changes: Past History and Present Status', *Massachusetts CPA Review* 60:3, 32–4, Summer 1986.

ENIS, CHARLES R., 'The Impact of Current Valued Data on the Predictive Judgments of Investors', *Accounting Organizations and Society* 13:2, 123–45, 1988.

EPSTEIN, M. J., *The Usefulness of Annual Reports to Corporate Shareholders*, Los Angeles Bureau of Economic and Business Research at Cal State University, 1975.

ESTES, R. N. and M. REIMER, 'A Study of the Effect of Qualified Audit Opinions on Bankers Lending Decisions', *Accounting and Business Research*, 250–9, Autumn 1977.

EYES, ALAN D. and BRUCE J. TABB, 'Bank Managers' Use of Financial Statements', *Accountants Journal*, 81–5, April 1978.

FAMA, E. and MacBETH, J. 'Risk, Return and Equilibrium: Empirical Tests', *Journal of Political Economy* 91:2, 601–36, May/June 1973.

FAMA, E., L. FISHER, M. JENSEN and R. ROLL, 'The Adjustment of

Stock Prices to New Information', *International Economic Review* 10:1–21, February 1969.

FAMA, EUGENE F., 'Efficient Capital Markets: A Review of Theory and Empirical Work', *Journal of Finance*, 383–417, May 1970.

——, 'Stock Returns, Expected Returns, and Real Activity', *Journal of Finance* 45:4, 1089–1108, September 1990.

——, 'Efficient Capital Markets: II', *Journal of Finance* 46:5, 1575–1617, December 1991.

FAMA, EUGENE F., and KENNETH R. FRENCH, 'Permanent and Temporary Components of Stock Prices', *Journal of Political Economy* 96:2, 246–73, April 1988.

——, 'The Cross Section of Expected Stock Returns', *Journal of Finance* 47:2, 427–65, June 1992.

FARRAGHER, EDWARD T. and ALAN REINSTEIN, 'Using the Statement of Cash Flows', *Real Estate Finance* 5:3, 59–64, Fall 1988.

FASB, *Economic Consequences of Financial Accounting Standards*, Stamford: FASB, July 1978a.

——, 'Objectives of Financial Reporting by Business Enterprises', *Statement of Financial Accounting Concepts No 1*, Stamford: FASB, 1978b.

——, Discussion Memorandum, *An Analysis of Issues Related to Reporting Funds Flows, Liquidity, and Financial Flexibility*, Stamford: FAS Board, 15 December 1980.

——, *Reporting Income, Cash Flows, and Financial Position of Business Enterprises*, Exposure Draft, FASB, 1981.

——, *Statement of Cash Flows*, Exposure Draft, FASB 1986.

FELDMAN, M. S., and J. G. MARCH, 'Information as Signal and Symbol', *Administrative Science Quarterly*, 171–86, 1981.

FERTAKIS, J. P., 'On Communication, Understanding and Relevance in Accounting Reporting', *Accounting Review*, 680–91, October 1969.

FESS, P. E., and J. WEYGANDT, 'Cash Flow Presentations – Trends, Recommendations', *Journal of Accountancy*, 52–9, August 1969.

FINANCIAL ANALYSTS' FEDERATION, 'News Report', *Journal of Accountancy*, 9–10, June 1964.

FINANCIAL EXECUTIVES RESEARCH FOUNDATION, 'The Funds Statement: How Can It Be Improved?', *Financial Executive*, 52–5, October 1984.

FINN, F. J., 'Internal Evaluation of Security Analysts' Research', University of Queensland working paper, February 1982.

FINNEY, H. A., 'The Statement of Application of Funds', *Journal of Accountancy*, 460–1, December 1923.

——, 'Statement of Application of Funds; A Reply to Mr Esquerre', *Journal of Accountancy* 39: 497–511, June 1925.

FIRTH, M. A., 'A Study of the Consensus of the Perceived Importance of Disclosure of Individual Items in Corporate Annual Reports', *Journal of Accounting*, 57–70, Fall 1978.

——, 'The Incidence and Impact of Capitalization Issues', Occasional Paper No. 3, London: The Institute of Chartered Accountants in England and Wales, 1974.

——, 'The Impact of Earnings Announcements on Share Price Behaviour of Similar Firm Types', *Economic Journal*, 296–306, June 1976.

——, 'Consensus Views and Judgment Models in Materiality Decisions', *Accounting Organizations and Society* 4:4, 283–95, 1979.

FITZGERALD, M. D., 'An Investigation into the Relationship Between Information Flows and Stock Market Prices', PhD Thesis, Manchester Business School, 1974.

——, 'A Proposed Characterisation of U.K. Brokerage Firms and Their Effects on Market Prices and Returns', in Edwin J. Elton, and Martin J. Gruber, eds, *International Capital Markets*, Amsterdam: North-Holland, 19758.

FORD, J. KEVIN, NEAL SCHMITT, SUSAN L. SCHECHTMAN, BRIAN M. HULTS and MARY L. DOHERTY, *Organizational Behavior and Human Decision Processes* 43:1, 75–117, February 1989.

FOSTER, G., 'Intra Industry Information Transfers Associated with Earnings Releases', *Journal of Accounting and Economics*, 201–32, December 1981.

FOWLER, D. J., C. RORKE and A. L. RIDIN, 'Thin Trading, Errors in Variables, and the Market Model', Working Paper 77–47, Faculty of Management, McGill University, Canada, October 1977.

FRANK, W., 'An Empirical Analysis of International Accounting Principles', *Journal of Accounting Research*, 593–605, Autumn 1979.

FRANZ, DAVID P., and JAMES B. THIES, 'Intertemporal Divergence Among Cash Flow, Working Capital, and Income from Operations', *Review of Business and Economic Research* 23:2, 18–28, Spring 1988.

FREEMAN, R. N., 'The Disclosure of Replacement Cost Accounting Data and Its Effect on Transaction Volumes: A Comment', *Accounting Review*, 177–80, January 1981.

FRIEDLAND, JONATHAN, 'A Call to Account', *Far Eastern Economic Review*, 9 November 1989.

FRISHKOFF, PAUL, PATRICIA A. FRISHKOFF and MARINUS J. BOUWMAN, 'Use of Accounting Data in Screening by Financial Analysts', *Journal of Accounting Auditing and Finance* 8:1, 44–53, Fall 1984.

FULLER, RUSSELL J., and JOHN L. KLING, 'Is the Stock Market Predictable?', *Journal of Portfolio Management* 16:4, 28–36, Summer 1990.

GAFFIKIN, M. J. R. 'The Methodology of Early Accounting Theorists', *Abacus* 23:1, 17–30, 1987.

GAHARAN, CATHERINE INNES GREEN, 'A Comparison of the Effectiveness of the Operating Funds Flow Measures of Cash, Net Quick Assets, and Working Capital in Predicting Future Cash Flow', PhD Dissertation, The Louisiana State University and Agricultural and Mechanical College, 1988.

GAHLON, JAMES M., and ROBERT L. VIGELAND, 'Early Warning Signs of Bankruptcy Using Cash Flow Analysis', *Journal of Commercial Bank Lending* 71:4, 4–15, December 1988.

GARDELLA, ROBERT, 'The Development of Accounting in the West, China and Japan', *Academy of Accounting Historians* working paper no. 60 issued 1983 then reissued in their collected papers, Vol. 3, ed. A. C. Bishop and D. R. Richards in 1984.

GENTRY, JAMES A., PAUL NEWBOLD and DAVID T. WHITFORD,

'Predicting Bankruptcy', *Financial Analysts Journal* 41:5, 47–55, September/October 1985a.

——, 'Classifying Bankrupt Firms with Funds Flow Components', *Journal of Accounting Research* 23:1, 146–60, Spring 1985b.

——, 'Funds Flow Components, Financial Ratios and Bankruptcy' *Journal of Business Finance and Accounting* 14:4, 595–606, Winter 1987.

GHOSE, T. K., *The Banking System of Hong Kong*, Singapore:Butterworths, 1987.

GIACOMINO, D. E. and D. E. MIELKE, 'Preparation and Use of Cash Flow Statements', *CPA Journal*, 30–5, March 1987.

——, 'Using the Statement of Cash Flows to Analyze Corporate Performance', *Management Accounting* 69:11, 54–7, May 1988.

GIBBONS, J. D., *Nonparametric Statistical Inference*, New York: Marcel Dekker, 2nd edition, 1985.

GIBSON, CHARLES H. and MERRY M. KRUSE, 'The Statement of Changes is Changing', *Woman CPA* 46:4, 24–8, October 1984.

GIBSON, CHARLES H., T. P. KLAMMER and S. A. REED, 'The Cash Flow Statement', *CPA Journal* 56:11, 18–38, November 1986.

GIESE, J. W. and T. P. KLAMMER, 'Achieving the Objectives of APB Opinion No 19', *Journal of Accountancy* 137:3, 54–61, March 1974.

GLAUTIER, M. W., G. UNDERDOWN and A. C. CLARK, *Basic Accounting Practice*, London: Pitman, 128–147, 1978.

GOLDBERG, L. R., 'The Funds Statement Reconsidered', *Accounting Review*, 485–91, October 1951.

——, 'Man Versus Model of Man: A Rationale, Plus Some Evidence, for A Method of Improving on Clinical Inferences', *Psychological Bulletin*, 422–32, June 1970.

GOLDSTEIN, K. M., 'Cognitive Style: Five Approaches', Ch. 5 of *Integrative Complexity*, 136–72, 1978.

GOLUB, S. J. and H. D. HOFFMAN, 'Cash Flow: Why It Should be Stressed in Financial Reporting', *Financial Executive* 52:2, 34–40, February 1984.

GOMBOLA, M. J. and J. E. KETZ, 'A Note on Cash Flows and Classification Patterns of Financial Ratios', *Accounting Review*, 105–14, January 1983.

GONEDES, NICHOLAS J., 'Evidence on the Information Content of Accounting Messages: Accounting Based and Market Based Estimates of Systematic Risk', *Journal of Financial and Quantitative Analysis*, 407–44, July 1973.

——, 'Capital Market Equilibrium and Annual Accounting Numbers: Empirical Evidence', *Journal of Accounting Research*, 26–62, Spring 1974.

——, 'A Note on Accounting-Based and Market-Based Measures of Systematic Risk', *Journal of Financial and Quantitative Analysis*, 355–65, June 1975.

GONEDES, N. J. and N. DOPUCH, 'Capital Market Equilibrium, Information Production and Selective Accounting, Techniques: Theoretical Framework and Review of Empirical Work', *Journal of Accounting Research* Supplement no. 12, 48–169, 1974.

GOODRICH, PETER SPANG, 'Grouping National Accounting Policies:

A Q Factor Analysis', Leeds University School of Economic Studies, Discussion Paper No. 96, July 1980.

——, 'A Typology of International Accounting Principles and Policies', *AUTO Review*, 1982.

——, 'Cross National Financial Accounting Linkages: An Empirical Political Analysis', *British Accounting Review* 18:2, 42–60, 1986.

GOODSTADT, LEO, 'The End of Personal Guarantees?', *Far East Economic Review*, 6 November 1986.

GORDON, M. J., 'Postulates and Research in Accounting', *Accounting Review*, 251–63, April 1964.

GOVINDARAJAN, V., 'The Objectives of Financial Statements: An Empirical Study of the Use of Cash Flows and Earnings by Security Analysts', *Accounting Organizations and Society* 5:4, 383–92, 1980.

GRACI, S. P., 'Effects of the Statement of Changes in Financial Position on the Short Term Loan Decision', PhD Dissertation, University of Arkansas, 1982.

GRANIT, R. and C. G. PHILLIPS, 'Excitatory and Inhibitory Processes Acting upon Individual Purkinje Cells of the Cerebellum in Cats', *Journal of Physiology* 133: 520–47, 1956.

GRANT, EDWARD B., 'Market Implications of Differential Amounts of Interim Information', *Journal of Accounting Research*, 255–68, Spring 1980.

GRAY, S. J., 'Segment Reporting and the EEC Multinationals', *Journal of Accounting Research*, 242–53, Autumn 1978a.

——, 'Management Forecasts and European Multinational Company Reporting', *Journal of International Business Studies*, 21–32, Fall 1978b.

——, 'Statistical Information and Extensions in European Financial Disclosure', *International Journal of Accounting*, 27–40, Spring 1978c.

——, 'The Impact of International Accounting Differences from a Security Analysis Perspective: Some European Evidence', *Journal of Accounting Research*, 64–76, Spring 1980.

——, 'International Accounting: A Review of Academic Research in the United Kingdom', *International Journal of Accounting* 19:1, 15–32, 1985.

——, 'Towards a Theory of Cultural Influence on the Development of Accounting Systems Internationally', *Abacus* 24:1, 1–15, 1988.

GRAY, S. J., L. G. CAMPBELL and J. C. SHAW, *International Financial Reporting*, Chapter 4, pp. 189–221, Basingstoke: Macmillan, 1984.

GREEN, WILMER L., *History and Survey of Accountancy*, New York: Standard Press Texts, 29–30, 128, 1930.

GREENBERG, ROBERT R., G. L. JOHNSON and K. RAMESH, 'Earnings Versus Cash Flow as a Predictor of Future Cash Flow Measures', *Journal of Accounting Auditing and Finance* 1:4, 266–77, Fall 1986.

GUL, FERDINAND A., 'The Effects of Uncertainty Reporting on Lending Officers' Perceptions of Risk and Additional Information Required', *Abacus* 23:2, 172–9, 1987.

HAGERMAN, R. L., 'The Efficiency of the Market for Bank Stocks: An Empirical Test', *Journal of Money, Credit and Banking*, 846–55, August 1973.

HAKANSSON, NILS, 'Empirical Research in Accounting, 1960–70: An Appraisal', in N. DOPUCH and L. REVSINE, eds, *Accounting*

Research, 1960–70: A Critical Evaluation, Urbana, IL: Center for International Education and research in Accounting, 137–73, 1973.

HALL, S. 'The Rediscovery of Ideology: Return of the Repressed in Media Studies', in M. Gurevitch, T. Bennett, J. Curran and J. Curran and J. Woolacott, eds, *Culture, Society and Media*, London: Methuen, 59–60, 1982.

HAMMAD, AHMED HANY, 'The Relationship of Alternative Accounting Signals to Market Beta and to Changes in Security Prices', PhD Dissertation, North Texas State University, 1983.

HAN KAN HONG, 'The Funds Statement and Cash Flows', *SES Journal*, Singapore, 16–21, October 1981.

HARMON, W. KEN, 'Earnings Versus Funds Flows: An Empirical Investigation of Market Reaction', *Journal of Accounting Auditing and Finance* 8:1, 24–34, Fall 1984.

HARRISON, G. L. and J. L. McKINNON, 'Cultural and Accounting Change: A New Perspective on Corporate Reporting Regulation and Accounting Policy Formulation', *Accounting Organisations and Society* 11:3, 1986.

HARRISON, T., 'Different Market Reactions to Discretionary and Non Discretionary Accounting Changes', *Journal of Accounting Research*, 84–107, Spring 1977.

HASSANLI, E., 'Predictors of Cash Flows', *Journal of Business Forecasting* 7:3, 8–10, Fall 1988.

HAWKINS, DAVID F., 'The Development of Modern Financial Reporting Practices Among American Manufacturing Corporations', *Business History Review* 37: 135–68, Autumn 1963.

HAWKINS, DAVID F. and WALTER J. CAMPBELL, *Equity Valuation: Models, Analysis and Implications*, New York: Financial Executives Research Foundation, 1978.

HAYES, J. R., 'Human Data Processing Limits in Decision Making', in E. Bennett, ed., *Information System Science and Engineering. Proceedings of the First Congress on the Information Systems Sciences*, New York: McGraw-Hill, 1964.

HEATH, LOYD C., *Financial Reporting and the Evaluation of Solvency*, Accounting Research Monograph No. 3, New York: AICPA, 1978a.

——, 'Let's Scrap the Funds Statement', *Journal of Accountancy* 146:4, 94–103, October 1978b.

——, 'Is Working Capital Really Working?', *Journal of Accountancy* 148: 55–62, August 1980.

——, 'Cash Receipts and Payments Versus Income Reconciliation', *Cash Flow Accounting Conference Proceedings*, 164–71, 1982.

——, 'Cash Flow Reporting: Bankers Need a Direct Approach', *Journal of Commercial Bank Lending*, February 1987, reproduced in RMA, *Cash Flow*, Philadelphia: Robert Morris Associates, 9–19, 1989.

HENDRICK, C., J MILLS and C. A. KIESLER, 'Decision Time As A Function of the Number and Complexity of Equally Attractive Alternatives', *Journal of Personality and Social Psychology* 8: 313–18, 1968.

HENDRIKSEN, E. S., *Accounting Theory*, Homewood, IL: R. D. Irwin, 3rd edition, 1977.

HENRY, EVAN J., 'A New Funds Statement for Greater Disclosure', *Journal of Accountancy* 139:4, 56–62, April 1975.

HICKS, BARRY E., 'The Cash Flow Basis of Accounting', Cash Flow Accounting: Papers of the International Conference on Cash Flow Accounting held in August 1980, eds Barry E. Hicks and Pearson Hunt, Laurentian University, Sudbury, Ontario, Canada, 1981.

HILTEBEITEL, KENNETH MERRILL, 'The Accounting Standards Overload Issue: An Empirical Test of the Effect of Four Selected Financial Accounting Standards on the Lending Decisions of Bankers', PhD Dissertation, Drexel University, 1985.

HO, SHIH-JEN KATHY, 'The Usefulness of Cash Flows Relative to Accrual Earnings: A Security Valuation Study', PhD Dissertation, Syracuse University, 1988.

HODGMAN, D. R., *Commercial Bank Loan and Investment Policy*, University of Illinois Bureau of Economic and Business Research, 1963.

HOFFMAN, P. J., 'The Paramorphic Representation of Clinical Judgement', *Psychological Bulletin* 47:116–31, 1960.

HOFSTEDE, G., *Culture's Consequences*, Beverly Hills: Sage, 1980.

——, 'Dimensions of National Cultures in Fifty Countries and Three Regions', in J. B. Deregowski, S. Dziurawiec and R. Annis, eds, *Explorations in Cross Cultural Psychology*, Zurich: Swits and Zeitlinger, 1983.

——, 'Cultural Dimensions in Management and Planning', *Asia Pacific Journal of Management*, January 1984.

HOGARTH, R., and S. MAKRIDAKIS, 'Forecasting and Planning: An Evaluation', *Management Science*, 115–38, February 1981.

HOLLOWAY, NIGEL, 'A Numbers Problem', *Far Eastern Economic Review*, 74–5, 9 November 1989.

HOLMES, GEOFFREY, 'Standardise Funds Statements', *Accountancy* 87:995, 88–94, July 1976.

HONG, HAI, GERSHON MANDELKER and ROBERT KAPLAN, 'Pooling versus Purchase: The Effects of Accounting for Mergers on Stock Prices', *Accounting Review*, 31–47, January 1978.

HOOPER, P. and J. PAGE, 'Better Financial Statements for Corporate Valuation', *Management Accounting*, 52–6, September 1979.

HOSHOWER, LEON B., and JOSEPH A. VERSAGGI, 'Financial Statement Users' Interpretations of Accounting Data', *Ohio CPA Journal* 44:2, 31–4, Spring 1985.

HUNT, J. McV., 'Motivation Inherent in Information Processing and Action', in C. J. Harvey, ed., *Motivation and Social Interaction; Cognitive Determinants*, New York: Ronald Press, 35–94, 1963.

HUSBAND, GEORGE R., 'The Corporate Entity Fiction and Accounting Theory', *Accounting Review* 133:3, 242, September 1938.

HUSBAND, G. R. and D. E. THOMAS, *Principles of Accounting*, 609, Boston: Houghton Mifflin, 1935.

IASC, 'Statement of Changes in Financial Position', *IAS no 7*, London, 1977.

——, 'Survey of the Use and Application of International Accounting Standards 1988', London: International Accounting Standards Committee, 1988.

——, *Framework for the Preparation of Financial Statements*, reproduced pp. 22–9 of the *Certified Accountant*, October 1989.

ICAA – Institute of Chartered Accountants in Australia, *Statements of Source and Application of Funds*, Technical Bulletin F1, Sydney: ICAA, 1971.

IJIRI, Y., 'Recovery Rate and Cash Flow Accounting', *Financial Executive*, 54–60, March 1980.

IP, P. N., 'Betas of Hong Kong Stocks and Their Investment Value', *Hong Kong Economic Journal*, 61–7, April 1982.

IRISH, R. A., 'The Evolution of Corporate Accounting', *The Australian Accountant* 17: 480–501, November 1947.

IRVINE, BRUCE V., 'Setting Accounting Standards for the World', *CMA Magazine* 62:3, 13–17, April 1988.

ISELIN, ERROL R., 'The Effects of Information Load and Information Diversity on Decision Quality in a Structured Decision Task', *Accounting, Organizations and Society* 13:2, 147–64, 1988.

ISMAIL, B. E. and J. C. RAE, 'Improving Funds Flow Forecasts', *Journal of Business Forecasting* 3:3, 11–14, Autumn 1984.

JACOB, RUDOLPH AUBREY, 'The Time Series Behavior and Informational Content of Selected Cash Flow Variables', PhD Dissertation, New York University Graduate School of Business Administration, 1987.

JACOBS, BRUCE and R. S. KAPLAN, 'Accounting Alternatives and the Steady State Rates of Return of Stock Prices', Carnegie-Mellon University working paper 54–74–75 presented to the Stanford Research Seminar of 1975.

JACOBY, J., D. MAZURSKY, T. TROUTMAN and A. KUSS, 'When Feedback is Ignored: Disutility of Outcome Feedback', *Journal of Applied Psychology* 69: 531–45, 1984.

JACOBY, J., D. E. SPELLER and C. A. KOHN, 'Brand Choice Behavior as a Function of Information Load', *Journal of Marketing Research* 11: 63–9, 1974.

JAEDICKE, R. K. and R. T. SPROUSE, *Accounting Flows: Income Funds and Cash*, Englewood Cliffs, NJ: Prentice Hall, 78–135, 1965.

JAFFE, JEFFREY F., 'Special Information and Insider Trading', *Journal of Business*, 410–28, July 1974.

JAFFE, JEFFREY, DONALD B. KEIM and RANDOLPH WESTERFIELD, 'Earnings Yields, Market Values, and Stock Returns', *Journal of Finance* 44:1, 135–48, March 1989.

JENSEN, M. C. and W. MECKLING, 'The Theory of the Firm: Managerial Behavior, Agency Costs and Ownership Structure', *Journal of Financial Economics*, 305–60, October 1976.

JICPA, *Corporate Disclosure in Japan – Overview*, Japan Institute of CPAs, 1987.

JOHNSON, E. J., *Expertise and Decision Under Uncertainty; Performance and Process*, working paper, Carnegie Mellon University, 1985.

JONG HYEON HUH, 'The Traditional Accounting Systems in the Oriental Countries – Korea China Japan', *Academy of Accounting Historians working paper 22*, 1976 and in their working paper collection, ed. N. Coffman, Vol. 2, issued in 1979.

JOYCE, E. J., 'Expert Judgement in Audit Program Planning', *Journal of Accounting Research Supplement*, 29–60, 1976.

JOYCE, E. J. and G. C. BIDDLE, 'Are Auditors' Judgements Sufficiently Regressive?', *Journal of Accounting Research*, Autumn 1981.

KAMAROTOU, H., and J. O'HANLON, 'Informational Efficiency in the UK, US, Canadian and Japanese Equity Markets: A Note', *Journal of Business Finance and Accounting* 16:2, 183–92, Spring 1989.

KAN, NELSON, 'The Need Hierarchy of Small/Medium Chinese Trading/Manufacturing Firms and its Implications on the Strategy of Local Chinese Banks', MBA Dissertation, Hong Kong University, 1985.

KAPLAN, ROBERT S., 'The Information Content of Financial Accounting Numbers: A Survey of Empirical Evidence', in R. A. ABDEL-KHALIK and T. F. KELLER, eds, *The Impact of Accounting Research on Practice and Disclosure*, Durham, NC: Duke University Press, 134–73, 1978.

KAPLAN, R. S. and RICHARD ROLL, 'Investor Evaluation of Accounting Information: Some Empirical Evidence', *Journal of Business*, 225–57, April 1972.

KEANE, S. M., *Stock Market Efficiency: Theory, Evidence, Implications*, Oxford: Philip Alan, 1983.

KEIM, D. B., 'Size Related Anomalies and Stock Return Seasonality: Further Empirical Evidence', *Journal of Financial Economics*, 13–32, June 1983.

KELLER, KEVIN LANE and RICHARD STAELIN, 'Effects of Quality and Quantity of Information on Decision Effectiveness', *Journal of Consumer Research* 14:2, 200–13, September 1987.

KEMPNER, J. J., 'The Statement of Application of Funds in Modern Corporate Accounting Practice', Doctoral Dissertation, 114, Ohio State University, 1956.

KENLEY, W. J. and G. J. STAUBUS, 'Funds Statements', Chapter 5 of *Objectives and Concepts of Financial Statements: Accounting Research Study No. 3*, Melbourne: Accounting Research Foundation, 27–8, 1972.

KETZ, J. E., 'New Look of the Funds Statement', *FE: The Magazine for Financial Executives* 1:74–6, January/February 1985.

KETZ, J. E. and R. F. KOCHANEK, 'Funds Flow Statements', *Financial Executives*, 34–41, July 1982.

KETZ, J. EDWARD and JAMES A. LARGAY III, 'Reporting Income and Cash Flows from Operations', *Accounting Horizons* 1:2, 9–17, June 1987.

KHAMBATA, FARIDA and DARA KHAMBATA, 'Emerging Capital Markets: A Case Study of Equity Markets in India', *Journal of Developing Areas* 23:3, 425–37, April 1989.

KIDDER, LOUISE H., *Research Methods in Social Relations*, 122–43, New York: Holt Saunders International, 4th edition, 1981.

KIGER, JACK E., 'An Empirical Investigation of NYSE Volume and Price Reactions to the Announcement of Quarterly Earnings', *Journal of Accounting Research*, 113–28, Spring 1972.

KIM, JAE-IL, 'The Effects of Information Heterogeneity on Decision Making Processes in the Buying Center', PhD Dissertation, University of California, Berkeley, 1986.

KIRKMAN, P. R. A., 'What Can We Learn from Published Accounts in the USA?', *Accounting and Business Research*, 329–34, Autumn 1971.

KISTLER, LINDA H., and JOHN G. HAMER, 'Understanding the New Statement of Cash Flows', *Corporate Accounting* 6:1, 3–9, Winter 1988.

KLAMMER, THOMAS P., and SARAH REED, 'Operating Cash Flow Formats: Does Format Influence?', *Journal of Accounting & Public Policy* 9:3, 217–35, Fall 1990.

KLEMMER, E. T. and P. F. MULLER, 'The Rate of Handling Information in Key Pressing Responses to Light Patterns', *Human Factors Operations Research Lab Memo 34*, March 1953.

KOCH, BARRY, 'Funds Statements', Part II, Chapter 6, 113–28 of the *World Survey of Published Accounts*, ed. D. J. Tonkin, London: Lafferty Publications, 1989.

KOCHANEK, RICHARD and CORINE T. NORGAARD, 'Funds Statements: Why the Focus Has Changed from Working Capital to Cash Flow', *FE: The Magazine for Financial Executives* 3:1, 27–30, January 1987.

KOHLER, E. L. and P. L. MORRISON, *Principles of Accounting*, 337–9, New York: McGraw-Hill, 2nd edition, 1931.

KORIAT, A., S. LICHTENSTEIN and B. FISCHOFF, 'Reasons for Confidence', *Journal of Experimental Psychology: Human Learning and Memory*, 107–18, March 1980.

KOZUMA, YOSHINAO, 'Accounting and Reporting: Regulation and Practice', in F. D. S. CHOI and K. HIRAMATSU, eds, *Accounting and Financial Reporting in Japan*, 38–53, Wokingham: Van Nostrand Reinhold, 1987.

KRASNOFF, MITCHELL M., 'Recognition and Measurement – The End of the FASB's Conceptual Framework Project', *Corporate Accounting* 3:3, 67–70, Summer 1985.

KREUZE, JERRY G., 'Tracking a Client's Cash Flow: Understanding the New Reporting Proposal', *National Public Accountant* 32:3, 16–18, March 1987.

LACLAU, E., *Politics and Ideology in Marxist Theory*, London: New Left Books, 1977.

LAFFERTY, M. and D. CAIRNS, *Financial Times World Survey of Annual Reports 1980*, London: Financial Times Business Information, 1980.

LAPPIN, J. S. and K. DISCH, 'The Latency Operating Characteristic, I: Effects of Stimulus Probability on Choice Reaction Time', *Journal of Experimental Psychology* 92: 419–27, 1972.

——, 'The Latency Operating Characteristic, II: Effects of Visual Stimulus on Choice Reaction Time, *Journal of Experimental Psychology* 93, 367–72, 1972b.

——, 'The Latency Operating Characteristic III, Temporal Uncertainty Effects, *Journal of Experimental Psychology* 98: 279–85, 1973.

LARGAY, J. A. and C. P. STICKNEY, 'Cash Flows, Ratio Analysis and the W. T. Grant Bankruptcy', *Financial Analysts Journal*, 50–4, July/August 1979.

LAU, AMY HING LING, 'On the Prediction of Firms in Financial Distress with an Evaluation of Alternative Funds Flow Concepts', PhD Thesis, Washington University, 1982.

LAU, E., 'Hong Kong Stock Market from the International Investment Perspective', paper for the City Polytechnic Conference 'Investment in Hong Kong', Hong Kong, June 1987.

LAU, SHEILA C., S. R. QUAY, and C. M. RAMSEY, 'The Tokyo Stock Exchange and the Capital Asset Pricing Model', *Journal of Finance*, 507–14, May 1974.

LAUGHLIN, R. C. and A. G. PUXTY, 'Accounting Regulation: An Alternative Perspective', University of Sheffield discussion paper, March 1982.

LAW, C. K., 'The Efficiency of the Hong Kong Stock Market', *Hong Kong Economic Journal Monthly* 28:47–8, 1979.

——, 'A Test of the Efficient Market Hypothesis with Respect to the Recent Behaviour of the Hong Kong Stock Market', *Developing Economies* 20:61–72, 1982.

LAW, C. K. and K. W. AU YEUNG, 'A Test of Takeovers and Pricing Efficiency of Hong Kong Stock Market', in Y. K. HO and C. K. LAW, eds, *The Hong Kong Financial Markets: Empirical Evidence*, Kowloon, Hong Kong: University Printer and Publisher, 193–210, 1983.

LAWSON, G. H., 'Cash Flow Accounting', *The Accountant*, 586–9, 28 October 1971, and 620–2, 4 November 1971.

——, 'A New Approach to Cash Flow Analysis', *The Accountant*, 13–20, 10/17 February 1983.

——, 'The Measurement of Corporate Performance on a Cash Flow Basis: A Reply to Mr Eggington', *Accounting and Business Research* 15:58, 99–107, Spring 1985.

LEE, C. JEVONS, 'Fundamental Analysis and the Stock Market', *Journal of Business Finance and Accounting* 14:1 131–41, Spring 1987.

LEE, G. A., *Modern Financial Accounting*, London: Thomas Nelson, 176–81, 1975.

LEE, T. A., 'The Relevance of Accounting Information Including Cash Flows', *The Accountants Magazine* 76:1, 30–4, January 1972a.

——, 'The Nature and Purpose of Cash Flow Reporting', *The Accountants Magazine* 76:4, 198–200, April 1972b.

——, 'The Contribution of Fisher to Cash Flow Accounting: A Resolution of the Accounting Entity Dilemma', *Journal of Business Finance and Accounting* 6:3, 321–30, Autumn 1979.

——, 'Reporting Cash Flows and Realisable Values', *Accounting and Business Research*, Spring 1981a.

——, 'Support for Cash Flow Accounting', *The Accountants Magazine* 85: 146, 162, May 1981b.

——, 'Cash Flow Accounting and the Corporate Financial Report', in M. BROMWICH and A. G. HOPWOOD, eds, *Essays in British Accounting Research*, 63–78, London: Pitman, 1981c.

——, 'Cash Flow Accounting and the Allocation Problem', *Journal of Business Finance and Accounting* 9:3, 341–53, Autumn 1982.

——, 'SSAP10 and Cash Flow Analysis', *Accountants Magazine*, 232–3, June 1984a.

——, *Cash Flow Accounting*, New York: Van Nostrand Reinhold, 1984b.

——, 'Cash Flow Accounting, Profit and Performance Measurement: A Response to a Challenge', *Accounting and Business Research* 15:58, 93–7, Spring 1985.

——, 'Restricting the Domain and Potential of Cash Flow Accounting', *Accounting and Business Research* 20:80, 355–8, Autumn 1990.

——, 'Making cash flow statements useful', *Accountancy*, 35, April 1992.

LEE, T. A. and D. P. TWEEDIE, *The Private Shareholder and the Corporate Report*, Institute of Chartered Accountants in England and Wales, 1977.

——, *The Institutional Investor and the Corporate Report*, London: ICAEW, 1981.

LEHMAN, CHERYL and TONY TINKER, 'The Real Cultural Significance of Accounts', *Accounting Organizations and Society* 12:5, 503–22, 1987.

LeROY, STEPHEN F., 'Capital Market Efficiency: An Update', *Federal Reserve Bank of San Francisco Economic Review* Issue 2, 29–40, Spring 1990.

LEV, BARUCH, *Financial Statement Analysis: A New Approach*, Englewood Cliffs, NJ: Prentice Hall, 1974.

LEV, BARUCH and J. A. OHLSON, 'Market Based Empirical Research in Accounting: Review, Interpretation and Extension', *Journal of Accounting Research Supplement: Current Research Methodologies in Accounting: A Critical Evaluation*, Vol. 20, 1982.

LI, STEPHEN C. Y., 'Market Reaction to Company Report Announcements in the Hong Kong Stock Exchange', Department of Economics and Finance Research Paper 20, City Polytechnic of Hong Kong, June 1990.

LIBBY, R., 'Accounting Ratios and the Prediction of Failure: Some Behavioral Evidence', *Journal of Accounting Research*, 150–61, Spring 1975.

——, 'Man versus Model of Man: Some Conflicting Evidence', *Organizational Behavior and Human Performance*, 1–12, June 1976.

——, 'Bankers' and Auditors' Perceptions of the Message Communicated by the Audit Report', *Journal of Accounting Research*, 99–122, Spring 1979a.

——, 'The Impact of Uncertainty Reporting on the Loan Decision', *Studies in Auditing – Selections from the Research Opportunities in Auditing Program; Supplement to the Journal of Accounting Research*, 35–57, 1979b.

——, *Accounting and Human Information Processing: Theory and Applications*, Englewood Cliffs, NJ: Prentice Hall, 1981.

LIBBY, R. and R. K. BLASHFIELD, 'Performance of a Composite as a Function of the Number of Judges', *Organizational Behavior and Human Performance*, 121–9, April 1978.

LIBBY, R., and B. L. LEWIS, 'Human Information Processing in Accounting: The State of The Art', *Accounting Organizations and Society* 4: 245–68, 1977.

LIBBY, ROBERT and BARRY L. LEWIS, 'Human Information Processing Research in Accounting: The State of the Art in 1982', *Accounting Organizations and Society* 7:3, 231–85, 1982.

LINTNER, J., 'The Valuation of Risky Assets and Selection of Risky

Investments in Stock Portfolios and Capital Budgets', *Review of Economics and Statistics*, 13–37, February 1965.

LINTNER, JOHN and ROBERT GLAUBER, 'Higgledy Piggledy Growth in America', University of Chicago 1967 working paper, reprinted in James Lorie and Richard Brealey, eds, *Modern Developments in Investment Management*, New York: Praeger, 1972.

LIPE, R., 'The Information Contained in the Components of Earnings', *Journal of Accounting Research* 24:37–64, 1986.

LITTLETON, A. C., 'The Antecedents of Double Entry Bookkeeping', in his *Accounting Evolution to 1900*, New York: Russell & Russell 1966 reprint of 1933 edition, 13–21.

——, *Structure of Accounting Theory*, AAA, 1953.

LIU, CHAO M., 'Variation in Accounting Information Load: The Impact of Disclosure Requirements of FASB Statement No 33 on Cash Flow Predictions of Financial Analysts', PhD Dissertation, North Texas State University, 1982.

LIVNAT, JOSHUA and PAUL ZAROWIN, 'The Incremental Information Content of Cash Flow Components', *Journal of Accounting and Economics* 13: 25–46, 1990.

LORD, C. G., I. ROSS and M. R. LEPPER, 'Biassed Assimilation and Attitude Polarization; The Effect of Prior Theories of Subsequently Considered Evidence', *Journal of Personality and Social Psychology*, 2098–109, November 1979.

LUSK, E. J., 'A Test of Differential Performance Peaking for a Disembedding Task', *Journal of Accounting Research*, 286–94, Spring 1979.

MacALLISTER, D. W., T. R. MITCHELL and L. R. BEACH, 'The Contingency Model for the Selection of Decision Strategies: An Empirical Test of the Effects of Significance, Accountability and Reversibility', *Organizational Behavior and Human Performance* 24: 228–44, 1979.

McCASLIN, T. E. and K. G. STANGA, 'Similarities in the Measurement Needs of Equity Investors and Creditors', *Accounting and Business Research*, 151–6, Spring 1986.

McCOMB, DES, 'The International Harmonization of Accounting: A Cultural Dimension', *International Journal of Accounting*, 1–16, Spring 1979.

McDONALD, JOHN G., 'French Mutual Fund Performance: Evaluation of Internationally Diversified Portfolios', *Journal of Finance*, 1161–80, September 1972.

McDONALD, JOHN G. and A. K. FISHER, 'New Issue Stock Price Behaviour', *Journal of Finance*, 97–102, March 1972.

McGILL, W. J., 'Serial Effects in Auditory Threshold Judgements', *Journal of Experimental Psychology* 53:5, 297–303, 1957.

McKINNON, JILL L., CARRICK A. MARTIN and GRAHAM A. PARTINGTON, 'Clarifying Funds Statements – The Two Entity Test', *Accounting and Finance* 23:1, 79–88, May 1983.

McMONNIES, P. N., 'Should Financial Reports be Scrapped?', *The Accountants Magazine*, 487–8, December 1984.

McMONNIES, PETER N., ed., *Making Corporate Reports Valuable*, Edinburgh, ICAS: 1989.

McNAMARA, T., *Numeracy and Accounting*, Plymouth, UK: M & E Becbooks, 315–18, 1979.

McNICHOLS, M. and J. MANEGOLD, 'Financial Disclosure and the Behavior of Security Prices: An empirical investigation', UCLA working paper, February 1982.

MAHONEY, JOHN J., MARK V. SEVER and JOHN A. THEIS, 'Cash Flow: FASB Opens the Floodgates', *Journal of Accountancy* 165:5, 26–38, May 1988.

MAINGOT, MICHAEL, 'The Information Content of UK Annual Earnings Announcements: A Note', *Accounting and Finance*, 51–8, May 1984.

MAKSY, MOSTAFA M., 'Articulation Problems Between the Balance Sheet and the Funds Statement', *Accounting Review*, 683–99, October 1988.

MANIATIS, GEORGE C., 'The Reliability of the Equities Market to Finance Industrial Development in Greece', *Economic Development and Cultural Change*, 598–620, July 1971.

MARCH, JAMES G., 'Ambiguity and Accounting: The Elusive Link Between Information and Decision Making', *Accounting Organizations and Society* 12:2, 153–68, 1987.

MARCH, J. G., and J. P. OLSEN, 'The New Institutionalism: Organizational Factors in Public Life', *American Political Science Review* 734–49, 1984.

MARCH, J. G. and G. SEVON, 'Gossip, Information and Decision Making', in L. S. SPROULL and J. PATRICK CRECINE, eds, *Advances in Information Processing in Organizations*, Vol. I, Greenwich, CT: JAI Press, 1984.

MARINUCCI, SAM, 'Changes to Statement of Changes', *CA Magazine* 118:10, 68–72, October 1985.

MARLOWE, FANNIE LEE, 'Alternative Funds Flow Measures as Predictors of Failure', PhD Dissertation, Texas A & M University, 1984.

MARSH, P. R., 'An Analysis of Equity Rights Issues on the London Stock Exchange', PhD Thesis, London Business School, 1977.

MASON, A. K., *International Financial Reporting Standards*, ICRA 13, University of Lancaster, 1977.

——, *The Development of International Reporting Standards*, ICRA 17, University of Lancaster, 1978.

MASON, JULIAN, 'Funds Statements: Time to End the Confusion', *Accountancy* 94:1084, 95–9, December 1983.

MASON, P., *Cash Flow Analysis and the Funds Statement,* Accounting Research Study No. 2, New York: AICPA, p. 18, 1961.

MASON, R. O. and I. I. MITROFF, 'A Program for Research on Management Information Systems', *Management Science*, 475–87, January 1973.

MAURIELLO, J. A., *Intermediate Accounting*, New York: Ronald Press, 1950.

——, 'The All Inclusive Statement of Funds', *Accounting Review*, 347–58, April 1964.

MAUTZ, R. K., *An Accounting Technique for Reporting Financial Transactions*, University of Illinois Press, 1951.

MAY, GEORGE O., *Financial Accounting*, New York: Macmillan, 1943.

MAY, ROBERT, 'The Influence of Quarterly Earnings Announcements on Investor Decisions as Reflected in Common Stock Price Changes',

Journal of Accounting Research Supplement: Empirical Research in Accounting 9: 119–63, 1971.

MEAR, ROSS, and MICHAEL A. FIRTH, 'Cue Usage and Self Insight of Financial Analysts', *Accounting Review* 62:1, 175–82, January 1987.

MEEK, G. K. and S. J. GRAY, 'Globalization of Stock Markets and Foreign Listing Requirements: Voluntary Disclosures by Continental European Companies Listed on the London Stock Exchange', *Journal of International Business* 20:2, 315–36, Summer 1989.

MESSIER, W. F., 'An Analysis of Expert Judgement in the Materiality/ Disclosure Decision', working paper, University of Florida, 1979.

MIELKE, DAVID E. and DON E. GIACOMINO, 'Cash Flow Reporting: A Step toward International Harmonization', *International Journal of Accounting* 22:2, 143–51, Summer 1987.

MILLER, ALLIE F., 'An Empirical Study of the Effects of Information Formats on the Prediction of Financial Distress', PhD Dissertation, Arizona State University, 1986.

MILLER, D. E., *The Meaningful Interpretation of Financial Statements: The Cause and Effect Ratio Approach*, New York: American Management Association, 1972.

MILLER, D., and L. A. GORDON, 'Conceptual Levels and the Design of Accounting Information Systems', *Decision Sciences*, 259–69, April 1975.

MILLER, D. E., and D. B. RELKIN, *Improving Credit Practice*, American Management Association, 1971.

MILLER, H., 'Environmental Complexity and Financial Reports', *Accounting Review*, 3–7, January 1972.

MINTZ, STEPHEN MICHAEL, 'A Comparison of Accounting Standard Setting in The International Environment and in the US', DBA Dissertation, George Washington University, 1978.

MITCHEM, CHERYL EVELYN DRAKE, 'A Cash Flow and Macroeconomic Model of Financial Distress (Bankruptcy)', PhD Dissertation, Virginia Commonwealth University, 1990.

MODIGLIANI, FRANCO; G. A. POGUE, M. S. SCHOLES, and B. H. SOLNIK, 'Efficiency of European Capital Markets and Comparison with the American Market', *Proceedings of the First International Congress on Stock Exchanges*, Milan, Italy, 1972.

MOK, H. M. K., KIN LAM and I. Y. K. CHEUNG, 'An Exploration of Risk and Return on Hong Kong Stocks', *Securities Journal*, 1–16, February 1990.

MOONEY, JULIAN LOWELL, 'A Comparison of Earnings and Cash Flow as Risk Measures During Differing Economic Conditions', PhD Dissertation, University of Georgia, 1989.

MOONITZ, M., 'Inventories and Statement of Funds', *Accounting Review* 18: 262–8, July 1943.

——, 'Reporting on the Flow of Funds', *Accounting Review*, 375–85, July 1956.

——, Preface, *Accounting Research Study, No. 2*, New York: AICPA, 1961.

MOONITZ, MAURICE, *Obtaining Agreement on Standards in the Ameri-*

can *Profession, Studies in Accounting Research* 8, Sarasota, FL: AAA, p. 28, 1974.

MORIARITY, S., 'Judgement Based Definition of Materiality', *Selections from the Research Opportunities in Auditing Supplement to Journal of Accounting Research*, 114–35, 1979.

MORRIS, R. C., 'Funds Statement Practices in the United Kingdom', *ICRA Occasional Paper No. 6*, Lancaster: International Centre for Research in Accounting, 1–13, 1974.

MORSE, D., 'Price and Trading Volume Reactions Surrounding Earnings Announcements: A Closer Examination', *Journal of Accounting Research*, 374–83, Autumn 1981.

MOSSIN, J., 'Equilibrium in a Capital Asset Market', *Econometrica*, 768–80, October 1966.

MOST, K. S., 'The Development of Accounting Thought', in his *Accounting Theory*, pp. 31–54, 2nd edition, Dayton, Ohio: Grid Publishing, 1982a.

——, 'The Statement of Changes in Financial Position', Chapter 15 in his *Accounting Theory*, 2nd edition, Dayton, Ohio: Grid Publishing, 1982b.

——, *International Conflict of Accounting Standards*, Research monograph 8 of the Canadian Certified General Accountants' Research Foundation, 1984.

——, 'The Great FAS 95 Mystery', working paper, College of Business Administration, Florida International University, 1990.

MOST, K. S. and L. S. CHANG, 'How Useful are Annual Reports to Investors?', *Journal of Accountancy*, 111–13, September 1979.

MUELLER, G. G., 'Accounting Principles Generally Accepted in the US Versus Those Generally Accepted Elsewhere', pp. 91–103 of *International Journal of Accounting*, Spring 1968, reproduced in S. J. Gray, ed., *International Accounting and Transnational Decisions*, 57–69, New York: Butterworths, 1983.

MUI, Y. M. and C. K. LAW, 'The Expectation and Adjustment Patterns of the Stock Prices to New Interest Rates Information in Hong Kong', in Y. K. YO and C. K. LAW, eds, *The Hong Kong Financial Markets: Empirical Evidence*, Kowloon, Hong Kong: University Printer and Publisher, 159–73, 1983.

MURDOCH, B. and P. KRAUSE, 'Further Evidence on the Comparative Ability of Accounting Data to Predict Operating Cash Flows', *Mid-Atlantic Journal of Business* 26:2, 1–14, Winter 1990.

MURPHY, G. J., *The Evolution of Corporate Accounting Reporting Practices in Canada*, Academy of Accounting Historians' Working Paper 20, 1979.

NAIR, R., 'Empirical Guidelines for International Accounting Data', *Journal of International Business Studies*, 85–7, Winter 1982.

NAIR, R. D. and W. G.FRANK, 'The Impact of Disclosure and Measurement Practices on International Accounting Classifications', *Accounting Review*, 426–45, July 1980.

——, 'The Harmonization of International Accounting Standards 1973–1979', *International Journal of Accounting*, 61–77, Fall 1981.

NEWELL, A., and H. A. SIMON, *Human Problem Solving*, Englewood Cliffs, NJ: Prentice Hall, 1972.

NG, D. S., 'An Information Economic Analysis of Financial Reporting and External Auditing', *Accounting Review*, 910–20, October 1978.

NIEDERHOFFER, VICTOR and PATRICK REGAN, 'Earnings Changes, Analysts' Forecasts and Stock Prices', *Financial Analysts Journal*, 65–71, May/June 1972.

NIXON, KEVIN J., 'FASB Statements on Consolidation, Cash Flows', *Commercial Lending Review* 3:3, 80–6, Summer 1988.

NOBES, C. W., 'A Judgemental International Classification of Financial Reporting Practices', *Journal of Business Finance and Accounting* 10:1, 1–19, 1983.

——, 'International Classification of Financial Reporting', in C. W. NOBES and R. H. PARKER, eds, *Comparative International Accounting*, Oxford: Philip Allan, 2nd edition, 174–87, 1981.

——, 'Another Look at the Draft Fifth', *Accountancy*, August 1984.

NOBES, C. W., and R. H. PARKER, *Comparative International Accounting*, Oxford: Philip Allan, 2nd edition, 1981.

NOBLE, HOWARD S., W. E. KARRENBROCK and H. SIMONS, *Advanced Accounting*, South West Publishing, 1941.

NURNBERG, HUGO, 'Issues in Funds Statement Presentation', *Accounting Review* 58:4, 799–812, October 1983.

——, 'Depreciation in the Cash Flow Statement of Manufacturing Firms: Amount Incurred or Amount Expensed', *Accounting Horizons* 3:1, 95–101, March 1989.

OFFICER, R. R., 'Seasonality in Australian Capital Markets: Market Efficiency and Empirical Issues', *Journal of Financial Economics* 2:29–51, 1975.

O'LEARY, CAROLYN D., 'Cash Flow Reporting Part 1: An Overview of SFAS 95', *Journal of Commercial Bank Lending* 70:9, 22–8, May 1988.

ONKEN, J., R. HASTIE and W. REVELLE, 'Individual Differences in the Use of Simplification Strategies in a Complex Decision Making Task', *Journal of Experimental Psychology: Human Perception and Performance* 11: 14–27, 1985.

OSKAMP, S., 'Overconfidence in Case Study Judgements', *Journal of Consulting Psychology*, 261–5, 1965.

OU AI JINAN, JANE, 'The Information Content of Non Earnings Accounting Numbers as Earnings Predictors', PhD Dissertation, University of California, Berkeley, 1984.

OU, J. A. and S. H. PENMAN, 'Financial Statement Analysis and the Prediction of Stock Returns', *Journal of Accounting and Economics* 11: 295–329, 1989.

PACHELLA, ROBERT G., 'The Interpretation of Reaction Time in Information Processing Research' in Barry H. Kantowitz, ed., *HIP: Tutorials in Performance and Cognition*, Hillsdale, NJ: Erlbaum, 1974.

PALACIOS, JUAN A., 'The Stock Market in Spain: Tests of Theory,' in E. J. Elton and M. J. Gruber, eds, *Efficiency and Capital Market International Capital Markets*. Amsterdam: North-Holland, 114–49, 1975.

PANKOFF, L. D. and R. VIRGIL, 'Some Preliminary Findings from a Laboratory Experiment on the Usefulness of Financial Accounting Information to Securities Analysts', *Journal of Accounting Research Supplement*, 1–48, 1970.

PARTINGTON, G., J. McKINNON and C. MARTIN, 'Funds Statements and the Two Entity Test: A Response', *Abacus* 22:1, 39–44, March 1986.

PATELL, JAMES, 'Corporate Earnings Forecasts: Empirical Tests and Consumption-Investment Model', PhD Dissertation, Carnegie-Mellon University, 1976.

PATELL, J. and WOLFSON, M. A., 'Anticipated Information Releases Reflected in Call Option Prices', *Journal of Accounting and Economics*, 117–40, August 1979.

PATON, W. A., *Essentials of Accounting*, New York: Macmillan, 803, 1938.

——, *Accounting Theory with Special Reference to the Corporate Enterprise*, New York: Ronald Press, 1922, reprinted by Accounting Studies Press, 1962.

PATON, W. A. and A. C. LITTLETON, *An Introduction to Corporate Accounting Standards*, Chicago: American Accounting Association, Ronald Press, 1940.

PATZ, DENNIS and JAMES BOATSMAN, 'Accounting Principle Formulation in an Efficient Markets Environment', *Journal of Accounting Research*, 3392–403, Autumn 1972.

PAUTLER, H. A., 'An All Purpose Funds Statement: Basis and Development', *NAA Bulletin*, 3–14, February 1963.

PAYNE, JOHN W., 'Task Complexity and Contingent Processing in Decision Making: An Information Search and Protocol Analysis', *Organizational Behaviour and Human Performance* 16: 366–87, 1976.

PERCY, M. and D. J. STOKES, 'Further Evidence on Empirical Relationships between Earnings and Cash Flows', *Accounting and Finance* 32:1, 27–42, 1992.

PERERA, M. H. B., 'Towards a Framework to Analyse the Impact of Culture on Accounting', *International Journal of Accounting* 24:1, 42–56, 1989.

PEW, R. W., 'The Speed Accuracy Operating Characteristic: Attention and Performance II', *Acta Psychologica* 30: 16–26, 1969.

PHILLIPS, T. R. JR, 'An Empirical Investigation and Analysis of the Usefulness of Selected Revisions in Concept, Form and Content of the Statement of Changes in Financial Position', PhD Dissertation, Georgia State University, 1984.

PINCHES, GEORGE C., 'Discussion', *Journal of Finance*, 523–6, May 1974.

POGUE, GERALD A., and B. H. SOLNIK, 'The Market Model Applied to European Common Stocks: Some Empirical Results', *Journal of Financial and Quantitive Economics*, 917–44, December 1974.

PRAETZ, P. D., 'Australian Share Prices and the Random Walk Hypothesis', *Australian Journal of Statistics* 11:3, 123–39, 1969.

PRATT, JAMIE and GIORGIO BEHR, 'Environmental Factors, Transaction Costs, and External Reporting: A Cross National Comparison', *International Journal of Accounting* 22:2, 1–24, 1987.

PRATT, J. and H. H. CHRISMAN, 'Teaching the Statement of Changes etc.', *Accounting Review* 57:3, 794–805, October 1982.

PRESSLY, THOMAS RICHARD, 'An Empirical Study of Investor Use of Statement of Cash Flows Information in Stock Price Prediction Decisions', PhD Dissertation, Kent State University, 1989.

PREVITS, GARY JOHN, 'Frameworks of American Financial Accounting Thought: An Historical Perspective to 1973', *Accounting Historians Journal* 11:2, 1–18, Fall 1984.

PRICE WATERHOUSE INTERNATIONAL, 'Accounting Principles and Reporting Practices', London: PWI, 1973 and 1975.

——, *Accounting Principles and Reporting Practices: A Survey in 46 Countries*, London: Price Waterhouse and the ICAEW, 1976.

——, 'International Survey of Accounting Principles and Reporting Practices', London: PWI, 1979.

RAKES, G. K. and W. G. SHENKEN, 'User Responses to APB 19', *Journal of Accountancy*, 91–4, September 1972.

RAWSKI, E., *Education and Popular Literacy in Ching China*, Michigan University Press, 125–7, 1979.

RAYBURN, J., 'The Association of Operating Cash Flow and Accruals with Security Returns', *Journal of Accounting Research* 24: 12–38, 1986.

RAYBURN, JUDY and ROSS JENNINGS, 'The Association of Operating Cash Flows and Accruals with Security Returns/Discussion', *Journal of Accounting Research Supplement* 24, 112–37, 1986.

RAYMAN, R. A., 'Accounting Reform: Standardization, Stabilization or Segregation', *Accounting and Business Research* 1:4, 300–8, Autumn 1971.

RECKERS, PHILIP M., DAN C. KNEER, WALLACE REED and MARIANNE M. JENNINGS, 'Materiality: Are Bankers More Concerned than CPAs?', *Journal of Commercial Bank Lending* 67:1, 14–27, September 1984.

REGAZZI, J. H., 'Why Aren't Financial Statements Understood?', *Journal of Accountancy*, 48–55, April 1974.

REID, W. and D. R. MYDDLETON, *The Meaning of Company Accounts*, Aldershot: Gower, 211–36, 1978.

REINGANUM, M. R., 'The Anomalous Stock Market Behavior of Small Firms in January: Empirical Tests for Tax Loss Selling Effects', *Journal of Financial Economics*, 89–104, June 1983.

REVSINE, L., 'Data Expansion and Conceptual Structure', *Accounting Review*, 704–11, October 1970.

RICHMAN, BRUCE, SHIRLEY JEFFREY and JAMES JAVORCIC, 'An Introduction to SFAS No 95 Statement of Cash Flows', *Real Estate Accounting and Taxation* 3:3, 4–12, Fall 1988.

RMA (abbreviation of ROBERT MORRIS ASSOCIATES), *Cash Flow*, Philadelphia: Robert Morris Associates, 1989 (reprints by the *Journal of Commercial Bank Lending*).

RO, B. T., 'The Information Content of Accounting', *Accounting Review* 1981.

ROBB, A. J., 'Funds Statements and the Two Entity Test', *Abacus* 21:1, 101–9, March 1985

ROBERTS, A. C. and D. GABHART, 'Statement of Funds: A Glimpse of the Future?', *Journal of Accountancy*, 49–54, April 1972.

ROBERTS, H. V., 'Stock Market Patterns and Financial Analysis: Methodological Suggestions', *Journal of Finance* 14:1–10, March 1959.

ROBINS, P. and F. MITCHELL, 'Funds Statement Needs Revision', *Accountancy Age* p. 18 of 21 and 28 February and p. 27 of 28 March 1985.

ROCKLEY, L. E., *The Meaning of Balance Sheets and Company Reports*, London: Business Books, pp. 84–108, 1975.

ROGERS, WAYMOND and LESTER W. JOHNSON, 'Integrating Credit Models Using Accounting Information with Loan Officers' Decision Processes', *Accounting and Finance*, 1–22, November 1988.

ROLL, R., 'A Critique of the Asset Pricing Theory's Tests, Part 1: On Part and Potential Testability of the Theory', *Journal of Financial Economics* 4:1, 129–36, 1977.

RONEN, J., I. SADAN and C. SNOW, 'Income Smoothing: A Review', *Accounting Review*, 11–26, Spring 1977.

ROSEN, L. S., 'Funds Statements – Prime Disclosure Vehicle of the 1980s?' *Canadian Chartered Accountant* 105:1, 48–53, July 1974.

ROSEN, L. S. and D. T. DE COSTER, 'Funds Statements: A Historical Perspective', *Accounting Review*, 124–36, January 1969.

ROSS, S. A., 'The Arbitrage Theory of Capital Asset Pricing', *Journal of Economic Theory* 13:3, 341–60, 1976.

——, 'The Determination of Capital Structure: The Incentive Signalling Approach', *Bell Journal of Economics* 8:23–40, 1977.

ROTHSTEIN, HOWARD G., 'The Effects of Time Pressure on Judgment in Multiple Cue Probability Learning', *Organizational Behavior and Human Decision Processes* 37:1, 83–92, 1986.

RUJOUB, MOHAMMAD A., 'An Empirical Investigation of the Discriminant and Predictive Ability of the Statement of Cash Flows (SFAS No. 95)', PhD Dissertation, University of Arkansas, 1989.

RUTHERFORD, B. A., 'The Use of Cash Flow Reports', *Abacus*, 30–50, June 1982a.

——, 'The Interpretation of Cash Flow Reports and Other Allocation Problems', *Abacus*, 40–9, June 1982b.

——, 'Cash Flow Reporting and Distributional Allocations: A Note', *Journal of Business Finance and Accounting* 10:2, 313–16, Summer 1982c.

SID, *The Role of Accountancy in Economic Development*, seminar of the Society for International Development, Washington DC, April 1976.

SALAMON, G. L. and E. D. SMITH, 'Corporate Control and Managerial Misrepresentation of Firm Information', *Bell Journal of Economics*, 319–28, Spring 1979.

SAMUELS, J. M. and J. OLIGA, 'Accounting Standards in Developing Countries', *International Journal of Accounting*, 18, Fall 1982.

SAMUELS, J. M. and A. G. PIPER, *International Accounting: A Survey*, Beckenham: Croom Helm, 1985.

SAMUELS, J. M., RICKWOOD and A. G. PIPER, *Advanced Financial Accounting* Maidenhead, Berks: McGraw-Hill, 1989.

SAN MIGUEL, J. G., 'Human Information Processing and its Relevance to Accounting: A Laboratory Study', *Accounting Organizations and Society*, 357–373, 1976.

SANDERS, THOMAS H., H. R. HATFIELD and U. MOORE, *A Statement of Accounting Principles*, American Institute of Accountants, 1938.

SARHAN, M. H., ARJAN T. SADHWANI and JEFFREY P. LESSARD,

'Changing from Working Capital to Cash Flow in the Funds Statement: An Empirical Investigation of Management Motives', *Akron Business and Economic Review* 18:1, 55–63, Spring 1987.

SAVICH, R. S., 'The Use of Accounting Information in Decision Making', *Accounting Review*, 642–52, July 1977.

SCHEPANSKI, A., 'Tests of Theories of Information Processing Behavior in Credit Judgment', *Accounting Review* 58:3, 581–99, July 1983.

SCHMANDT-BESSERAT, DENISE, 'Reckoning Before Writing', *Archaeology* 32:3, 23–31, 1979.

SCHNEIDER, SUSAN C., 'Information Overload: Causes and Consequences', *Human Systems Measurement* (Netherlands) 7:2, 143–53, 1987.

SCHREYOGG, G., 'Contingency and Choice in Organization Theory', *Organization Studies*, 305–26, 1980.

SCHRODER, HAROLD M., MICHAEL J. DRIVER and SIEGFRIED C. STREUFERT, *Human Information Processing: Individuals and Groups Functioning in Complex Social Situations*, New York: Holt, Rinehart and Winston, 1967.

SCHRODER, H. M. and O. J. HARVEY, 'Conceptual Organization and Group Structure', in O. J. Harvey, ed., *Motivation and Social Interaction – Cognitive Determinants*, New York: Ronald Press, 134–66, 1963.

SCHROEDER, ANGELIKA THERESA HELKE, 'Cash Flow Predictions Using Alternative Income Measures', PhD Dissertation, University of Colorado at Boulder, 1988.

SCHULTZ, J. J. JR, 'Discussion' (of the impact of uncertainty reporting on the loan decision), *Journal of Accounting Research Supplement* 17, 1979.

SCHWERT, G. WILLIAM, 'Stock Returns and Real Activity: A Century of Evidence', *Journal of Finance* 45:4, 1237–57, September 1990.

SCOTT, D. R., *The Cultural Significance of Accounts*, Homewood, IL: Henry Holt & Co, 1931.

SCOTT, G. M., *88 International Accounting Problems*, Sarasota, FL: AAA, 1980, in *SEC, Proceedings, Major Issues Conference*, Washington, DC: Securities and Exchange Commission, 1977.

SEC, *Accounting Series 117*, Washington, DC: SEC, October 1970.

SEC *Accounting Rules*, p. 3334, New York: Commerce Clearing House, 1971.

SECURITIES REVIEW COMMITTEE, 'The Operation and Regulation of the Hong Kong Securities Industry', Report of the Securities Review Committee, chaired by Ian Hay Davison, p. 21, May 1988.

SEED, ALAN H. III, 'Utilizing the Funds Statement', *Management Accounting*, 15–18, May 1976.

——, 'The Funds Statement: How Can it be Improved?', *Financial Executive* 52:10, 52–5, October 1984a.

——, *The Funds Statement: Structure and Use*, Morristown, NJ: Financial Executives' Institute, 1984b.

SENATRA, PHILLIP, 'The New Statement of Cash Flows: The Basic Rules', *Practical Accountant* 21:3, 28–39, March 1988.

SENDERS, JOHN W., 'Mental Workload' on p. 3 last verse, in P. A. Hancock and Najmedin Meshkati, eds, *Human Mental Workload; Advances in Psychology 52*, Amsterdam: North-Holland, Elsevier, 1988.

SHARPE, W. F., 'Capital Asset Prices: A Theory of Market Equilibrium under Conditions of Risk', *Journal of Finance*, 425–42, September 1964.

SHIELDS, M. D., 'Some Effects of Information Load on Search Patterns Used to Analyse Accounting Reports', *Accounting Organizations and Society* 5: 429–42, 1980.

——, 'Effects of Information Supply and Demand on Judgment Accuracy: Evidence from Corporate Managers', *Accounting Review*, 284–303, April 1983.

SHWARZBACH, H. and M. HIGGINS, 'Cash Flow from Operating Activities: An Analysis of Management Manipulation', paper presented to the 1992 annual meeting of the AAA, Washington, DC.

SIEBER, JOAN E., and J. T. LANZETTA, 'Conflict and Conceptual Structure as Determinants of Decision Making Behavior', *Journal of Personality* 32:4, 622–41, 1964.

SIEGEL, JOEL and ABE SIMON, 'The Statement of Changes in Financial Position: A Vital Clue to a Company's Financial Health', *National Public Accountant* 26:6, 22–6, June 1981.

SIEGEL, SIDNEY, *Nonparametric Statistics*, New York: McGraw-Hill, 1956.

SIMON, H. A. and K. KOTOVSKY, 'Human Acquisition of Concepts for Sequential Patterns', *Psychological Review*, 534–46, November 1963.

SIMON, H. A. and A. NEWELL, 'Thinking Processes', in D. H. Krantz, R. C. Atkinson, R. D. Luce and P. Suppes, eds, *Contemporary Developments in Mathematical Psychology*, Vol. 1, San Francisco: Freeman, 1974.

SIMS, MICHELE A. and DAVID CANTRICK-BROOKS, 'A Study of the Political Input into the Australian Accounting Standard Setting Process with Respect to AAS12 and AAS28', paper to the annual meeting of the Accounting Association of Australia and New Zealand, 1992.

SLOVIC, P., D. FLEISSNER and W. S. BAUMAN, 'Analysing the Use of Information in Investment Decision Making: A Methodological Proposal', *Journal of Business*, 283–301, April 1972.

SLOVIC, P. and S. LICHTENSTEIN, 'Comparison of Bayesian and Regression Approaches to the Study of Information Processing in Judgment', *Organizational Behavior and Human Performance* 6: 649–744, 1971.

SMITH, A. F., 'Funds Flow Statements Revamped', *Management Accounting (UK)* 63:10, 25–9, November 1985.

SMITH, CLIFFORD W. JR, 'Investment Banking and the Capital Acquisition Process', *Journal of Financial Economics* 15:3–29, 1986.

SMITH, E. D., 'The Effect of the Separation of Ownership from Control on Accounting Policy Decisions', *Accounting Review*, 707–23, October 1976.

SNOWBALL, DOUG, 'On the Integration of Accounting Research on Human Information Processing', *Accounting and Business Research*, 307–18, Summer 1980a.

——, 'Some Effects of Accounting Expertise and Information Load: An Empirical Study', *Accounting, Organizations and Society*, 323–8, 1980b.

SNOWBALL, DOUG, J. R. BETTMAN and E. J. JOHNSON, *Adaptive Strategy Selection in Decision Making*, working paper 62–85–86, Duke University, 1986.

SOLOMONS, DAVID, 'Economic and Accounting Concepts of Income', *The Accounting Review*, 374–83, July 1961.

SOMEYA, KYOJIRO, 'The Development of Funds Flow Accounting', in M. J. R. Gaffikin, ed., *Contemporary Accounting Thought: Essays in Honour of R. J. Chambers*, Sydney: Prentice-Hall, 1984.

SOMMERVILLE, PATRICIA MILLER, 'An Analysis of the Attitudes Towards Cash Flow Per Share and a Comparative Analysis of Accrual and Cash Basis Accounting in Explaining Cash Flow Per Share', PhD Dissertation, Saint Louis University, 1991.

SONDHI, ASHWINPAUL C., GEORGE H. SORTER and GERALD I. WHITE, 'Cash Flow Redefined: FAS 95 and Security Analysis', *Financial Analysts Journal* 44:6, 19–20, November/December 1988.

SORTER, GEORGE A., 'The Emphasis on Cash and its Impact on the Funds Statement – Sense and Nonsense', *Journal of Accounting Auditing and Finance* 5:3, 188–96, Spring 1982.

SPILLER, G. A. and R. L. VIRGIL, 'Effectiveness of APB Opinion No 19', *Journal of Accounting Research* 12:1, 112–22, Spring 1974.

SPRAGUE, CHARLES E., *The Philosophy of Accounts*, 1907, Scholars Book reprint 1972.

SPROUSE, R. T., 'The Balance Sheet – Embodiment of the Most Fundamental Aspects of Accounting Theory', in S. A. Zeff and T. F. Keller, eds, *Financial Accounting Theory*, New York: McGraw-Hill, 1971.

SSAP 10, 'Statement of Changes in Financial Position', reprinted in the *New Zealand Accountants Journal*, 225–7, July 1979.

STAMP, E., 'A First Step Towards a British Conceptual Framework', *Accountancy*, March 1972.

STANGA, K. G. and T. E. McCASLIN, 'Related Qualities of Useful Accounting Information', *Accounting and Business Research* 14:53, 35–42, Winter 1983.

STARK, M., 'Funds – Working Capital or Cash?', *Michigan CPA*, 23–5, May/June 1975.

STAUBUS, G., 'The Association of Financial Accounting Variables with Common Stock Values', *Accounting Review*, 119–24, January 1965.

STAUBUS, G. J., 'Cash Flow Accounting and Liquidity: Cash Flow Potential and Wealth', *Accounting and Business Research* 19:74, 161–9, Spring 1989.

STEPHENS, R. G., 'Accounting Disclosures for User Decision Processes', in Y. IJIRI and A. B. WHINSTON, eds, *Quantitive Planning and Control*, New York: Academic Press, 291–309, 1979.

STEWART, MORAG IRVINE, 'Information Overload in Multicriteria Decisions: An Investigation of a Load Reduction Strategy', PhD Dissertation, Arizona State University, 1988.

STREIGHTOFF, F. H., *Advanced Accounting*, 215, New York: Harper and Bros, 1932.

STREUFERT, S. C., 'Effects of Information Relevance on Decision Making in Complex Environments', *Memory and Cognition*, 224–8, 1973.

STREUFERT, S., M. CLARDY, M. J. DRIVER, M. KARLINS, H. M. SCHRODER and P. SUEDFELD, 'A Tactical Game for the Analysis of Complex Decision Making in Individuals and Groups', *Psychological Reports* 17:723–9, 1965.

STUDY GROUP ON THE OBJECTIVES OF FINANCIAL STATEMENTS, *Objectives of Financial Statements* [The Trueblood Report], New York: AICPA, pp. 20–37, 1973.

SUEDFELD, P., 'Attitude Manipulation in Restricted Environments; Conceptual Structure and Response to Propaganda', *Journal of Abnormal Psychology* 68:3, 242–6, 1964.

——, 'A Tactical Game for the Analysis of Complex Decision Making in Individuals and Groups', *Psychological Reports* 17:723–9, 1965.

SUMBY, W. H., D. CHAMBLISS and I. POLLACK, 'Information Transmission with Elementary Auditory Displays', *Journal of the Acoustical Society of America* 30:425–9, 1958.

SUMMERS, E. L., 'Observation of Effects of Using Alternative Reporting Practices', *Accounting Law Review*, 258–68, April 1968.

SUNDER, SHYAM, 'Relationships Between Accounting Changes and Stock Prices: Problems of Measurement and Some Empirical Evidence', *Journal of Accounting Research Supplement: Empirical Research in Accounting* 11:1–45, 1973.

——, 'Stock Price and Risk Related to Accounting Changes in Inventory Valuation', *Accounting Review*, 303–15, April 1975.

SWANSON, EDWARD P., 'Designing a Cash Flow Statement', *CPA Journal* 56:1, 38–45, January 1986.

SWANSON, E. P. and R. VANGERMEERSCH, 'The Statement of Financing and Investing Activities', *CPA Journal*, 32–9, November 1981.

SWIERINGA, R. J., T. R. DYCKMAN and R. E. HOSKIN, 'Empirical Evidence About the Effects of an Accounting Change on Information Processing', in T. H. Burns, ed., *Behavioral Experiments in Accounting II*, Ohio State University, 225–59, 1979.

SWIERINGA, R. J., M. GIBBINS, L. LARSSON and J. L. SWEENEY, 'Experiments in the Heuristics of Human Information Processing', *Studies on HIP in Accounting: Journal of Accounting Research Supplement* 14:159–87, 1976.

SWINNEY, D. A., 'Lexical Access during Sentence Comprehension: (Re)consideration of Context Effects', *Journal of Verbal Learning and Verbal Behavior* 18:645–59, 1979.

SYED, AZMAT A., PU LIU and S. D. SMITH, 'The Exploitation of Inside Information at the Wall Street Journal: A Test of Strong Form Efficiency', *Financial Review* 24:4, 567–79, November 1989.

TAGGART, J., 'Sacred Cows in Accounting', *Accounting Review* 28:3, 313–19, July 1953.

TAYLOR, MARTIN E., THOMAS G. EVANS and ARTHUR C. JOY, 'The Impact of IASC Accounting Standards on Comparability and Consistency of International Accounting Reporting Practices', *International Journal of Accounting* 22:1, 1–11, 1986.

TAYLOR, PAUL, 'Published Funds Statements and SSAP 10', *Accountancy* 90:1034, 95–8, October 1979.

THEIOS, J., 'The Locus of Cognition', Paper to the 13th Annual Meeting of the Psychonomic Society, November 1972.

THODE, S. F., R. E. DRTINA and J. A. LARGAY III, 'Operating Cash Flows: A Growing Need for Separate Reporting', *Journal of Accounting Auditing and Finance* 1:1, 46–61, Winter 1986.

THOMAS, A. L., *The Allocation Problem: Studies in Accounting Research* 3, American Accounting Association, 101, 108–9, 1969.

THOMAS, ANDREW P., 'The Contingency Theory of Corporate Reporting: Some Empirical Evidence', *Accounting Organizations and Society* 11:3, 253–70, 1986.

THOMAS, ARTHUR L., 'Cash Flow Reporting as Allocation Free Disclosure: A Polemic', Cash Flow Accounting: Papers of the International Conference on Cash Flow Accounting held in August 1980, eds Barry E. Hicks and Pearson Hunt, Laurentian University, Sudbury, Ontario, Canada, 1981.

THOMPSON, JAMES H. and THOMAS E. BUTTROSS, 'Return to Cash Flow', *CPA Journal* 58:3, 30–40, March 1988.

TRUEBLOOD, R. S., *Objectives of Accounting Statements [q. v. supra], Accounting Objectives Study Group*, American Institute of Certified Public Accountants, 1973.

TUCKMAN, B., 'Personality Structure, Group Composition and Group Functioning', *Sociometry* 27:469–87, 1964.

TVERSKY, A., 'Intransitivity of Preferences', *Psychological Review* 76:31–48, 1969.

——, 'Elimination by Aspects: A Theory of Choice' *Psychological Review* 79:281–99, 1972.

TVERSKY, A. and D. KAHNEMAN, 'Belief in the Law of Small Numbers', *Psychological Bulletin*, 105–10, August 1971.

——, 'Availability: A Heuristic for Judging Frequency and Probability', *Cognition Psychology*, 207–32, September 1973.

TWEEDIE, D. P., 'Cash Flows and Realisable Values: The Intuitive Concepts? An Empirical Test', *Accounting and Business Research* 8:29, 2–13, Winter 1977.

UGALDE, ERVIN, 'The Usefulness of SFAS 52 and SFAS 95 Requirements in Highly Inflationary Economies', MS Dissertation, Eastern Michigan University, 1991.

VAGA, TONIS, 'The Coherent Market Hypothesis', *Financial Analysts Journal* 46:6, 36–49, November/December 1990.

VALENZA, C. G., 'Cash Flow Controversy', *Bank Administration* 65:40–2, January 1989.

VAN HORNE, J. C., 'Optimal Initiation of Bankruptcy Proceedings by Debt Holders', *Journal of Finance* 31:897–910, 1976.

VATTER, WILLIAM J., 'Origins of the Fund Theory', *The Fund Theory of Accounting and its Implications for Financial Reports*, University of Chicago, pp. 1–13, 1947.

VICKNAIR, D. B., 'An Investigation of Users' Perceptions Concerning Corporate Funds Flow Information', DBA Dissertation, University of Tennessee, 1983.

VOLONINO, LINDA ANN, 'An Empirical Investigation of the Impacts of Information Load on Decision Quality and Decision Confidence in Multicriteria Decision Making', PhD Dissertation, State University of New York at Buffalo, 1988.

WAI, V. T. and H. T. PATRICK, 'Stock and Bond Issues and Capital Markets in Less Developed Countries', Washington, DC: IMF Staff Papers, March 1973.

WALDRON, MARILYN A., 'A Comparative Analysis of Accrual and Cash Basis Accounting in Predicting Cash Flows from Operations in the Oil and Gas Industry', DBA Dissertation, Louisiana Tech University, 1988.

WALKER, R. G., 'International Accounting Compromises: The Case of Consolidated Accounting', *Abacus*, 14, December 1978.

——, 'Funds Statements and the Interpretation of Financial Data – An Empirical Investigation', University of New South Wales School of Accountancy Working Paper Series No. 18, 1981.

——, 'Funds Statements and the Interpretation of Financial Data – An Empirical Investigation', in M. J. R. Gaffikin, ed., *Contemporary Accounting Thought: Essays in Honour of R. J. Chambers*, Sydney: Prentice-Hall, 125–48, 1984.

WALLACE, R. S. O. and P. A. COLLIER, 'The "Cash" in Cash Flow Statements: A Multi-country Comparison', *Accounting Horizons* 5:4, 44–52, December 1991.

WALTON, S., 'Students' Department', *Journal of Accountancy*, 231, March 1914.

WAN, H. Y., 'The Weak Form Test of the Efficiency of Hong Kong Stock Market', *Hong Kong Economic Journal Monthly* 16:54–6, 1980a.

——, 'The Instability of Beta Coefficients of Hong Kong Stocks', *Hong Kong Economic Journal Monthly* 42:9, 38–40, September 1980b.

WARREN, R. I., and J. WHITE, 'Cash Flow Information: Toward a More Useful Statement of Changes in Financial Position', *The National Public Accountant*, 10–34, February 1975.

WASNIEWSKI, DENNIS F., 'Statement of Cash Flows', *Business Credit* 90:8, 26–8, September 1988.

WATTS, R. L., 'Corporate Financial Statements: A Product of the Market and Political Processes', *Australian Journal of Management* 2:53–75, April 1977.

WATTS, R. L. and J. L. ZIMMERMAN, 'Towards a Positive Theory of The Determination of Accounting Standards', *Accounting Review* 53, January 1978.

——, 'The Demand and Supply of Accounting Theories: The Market for Excuses', *Accounting Review* 54, April 1979.

WEBER, M., *General Economic History*, New York: Collier, 170–4, 1961.

WEBER, R., 'Auditor Decision Making on Overall System Reliability: Accuracy, Consensus, and the Usefulness of a Simulated Decision Aid', *Journal of Accounting Research* 368–88, Autumn 1978.

WEIDLICH, W., 'The Statistical Description of Polarization Phenomena in Society', *British Journal of Mathematical and Statistical Psychology* 24:251–66, 1971.

WELSH, MARY JEANNE, 'An Experimental Research Study on the Effect of Recognition and Disclosure of Corporate Pension Plan Assets and Obligations on Investment Decisions', PhD Dissertation, Louisiana State University, 1987.

WENZEL, LOREN ALVIN, 'The Predictive Ability of Quarterly Accrual and Cash Flow Variables: A Multiple Time Series Approach (Forecasting)', DBA Dissertation, Memphis State University, 1990.

WHITMAN, J. D., 'What is the Standard of Accounting in Hong Kong?

A Comparison of Accounting and Stock Market Rates of Return to Shareholders 1976–1985', Proceedings of the Academy of International Business South East Asia Regional Conference, Hong Kong, June 1990.

WILKES, ROBERT E., 'A Banker Explains the Right Way to Get a Loan – Why Some Are Rejected', *Business Owner* 9:4, 10–12, April 1985.

WILLIAMSON, O. E., 'A Dynamic Stochastic Theory of Managerial Behavior', in A. Philips and O. E. Williams, eds, *Prices: Issues in Theory, Practice and Public Policy*, Philadelphia: University of Pennsylvania Press, 11–31, 1967.

——, *Markets and Hierarchies: An Analysis and Antitrust Implications*, London: The Free Press, 1975.

WILSON, D. A., 'A Note on Environmental Complexity and Financial Reports', *Accounting Review*, 586–8, July 1973.

WILSON, G. PETER, 'The Incremental Information Content of Accruals and Cash Flows after Controlling for Earnings', PhD Dissertation, Carnegie–Mellon University, 1985.

——, 'The Relative Information Content of Accruals and Cash Flows: Combined Evidence at the Earnings Announcement and Annual Report Date', *Journal of Accounting Research* 24:165–200, 1986.

——, 'The Incremental Information Content of the Accrual and Funds Components of Earnings after Controlling for Earnings', *Accounting Review* 62:293–321, 1987.

WONG, C. C., 'Market Anomalies of the Hong Kong Stock Market', MPhil Dissertation, Hong Kong University, 1989.

WONG, K. A. and K. S. KWONG, 'The Behavior of Hong Kong Stock Prices', *Applied Economics* 16:905–17, December 1984.

WOOD, F., *Business Accounting 2*, pp. 801–29, London: Longman, 1975.

WRIGHT, P., 'The Harassed Decision Maker: Time Pressures, Distractions, and the Use of Evidence', *Journal of Marketing Research* 44:429–43, 1974.

WRIGHT, W. F., 'Self Insight into the Cognitive Processing of Financial Information', *Accounting, Organizations and Society* 4:323–31, 1977.

—— 'Properties of Judgment Models in a Financial Setting', *Organization Behavior and Human Performance*, 73–85, February 1979.

WYATT, ARTHUR, 'International Accounting Standards: A New Perspective', *Accounting Horizons* 3:3, 105–8, September 1989.

YALLAPRAGADA, RAMMOHAN R. and ARLEENE P. BREUX, 'Financial Statement Analysis: Its Use in Lending Institutions', *National Public Accountant* 34:1, 32–7, January 1989.

YAM, STEPHEN, 'Accounting for Joint Ventures in China', *CMA Magazine* 60:4, 24–9, July/August 1986.

YELLOTT, J. I., 'Correction for Fast Guessing and the Speed Accuracy in Choice Reaction Time', *Journal of Mathematical Psychology* 8:159–99, 1971

YERKES, R. M. and J. B. DOBSON, 'The Relation of Strength of Stimulus to Rapidity of Habit Formation', *Journal of Comparative Neurological Psychology* 18:459–82, 1908.

YU, S. C., 'A Flow of Resources Statement for Business Enterprises', *Accounting Review*, 571–82, July 1969.

ZEGA, CHERYL ANN, 'The New Statement of Cash Flows', *Management Accounting* 70:3, 54–9, September 1988.

ZHOU ZHUNG HUI, 'Chinese Accounting Systems and Practices', *Accounting Organizations and Society* 13:2, 207–24, 1988.

ZIMMER, I., 'A Lens Study of the Prediction of Corporate Failure by Bank Loan Officers', *Journal of Accounting Research*, 629–36, Autumn 1980.

——, 'A Comparison of the Predictive Accuracy of Loan Officers and their Linear Additive Models', *Organizational Behavior and Human Performance*, 69–74, February 1981.

Name index

Subject index